HENCO FURNITURE HOUSE

Worth the Drive

The Journey of My Life

by
Tom Hendrix

Fred,

Congratulation on a well
lived productive life
in service to people,

Thanks

Tom Hendrix

DEDICATION

To Sherry Lynne, my wife and partner of 54 years, for your love and devotion. This book would not have happened without you.

To my loving family — my beautiful daughters, Susan and Leigh Anne, my supportive sons-in-law Patrick O'Connell and Stuart McWhorter; and the precious grandchildren they gave us, Sarah Catherine and Sean O'Connell, and Clayton, Thomas, Caroline, Marleigh and Layla McWhorter, for your encouragement, patience and being good listeners as I shared my stories.

Copyright © 2014 by Thomas Edward Hendrix. All rights reserved.

This book or any portion there of may not be reproduced or used in any manner whatsoever without the express written permission of the publisher except for the use of brief quotations in a book review.

Printed in the United States of America

First Printing, 2014 • Counce, Tennessee 38326

ISBN 978-0-9907576-1-0

www.mrhenco.com

Acknowledgement

I have often made the statement, I am like the little turtle that was found sitting on top of a fence post — I had a lot of help getting there. That statement is again so true. It is hard for me to begin to thank those who helped me with my book; those who encouraged me to record my experiences, offered comments and recollections, provided gracious support, proofed and assisted with the editing and design.

With great appreciation, I thank Mary Reed, Mike Reed and Ginger Williams. Your expertise and professionalism, in editing and shaping my manuscript, is commendable. I hope you can tell your friends "it was worth the drive."

George Donaldson, Bob and Pat Brooks, Chuck Few, Jack Hawkins, Gene Hébert, Elisabeth Jonas, Mark Kissel, Pat Kroken, Marvin Dabbs, Tom O'Neal and Joe Utsey — I sincerely thank you for your advice and help in regard to Henco Fundraising and Henco Furniture & Home Center. Jimmy Harrison and Steve Smith — thanks so much for your comments.

With sincere thanks to those of you who encouraged me to record my experiences, especially, before I forgot them — Dr. E. Claude Gardner, Russell Caldwell, Frank Rosenberg, Ken Marston, Dr. Matt and Carolyn Tomlin; and Estel Mills, Dr. Cavit Cheshier and John McConnico, who have inspired me time and again.

I am most grateful to the Reverend Dr. David Comperry for his thoughtful assistance.

Anders and Johan Widestrand and Spencer Cheng — thank you for your contributions and everlasting enrichments to our family and my journey.

Continued ... **3**

To Bill Avery, a big thank you for photographing me in the best light possible.

A hearty thanks goes to Ken Kiem for his introduction to Reed & Associates.

Without the dedicated associates who joined in my endeavors — Bible sales, Nasco, Henco, Princeton, Spectrum, Bolivar Aviation, Hendrix Orchard, The Swinery, Landmark Properties, M&H Emu Ranch, and Henco Furniture, my story could not have been told. Thank you.

If I have failed to recognize someone who helped me or if someone's name was not mentioned with whom I have associated through the years, I ask your forgiveness.

***

From Susan and Leigh Anne

As you read this book, our hope is that you will come to know Tom Hendrix as an inspiring, wonderful man. We call him Daddy, but others call him positive, determined, a risk-taker, a spirited businessman — the epitome of an entrepreneur. He is all that, but we also love him for inspiring us to experience experiences, to be confident, productive women, to be thoughtful wives and parents.

His unique ways of teaching life lessons has encouraged us to strive toward our full potential. When we were in college, we dreaded his letters written on Henco letterhead, but in hindsight, we have appreciated every word. As mothers, we find ourselves using many of his techniques to inspire and teach life lessons to our children.

We also hope that you will understand what an amazing woman he chose as his wife and partner for his journey. Sherry Lynne, as he lovingly calls her, is Mom to us. She is the embodiment of unconditional love. She is the heart of our family — patient, unselfish and supportive. We are proud to share our Daddy's story, the journey he has taken with our Mom and the family that we have created together. It has been and continues to be worth the drive!

— Susan Hendrix O'Connell and Leigh Anne Hendrix McWhorter

WHAT FRIENDS SAY ABOUT TOM HENDRIX

"I had the privilege of studying under Dr. Peter Drucker, the undisputed guru of American business. As I listened to Dr. Drucker explain the characteristics of successful entrepreneurship, Tom Hendrix's name kept coming to mind. I worked for Tom, selling Bibles door to door, when we were both in college. He inspired not only me, but many other young people to be a success in life. Read his book. It will be a blessing to you."

— Rev. Jimmy Latimer, Senior Pastor,
Redeemer Evangelical Church, Germantown, Tennessee

***

"Tom Hendrix is a rare human being who has lived a life that is unique in substance and impressive in style — a true role model. His autobiography is an inspiring story of one man's successful life, and it contains many, many nuggets of advice and guidance for anyone aspiring to achieve in their careers. He has truly made a difference over the years, and his autobiography will continue his brilliant legacy for future generations."

— Dr. Charles E. Smith, Chancellor Emeritus, University of Tennessee

***

"Tom's impact goes well beyond his tremendous entrepreneurial and financial success. He has served as a valuable mentor to countless successful careers. I've benefited greatly from Tom's inspirational example and wise counsel over the years. This book provides that unique benefit to other aspiring entrepreneurs and business leaders."

— Nelson Mills, President, Chief Executive Officer,
Columbia Property Trust

***

"*Tom Hendrix, an astute entrepreneur, has delineated his long journey of building a highly successful retail, upscale business. He personally planned and promoted a top-of-the-line furniture store that was attractive and affordable to thousands who came because it was 'worth the drive.' He did this with hard work, clear vision and competent leadership. The principles of marketing he practiced will help anyone who desires to be an entrepreneur. Congratulations on this volume of an exciting and joyful journey.*"

— E. Claude Gardner, President Emeritus, Freed-Hardeman University

***

"*Many times the quality of one's life journey depends on with whom you walk the road. Tom is a special person, businessman, role model and leader of men. I can't begin to tell you the number of young men upon whom he has had a lasting effect. His long-awaited book should be a welcome motivational tool for a successful, well-lived life.*"

— Russell Caldwell, Founder, Caldwell's Office Outfitters

***

"*Tom took an interest in me when I was a senior in High School and has been a mentor, encourager and role model. He inspired me to become an entrepreneur. I will forever be thankful for his encouragement.*"

— Rod Parker, Wealth Management Advisor, Northwestern Mutual

CHAPTERS

ADDENDUM

PROLOGUE

MR. HENCO

In 2006, we celebrated the 65th birthday of my wife, Sherry, with a family trip to New York City. A highlight of the trip was brunch at Tavern on the Green, the famous restaurant in Central Park. The place was busy, and we were standing outside waiting for our table to be ready.

A woman leaving the restaurant saw me and shouted "Mr. Henco! I've been to your store! My family shops there!" Then she gave me a big embrace.

My wife and daughters were used to my being recognized by strangers, but my son-in-law was astonished. I've been recognized in the Miami airport, at UT football games, walking down the street in Highlands, North Carolina, and many other places. A whole table of women stood up and clapped when I went to an IHOP in Memphis.

People recognized me from my television ads, as I invited them to visit Henco Furniture in Selmer, Tennessee. "It's worth the drive," I always told them.

These experiences are always special, and I always thank the person for shopping at Henco Furniture. Sherry and I built that business with zero retail furniture experience. In its heyday, we sold $1 million a month.

The birth of Henco Furniture, however, came long after other successes — and a few failures. I sold Bibles, Japanese water shoes (later to be known as flip-flops), stools and even memorial cemetery plots early in my career.

I built two national companies before Henco Furniture. I also owned an aviation school, raised emus and ran the largest peach orchard in Tennessee.

But that's getting ahead of my story.

CHAPTER 1

THE JOURNEY BEGINS, MY CHILDHOOD

"The lessons I learned on the farm and across the kitchen table
were the best part of my education."

Dad and I made a practice of walking over our farm fields and looking for areas that needed attention so we could prioritize our work. We lived in the Buena Vista community outside of Bethel Springs, Tennessee, on a 170-acre, poor red-dirt farm. Taking care of the land so we could get the most out of it was important. Though I was only about 12 years old, I was expected to work hard.

One spring day, before we began our plowing to prepare the land for crops, Dad stopped at the creek bottom — a four-acre, narrow strip of water-saturated land. He looked over at me.

"Tom, we've put up with this water problem too long," he said.

"We're going to do something about it starting Monday morning. You and I, with a shovel each and an axe to cut the roots, are going to cut a ditch from here to the end of the field. It'll give us a drainage ditch to dry out this field so we can have a fine crop of corn here."

"How long will it take for us to cut this ditch?" I asked.

"If we start early in the morning, work late and don't stop digging, we'll finish it in six days, by Saturday night."

"How big is this ditch going to be?" I asked again.

"Two or two-and-a-half feet wide and maybe two or two-and-a-half feet deep. That size should solve the water problem."

Monday morning, bright and early, Dad and I arrived with our shovels and axes. We began digging the ditch.

The first two days were the toughest. I had blisters on my hands that calloused by the weekend. I had to grit my teeth at times as I dug in competition with my father. Dad didn't consider this work; we simply were on a mission to grow more corn.

"Tom, we will be proud to come here and see a green field of corn with the highest yield on the farm after our work this week."

When Saturday evening arrived, we had reached the drainage ditch at the end of the field, completing our project. We hugged each other — mission complete. And I logged another life lesson from my father.

Dad may not have realized the important lesson he was teaching me, but he certainly communicated to me the good we were doing and how proud we would be of our week's work. The backbreaking labor was worth the blistered hands. Dad was one of the greatest influences in my life. Hard work for the good of the family was a great lesson. It would serve me well later as I became an entrepreneur.

***

That's why the story of my life begins with my father, Carlos Hendrix. In 1918, during World War I, the U.S. Army drafted him and sent him overseas to France and Germany. His duty was to manage the mules and horses that pulled and maneuvered the heavy gunnery into position for battle. The work suited him because he spent his life before the war on the family farm handling livestock and tilling the land. He spoke of the last shots he heard in battle — the last of a horrible war that raged for four years.

At the height of the conflict, Ora Baker, Dad's cousin, sent Dad the address and picture of a beautiful young lady named Icalena Hoover. Mrs. Baker suggested that Dad write to her. Icalena, who went by the name of Lena, welcomed the correspondence from her new friend, and my parents' love story began.

When the war ended, Dad's unit spent weeks marching back from the front lines in snow and rain with equipment and wagons with iron tires pulled by mules and horses. The roads were soft, and the mules and horses cut them into mud. The long march after the war was the most miserable time of Dad's army life, but it was worth the misery to provide freedom for his country.

As soon as Dad returned home, he went to see Mother. I have often thought about what that meeting was like — my parents seeing each other for the first time after having only communicated through letters.

The 25-mile trip from my father's family farm in Bethel Springs to my mother's home in Stantonville near Shiloh National Military Park was not easy. The journey took about

Carlos Hendrix in the Army

three and a half hours on horseback, regardless of the weather. Dad would start his ride early in the morning, arrive at the Hoover home at 9 or 10 a.m. and stay until the evening. Their courtship became serious, and they made plans for marriage about four months after Dad's army discharge on August 26, 1919.

Their wedding day was December 24, 1919 — Christmas Eve. The temperature was close to zero. Dad traveled to Stantonville by buggy. Mother's family heated stones to place at their feet, which helped keep them warm. They covered themselves in blankets and began their journey as a couple, planning a bright future together as they rode back to Bethel Springs.

On the way, they stopped at the home of R.W. Newsome, a McNairy County magistrate. The original plan was for the couple to step inside Mr. Newsome's home and exchange vows. But it was cold, and my parents were bundled warmly in the buggy. So Dad hollered as loud as he could for the preacher to come outside.

Icalena Hoover   *Carlos Hendrix*

"Get out and come in!" The preacher replied after stepping out of his home. Dad had another idea.

"Can you marry us right here in the buggy?"

"Carlos, we should go in," urged Mother.

"No. We can do this right where we are," Dad insisted.

Mr. Newsome honored his request. J.E. Maxedon witnessed. Dad gave Mr. Newsome a dollar for his service, beckoned his horse to gitty-up, and they rode off to start their new life together.

Mother and Dad lived with my grandparents, James Henry "Jimmy" and Sarah Frances Maxedon Hendrix, on the Hendrix family farm in a tiny log cabin with two bedrooms, a living room with a fireplace and a kitchen. The house had cracks in the floor and no insulation. Daylight found its way inside, and they stuffed whatever they had into the cracks to keep the cold air out. Over time, they added space to the house and made improvements. They built a new kitchen and sealed the inside walls with 12-inch, painted planks. They installed weatherboard on the outside walls. It was close quarters for a new bride and groom, but they made do until they could move into their own home.

Dad helped my grandfather farm. About 70 acres of the Hendrix farm were tillable. The economy was bad, and tools were meager. Mules turned the soil, hoes kept the grass from taking over the crop and jo-blades cut ditch banks. Dad also worked at sawmills, cut timber and hauled logs — whatever job he could find. The pay was 50 cents a day or less, and he worked 10 to 12 hours a day. But Dad was grateful to have the skills for all types of work. Everyone knew that when Carlos Hendrix was on the job, the work would get done.

After a few years, my parents rented a small house close to the farm. Mother later told us that moving into their own home was one of the happiest days of her life. Mother was fond of my grandparents and appreciated their generosity, but my parents needed their own place.

In a few years, Dad bought his father's 170-acre farm with money saved from his Army pay and his mustering-out pay as a down payment. He financed the balance through Selmer Bank & Trust in Selmer, Tennessee.

On December 5, 1921, my oldest brother, James Hoover, was born. He was named after his paternal grandfather and my mother's maiden name. Dr. Ernest Smith delivered the baby at my parents' home.

Both Dr. Ernest and my father were skilled hunters, and they became hunting buddies. Dr. Ernest used an automatic shotgun. Dad just had a double-bar-reled shotgun. Usually, Dad had the most birds at the end of the day. He would tell us about finding 12 or 15 coveys on a hunt, and they killed as many as they could for the dinner table. They were competitive, which made their hunts more productive and fun.

Quail hunting's practical aspect was to put food on the table. My father talked about killing more than 400 birds in a season. He was an excellent shot, and he had some of the best-trained bird dogs around.

Carlos after a quail hunt

Being invited to go quail hunting with Carlos was a special, most welcomed invitation. Our family relished our meals of tender fried quail deliciously cooked by Mother. She added hot biscuits and gravy, creamed potatoes and coleslaw. We had quail two or three times a week for breakfast with fried eggs, gravy and biscuits with molasses and butter.

***

Our family grew. My sisters, Etta Faye and Sarah Roslyn, were born in 1924 and 1926.

Tragedy struck in 1929 when lightning hit Dad's barn and burned it to the ground. Dad was fortunate to free the mules from the burning barn, but he lost the harvested crops and his first car, a black T-model Ford. Our family and nearby neighbors drew the well dry attempting to put the fire out. It was a tremendous setback, and it took my family years to fully recover. Later that year, Black Tuesday heralded the beginning of the Great Depression when the stock market crashed in October. It was the worst depression the country had ever seen. My brother, Carlton Smith, was born that December.

I was born two years and three months later on April 2, 1932 — in the middle of the Great Depression. My parents led our family through those difficult times in the only way they knew. They worked hard, and they made their children work hard.

Heartache occurred when my younger sisters Johnnie Lenora and Peggy Sue died. Johnnie was almost two when she died of colitis. Peggy Sue died when she was seven months old. The cause was not determined.

The economy was terrible, but our family fared better than most. We had no money, but we had plenty of food and clean clothes. My mother prepared good, nutritious food and took great pride in feeding her hungry family after a long day's work. We had a big vegetable garden, and she canned the harvest and filled the cellar. She put potatoes in a big round hole under the shed and covered them with hay for the long winter. She dried apples and peaches during the summer and stored them for later. She prepared hominy and kraut and preserved many other foods.

This was many years before electricity reached our farm. Mother cooked our meals on an old wood stove. We raised the windows for a better night's sleep on the hotter nights.

My mother washed our clothes with a rub board, drew water from the well and heated it in kettles over an outdoor fire. She hung the wet clothes on an outdoor clothesline and starched and pressed them with an iron heated from the wood stove. She churned buttermilk by hand and made and mended our clothes with a pedal sewing machine.

We learned family values from my parents as we sat at the long, rectangular table in the kitchen. My father sat at the head; my mother sat at the other end. We children sat along each side, enjoying our food with lively family conversation. Mother had a big pail of milk beside her, and as we passed our glasses down the table, she filled and refilled them, and the life lessons continued.

***

In large farm families, the older children looked after the younger children while the parents worked. Because my younger sisters, Peggy and Johnnie, had died, I was the baby of the family three times. I was already six when my sister, Alice Nell, was born and 10 when my brother, Lyndell Ray, came along. I was in high school by the time they were in elementary school, and to a great extent, they grew up after I left the farm.

Carlton was a little older than me, but we were joined at the hip. Together, we shucked the corn, fed the hogs, milked the cows, plowed the fields and trained the stubborn bull yearlings to pull our slide. We relied on each other, but we fought at times, as any two boys would. We were close friends, but we were very different. I was much more competitive about our farm work. Carlton liked school, and his handwriting was near perfect. He told me many times that he wanted to go to college so he wouldn't have to work as hard. Eventually he did just that, becoming the first in our family to get a higher education. He had his eye on something other than picking cotton. Mother and Dad loved us the same, but treated us differently. Dad would ask me to help him break the crazy two-year-old mules, but not Carlton.

Hoover was 11 years older than me. If Dad was not around, Hoover gave us instructions as we made the crop or did chores before heading out to catch the school bus. My older sisters, Etta and Roslyn, practically reared me. They changed my diapers, watched over me to keep me safe as I played and made sure I did my share of work. They were responsible, never goofing off like Carlton and me. They learned to cook at a young age and

Carlton and Tom

could prepare a meal as well as Mother. They were the most reliable in the family and had a very mature attitude toward anything we did. Day after day, they picked 300 pounds or more of cotton. They were instrumental as I developed good work habits, and I owe them a debt of gratitude.

We were poor, but my father was generous at times. I remember being at home one day while my siblings were in school, when Dad brought home a battery-operated radio. As a five-year-old boy, I was awed by this strange brown box. I had never seen nor heard a radio before. With big eyes, I watched attentively as the radio man explained to Mother how to use it. There was no sound coming out of it when Dad and the radio man went outside and decided where to put the radio aerial. I didn't understand how a wire across our garden would emit sound. Then the radio man came back inside the house and turned a black knob on the radio. A voice and music started coming out of the box. I played with the knobs all day until my siblings came home. I had seen a cow give birth to a calf and a hundred other interesting things in my young life, but nothing compared to this.

I couldn't wait to show Carlton how it worked. By the end of the day, I was an expert at operating the radio. We were the only family in the neighborhood with one. Mother made one phone call to a neighbor to tell her that we had a new radio and soon everyone knew. We had a party line telephone with six other families so, of course, everyone on the party line was listening. We had so many visitors that Dad had to limit the visits because they were beginning to interfere with family life.

That radio changed our lives, giving us a glimpse of the big wide world, much like today's Internet and technology has dramatically changed our children's lives.

***

In 1930s rural West Tennessee, most farming was done with mules. Dad had bought his first pair of mules about a year after he was married.

Dad began teaching me how to work the mules when I was young.

"This mule can hurt or cripple you for life, so don't ever be in a position that he can kick you," Dad told me. "Always keep your eyes on his head. If he backs his ears, he is irritated and is apt to kick. A mule reacts to surprise, so call his name as you get close. Don't surprise him."

One of my responsibilities at the age of five, before I started school, was to sit on a tow sack filled with hay and drive two mules pulling the disc harrow across the field while my father cut ditch banks nearby. Dad made sure the mules I drove were gentle and predictable.

Tom, barefooted, plowing with mules

Carlton and I worked one plow together in the early days. One of us drove the pair of mules, and the other held the plow turning the soil. When we reached the end of the row, both of us helped turn the plow. When I was 12, I could do it myself. I geared-up a pair of mules and hooked them to a two-horse turning plow to prepare for planting. I walked barefoot 10 to 12 hours a day turning the soil. To free my hands to maneuver the big plow, I placed the lines around my back. It took a lot of concentration to keep the plow at a proper angle to turn the soil to a proper depth, and to keep the mules from misbehaving so they would march in a straight row.

As Carlton and I turned the soil with our plows, we unearthed little creatures. Red worms, grub worms and a variety of bugs would appear, and the birds would swarm down for their breakfast or lunch. The male black birds with their bright orange spots on their wings were my favorite to watch. The little killdeers ran faster than any of the other visiting birds. I called them the 30-mph birds. We even turned up beds of tiny mice with the plow, and the birds swooped down to grab them, which didn't make me happy.

Almost every day, as I walked barefoot behind the plow, I uncovered a snake and jumped two feet into the air. Occasionally, if I saw a poisonous-looking snake slithering across our path, I would stop plowing, grab a stick and kill it. The plowing days were long and took a lot of energy and concentration, but observing nature made them more interesting.

When the sun began to set, we called it a day, unhooked the mules from the plow and headed to the creek so they would get a big belly of water. We returned to the barn, removed their gear and bridles, fed them and turned them into the stable for a night's rest.

Then, Carlton and I would milk the cows and feed the rest of the stock. Routinely, our last stop would be the hog lot where we fed the hogs a big bucket of corn and two big buckets of water. After the hogs, we filled Mother's wood box by the stove in the kitchen. Then it was time to clean up for supper.

We all gathered around the dinner table, finding our special seats and chattering about what happened that day. It was a fun time. In most cases, our workday was a celebration. Dad and Mother praised us for jobs well done. Dad, especially, had a way of instilling pride in our accomplishments, which made us proud to share our successful day with the family.

A productive day required concentration and efficiency, and Dad expected a good report when we sat down for supper. He had high expectations, and he expected us to live up to those expectations. We gave him a work report at every evening meal. My father had plowed the fields many times, and he knew where the mules should be at the end of the day. We had to keep moving to accomplish the day's work so we could give a good report. We were, no doubt, competitive as a family, and we were challenged to see who could do the most work. It was a great lesson for us to take through life.

***

When I started school, I learned we had to get up early, especially in the winter months. We woke well before daylight to milk the cows and feed the stock. Then we walked a mile to catch the school bus, rain or sunshine, hot or cold. The old bus was a truck with a wooden box built with benches down each side and another in the middle. Bethel Springs School was only six miles from our house, but the trip took 45 minutes as the truck weaved its way over narrow roads on its route.

On warm days after school, Mother stopped us as we walked in the door.

"Change your clothes and put your shoes aside," she instructed.

And then we headed out the door, barefooted, to do our chores. We saved our shoes for school and church, although we would even go to school barefooted when it was warm.

***

Not all the farm work was fun, especially de-horning the cattle and castrating the young bulls. But it was necessary to protect the cows from hurting each other. The beef herd, more so than the dairy cows, grew large, long and sharp horns, and the bulls could be vicious. Dad gave us notice about the impending task before we left for school.

"Boys, I have a project I want you to help me with after school," he said.

"I'll have everything in place so we can complete the job this evening."

Thoughts of our evening project often crossed my mind at school that day. I was not looking forward to it. When it was time, we drove the cows into a stanchion that closed around their necks, just behind their heads. We cut the horns at the base, and blood spurted out onto the barn's wall. Then we applied medication. For each cow, it was over in a minute or two. But I had sympathy, especially for castrating the young bulls when I thought about how that would feel without a painkiller. To this day, I don't like the thought of it.

***

In the early years of his marriage, Dad worked for 50 cents a day. After he purchased his first pair of mules, he could earn more money. Our financial picture began to change when he decided to clear some bottomland to increase the tillable area for his row crops. Dad had four mules and enough equipment to haul logs for a much better income than most people in our part of the country. With this extra income, he could hire the help to clear the land.

Dad had more people than he could hire at 50 cents per day working 10 or 12 hours. They cleared the land with rudimentary tools like cross-cut saws. Two men pulled the saw back and forth for hours, cutting the trees to the ground. Then they sawed the tree into log lengths for the best prices. Dad had three or four saws running, with other people chipping the trees with sharpened axes to fell them to the desired spot. They also would cut off the tree limbs and treetops for firewood, piling and burning the brush.

Dad hauled the huge logs with his powerful mules to a nearby sawmill. After the clearing operation got underway, the income from the logs would more than pay his labor cost. It also helped pay the bank for the loan on the farm.

Dad made sure he matched the people to the work for which they were best suited to get the most done. He was a good leader with high expectations. He commanded the respect of the men because they knew he would not ask them for something he wouldn't do.

Even though they were making only 50 cents a day, it was a job that would put bread on a family's table, and not many jobs were available during the depression. For the men, it was great to help Carlos clear his land for more cropland because he was one of the few who had the extra money to hire people.

Listening to Dad tell this story about clearing the land, I realized that the tools we possess determine the wealth of our nation. If we improve our tools, we improve our productivity and standard of living. Back then, people worked long hours with axes or cross-cut saws, for low pay. Today's gas-powered chain saws are 30 or 40 times more productive, which means higher wages and a better standard of living. We owe the people of that time a debt of gratitude for the backbreaking work they did. We made progress with each generation to put us where we are today.

***

One of my fond memories was Dad hitching mules to the wagon for the 3.5-mile walk to Buena Vista Methodist Church. Mother and Dad would sit on the spring seat in the front of the wagon. We sat in the back on hay covered with a handmade quilt so we would not soil our church clothes. When we arrived at church, Dad chained the tongue of the wagon to a tree, took the bridles off the mules and gave tham a block of hay to eat.

He was an elder, and we arrived early in the winter months to build a fire to warm the church. He passed the collection plate for the congregation's dimes, quarters and occasional dollar bills. When Dad set the plate on the bench in front of the pulpit, he would contribute a couple of dollars, too. He wore his blue serge suit, the white shirt Mother had heavily starched and ironed and Florsheim shoes. My father was a well-dressed man, and both of my parents set good examples. I was proud of them.

Church was important; values were important. The way my father took pride in the way he wore his clothes was a lesson to me.

Buena Vista Methodist Church

Through the years, I made a point of following moral values and making a good impression by being well dressed.

***

Because we used mules so much in those days, it was important that we train a young pair of two-year-olds each year to prepare them for work on the farm or logging. A young mule not familiar with any part of the process fought the unfamiliar gear, hitches and wagons. After they settled down with the gear, we led them to the wagon, which was chained to a tree by the wagon tongue.

This is when things got exciting.

Maneuvering the wild mules beside the wagon tongue to hitch them took some time. The animals were 10 times bigger than we were, and that made it a real contest. With determination, we hitched them up and unchained the wagon from the tree. The mules lunged in every direction, trying to run away. Dad kept a tight grip on the lines, doing his best to control them, and I held a side line from the wildest mule to help Dad. In the first 10 or 15 minutes, the mules did whatever they could to break free. But they eventually settled down. After two or three hours, they began to behave themselves.

Carlos and his mules

After a week, the mules accepted their new way of life, and we could teach them commands: start and stop, go left or right, and back up. This took some time, but Dad and I were persistent. We wanted well-trained mules because it saved so much time when they responded to verbal commands. Hauling logs is where we did the fine tuning. We constantly moved in every direction as we bunched the logs. And our well-trained mules paid big dividends.

Mr. Kenneth Woods, who lived in Henderson about 20 miles from our farm, had a mule auction barn that was a sizeable operation. All the mules that men ran through the ring had big white tags and black numbers on their backs identifying them to their owners.

Most years, Dad had four to six well-trained mules in their prime about four or five years old. And most years, he had a pair to sell. Mr. Woods' mule auction was well attended and was the best place in our area to sell them. Mr. Woods knew my father's reputation, and he always looked forward to him attending the auction.

When the sale began, men in the center ring cracked whips to move the mules as they were shown and sold. Mr. Woods, with his booming voice, was the auctioneer, and he worked to get the best possible price. It would take only a couple of minutes to sell each one.

When Dad led his pair of mules into the ring, their bridles sparkled with fancy red tassels, and their hair shined with a silky gloss. He fed them a special sweet feed with molasses to give their coats a silky sheen. Mr. Woods stepped into the ring and announced to the crowd that Carlos Hendrix had a pair of his fine mules trained to understand verbal commands from his logging operation. After the lively banter, Carlos' pair sold for around $700 — a prime price.

I knew my parents loved me, though my father never outwardly expressed it. I would hear him talk about me when our neighbors would come to visit some nights, and I pretended to sleep under the table.

"When I am breaking young mules to work, I had just as soon have Tom helping me as any grown man," Dad said to his company. "He always seems to be at the right place at the right time. And, he would not miss the excitement — the mules bucking, acting crazy, trying to run away is what he likes most. If we have a mean unruly cow, Tom will milk her, regardless."

The affirmation let me know that my father was proud of me. These conversations inspired me to take a gutsy approach to life. I hauled logs with my father and worked the mules with mule talk. The neighbors came to watch our mules perform, listening to my commands. I took great pride in being what people referred to as a good mule skinner. We had great respect for our mules.

We were tough but fair with great expectations. Certain tones in our voice meant different things to them, and they knew when we expected great things.

***

We never had a dull moment growing up on the farm, looking after the stock and hauling logs in the winter. Sure, at times, I wondered why we had to work all of the time. It would have been nice to play more like some of my friends. But, even with all of the work, we were a happy family with a lot of laughter in our home. And when we did play, Dad made us earn it.

Carlton and I did not have a bicycle like some of the other kids, and we wanted one. One morning in early fall as we were digging sweet potatoes, Carlton made a plan.

"Tom, why don't you ask Dad for a bicycle?"

So, at our noon meal when we were all relishing Mother's good food, I obliged my brother.

"Dad, Carlton and I want a bicycle," I said.

Everything fell quiet, but finally, the answer came.

"If you boys will continue to work hard getting these sweet potatoes out of the ground, we might get you a bicycle."

Carlton and I became a couple of moles going after those potatoes that afternoon. As promised, Dad felt we had worked hard, and on Saturday we went to Selmer to get a bicycle.

Because we did not have a truck to get the bicycle home, Dad asked one of our neighbors to let me ride to Bethel Springs in the back of his pickup with the bike. I was to ride it the rest of the way home. The only problem was that I didn't know how to ride a bicycle, and we lived five miles away. But I persuaded my father that I would learn and manage. Before long, through trial and error, I could stay upright. Everything went well until the bicycle chain caught my pant leg. I was wearing my best church clothes. To free my pants from the chain, I had to cut them loose. So I took my little knife out of my pocket and cut a big round hole in my pants. I knew Mother would not be happy, but I gave her the piece of cut fabric, and she mended my pants. They were ready for church on Sunday. Carlton and I had a new bicycle, and we were happy.

***

Good fortune came our way around 1942 when I was 10. Mr. Theo Whitehurst had a tract with about 1 million board feet of virgin pine timber on rugged terrain, and he asked Dad to haul the logs to the sawmill. Mr. Theo knew Dad was the perfect man for the difficult job, and Dad wanted to make the most of the opportunity. Mr. Theo paid a premium to harvest the trees from the steep hills because he had a high-speed sawmill to cut the logs into wide widths to sell at a premium.

Dad knew mules would have a difficult time pulling the heavy loads over the steep hills, so he bought two 1934-model Ford trucks. He stripped off the factory truck beds and installed specially designed beds to accommodate the large logs. He also modified the trucks for the lowest gearing system available. The loaded trucks would move slowly up the steep hills with a heavy load of logs. This was a first for that time. In fact, Mr. Theo doubted that Dad's trucks would be able to handle the tough terrain.

Dad hired Horry Carothers as a driver at $1.25 per day. Horry was the most skilled truck driver Dad could find. He was honest and dependable, and he promised to take care of the trucks with regular maintenance. The trucks worked well. While Horry drove to the sawmill, the logging crew loaded another truck that was ready for the haul when he returned.

Dad moved the timber and made some much needed money. He could see the sun breaking through the clouds and felt that his family's hard work was coming to fruition. The large tract of timber changed our financial situation quickly. Dad understood logging, and Mr. Theo knew Dad would keep his sawmill running with plenty of logs to make it profitable for everyone.

The logging operation was successful and helped our family immensely. After working and saving for several months, Dad walked into the Selmer Bank & Trust in his bib overalls to pay the farm loan off in full. The banker handed him his deed and shook his hand. Dad was free and clear of debt, and the entire family celebrated because we all had a hand in paying off the farm. I am so grateful to my family for having an optimistic, can-do attitude, which they passed to their children. A wonderful, can-do attitude that helps you overcome hardship is quite a gift.

***

In 1943, Dad built a new barn, which he desperately needed. In 1945, Dad fulfilled my mother's dream of a new home. They worked on the plans for a long time to make sure it fit their budget and their family. Homes were not financed back then. Abner Garrison agreed to build the house for $600, and Dad, being in the timber business, provided the lumber he had been setting aside to keep the cost down. Dad had a special grader with a scoop that was pulled by our mules to grade the space for the house. The site for the house had been a pig lot for many years, and the ground was as hard as a rock. The carpenters arrived the following week to stake out the house for its foundation. The project was underway.

The new Hendrix house was only 1,000 or 1,200 square feet, but it was the nicest home in our Buena Vista community. Our neighbors watched the construction with interest and came to see Mother and Dad's completed new home. It had modern conveniences, but no electricity.

Dad bought a new Ford tractor. It had two 14-inch turning plows, a disc harrow and a cultivator to plow the row crops. It changed our farm life overnight.

With the tractor's headlight, we could run 24 hours per day in the spring, turning the soil and preparing the fields for planting our row crops. I drove the tractor after school many times until midnight, and then another member of the family relieved me. It was a new day on the Hendrix farm.

Most of our neighbors had not purchased a tractor by that time, and it gave us an opportunity to earn extra money preparing their fields for crops. We kept the tractor running every hour possible to offset its cost. I could not get enough of it. I practiced my driving skills and raced to change the gears as I turned at the end of a row. It made planting the crops a lot more fun.

The tractor gave us more time to haul logs, and that increased the family's cash flow. With more cash, Dad eyed a new, light blue, top-of-the-line Chevrolet with all the extras. It was a beautiful car, and it drove like a dream. The new car gave us more room for our big family, and we were proud to drive it into town or church.

Dad's tractor worked so well on the farm that he decided to pull our big log wagons to haul more logs. Our new tools gave us a more productive way of life. All of a sudden, our farm was less labor intensive. We did not cut back on our hours, but we were getting a lot more done.

***

Dad wanted us to grow up to be responsible people, and he gave us as much responsibility as we could handle. As we grew, he increased our responsibilities. Mother would sometimes object.

"Carlos, you are going to get those boys killed," she said.

"They understand danger when they see it," he replied. "They are learning responsibility."

Keeping wood cut and the kitchen box full at all times for the fireplace was a job for Carlton and me. We cut most of our wood from timber on our farm on Saturdays, in all kinds of weather. On Saturdays during the spring, one of our jobs was to cut off our ditch banks. With this assignment, Dad gave us each a jo-blade to cut away the bushes on the banks and a file to keep the blades sharpened. Dad bought each of us a pair of gumboots to wear to wade through the briars and the water as we cut the lower brush. The gumboots also protected us from snakes.

Once when I was in the seventh grade, I decided to sharpen both of our jo-blades with our file. When I finished sharpening Carlton's blade, I handed it to him and walked past as he made a swing at a small bush. The blade cut through the bush and then into the back of my foot, cutting into my bone. Blood began gushing out of my boot.

Carlton gasped when he saw what happened.

"Tom, I think I am going to faint," he said.

"This is no time to faint," I screamed. "Run, get the tractor and take me out of this field. Hurry!"

I was losing blood fast. Carlton returned in about 10 minutes, and I climbed onto the tractor. When we got to the house, Mother and Dad were returning from town and, hurriedly, took me to the Webb-Williamson Hospital in Jackson. I needed surgery and stayed overnight. The doctor gave me a pair of crutches, and I got so good on the crutches that I could jump off our three-foot stage at school and land on one foot, not missing a step. In fact, I liked to show-off using my skills with the crutches. I was on crutches for four to six weeks as I healed.

***

Living on the farm was an adventure. I liked the life because we always had something to look forward to. We produced our own food, as did many other rural families in the South. We only needed to buy the basics. For everything else, we depended on our vegetable garden, fruit trees and livestock. We took corn to the gristmill for our cornmeal. We grew peanuts and picked them in early fall for a family treat during the winter months. We enjoyed watermelons during the summer.

Dad was well-known for his big Stone Mountain watermelons. Some were 50 to 70 pounds, and they were the best-tasting watermelons you could put in your mouth. We could hardly wait to pull that first watermelon each season. When we did, we put the word out to the neighbors and our cousins in the city to come over on weekends and help us celebrate "watermelon time."

Dad sliced them into large pieces — more than we could eat. We sat in a large circle, told fun stories and laughed heartily as watermelon juice ran down our chins. Dad was a gracious host. He always put a Stone Mountain watermelon in the back of their car or truck as our friends and family headed home.

The melons also were a big cash crop. During the season, Dad approached us early in the morning. "Boys, let's go pull a load of watermelons."

We headed to the field, and Dad walked along the hills thumping melons and listening for the sound only a ripe melon can make. If it had the ripe sound, he pulled it from the vine and turned it over to the opposite side, which was white. The white sides made it easier for us to spot the pulled melons as we moved through the field.

It was quite a workout picking up melons from the ground, carrying them across the field and loading them into the truck. Then we drove to Selmer and sold them. Dad cultivated regular customers who expected him on the court square with his tasty melons during each season. Dad walked into businesses on Main Street. He told them the price, and they paid him. He delivered his melons like delivering milk or eggs. And he saved some seeds from the prized Stone Mountain watermelons for the next season, keeping the tradition going.

When fall came around, we got excited for another eventful and busy activity: hog-killing day. We picked a cold day to prevent meat spoilage and invited our neighbors to help with the process. To meet the needs of our large family, we killed three or four hogs. Each weighed 300 pounds or more. First, we built a roaring fire underneath three big black iron pots with water drawn from the well. We heated the water to a temperature hot enough to scald a hog's carcass. That allowed us to clean and scrape off the hair, producing a hide free of germs.

Dad came out of the house with his .22 rifle. He knew exactly where to aim to bring the hog down without a squeal. We created a production line. Someone came behind my father and slit the hog's throat so the blood would drain. Someone else slit the hog's back legs and attached a single tree hook behind its tendons to raise and lower it in and out of the barrel of hot water. The carcass remained in the hot water a few minutes. Then we scraped the hog's hide clean, removing the hair with a sharp butcher knife. We hoisted the carcass back into the air and removed the internal organs, separating out the edible parts. If done properly, there was little to discard.

After we gutted the hogs, we moved the carcasses to a large, sturdy table where we cut them up into hams, shoulders, tenderloins and smaller cuts. The shoulders and hams made their way to the smoke house to be salted down to cure for a period of time depending on the weather. The salt preserved the meat so it could be eaten throughout the year. Dad made sure the hams were preserved, but not too salty.

One of the good parts of hog-killing day was the interaction and conversation. Laughter filled the air as we worked and shared news of the community, giving us a chance to catch up on the neighborhood gossip. Mother and my two older sisters prepared a noon meal, pan frying fresh pork tenderloin slices with plenty of baked biscuits, vegetables, pies and cakes. At the end of the long day, when all the meat was cut for its intended use, we gave a generous portion to our neighbors for their help.

Another annual fall activity was the family hunt for chestnuts and muscadines. It was a challenge to climb the tall trees and shake the muscadines to the ground. After we filled our buckets with muscadines, we filled our tow sacks with chestnuts.

At the end of summer, our family cut and stripped sorghum to take to the sorghum mill to make molasses. The mill operator pressed and ground the stalks to extract the juice. A mule pulled the wheel in a circular motion as the stalks were fed to the crusher. Then the juice was funneled to big vats and cooked until the syrup was thick.

I always enjoyed going to the mill and watching the mule walk in circles as the juice was extracted from the stalks. It was a special treat to dip the piece of the cane stalk into the vat of hot syrup and taste the new molasses. In some years, we would make 20 or 30 gallons of molasses. We gave some to the mill operator and some to family members and friends. We had molasses every morning for breakfast, with Mother's hot biscuits, as an important source of iron.

***

Our farm was like a big zoo — something different each day. When I opened my eyes in the morning, after a sound night's sleep, I would wonder if the cow had her new calf. I would jump out of bed, pull on my overalls, and run to the barn barefooted as fast as I could to hopefully see the newborn. It was a great way to start the day.

Sometimes, we assisted with the birth. Dad always kept a bull or two, and nearby farmers would bring their cows for the bulls to breed. It was an exciting time, and we learned a little about the birds and bees.

One day, when Carlton and I were six and eight years old, our family went to see my grandparents in Stantonville. Grandmother Hoover gave Carlton and me two White Rock hens. Later, Mother gave us the eggs to set the hens for baby chickens. When they hatched, we had 30 or more chickens. We looked out for our chickens, making sure they had the best food available, and soon they were full grown.

We sold them for $7 and bought a female calf from our neighbor. She later had a calf, and our herd expanded. After a few years, we had a pasture full of calves and cows. Because we wanted to show them at the county fair for a blue ribbon, we sold all we had and divided the money to buy two heifers that could win the judging contest. Carlton and I went our own way to see who could manage for the best result. I guess I got lucky. At every show I entered, I won a blue ribbon. I won Junior Champion at the West Tennessee State Fair and received the Grand Champion award in showmanship for the Mid-South Fair in Memphis. My picture with my cow was in the Memphis *Commercial Appeal* newspaper.

Unfortunately, our cows contracted Brucellosis or Bang's disease, which affected their reproduction and forced us to sell them for slaughter prices. If they had not contracted the disease, we could have sold them for maybe $1,500 or $2,000.

"This is a lesson for you boys," my father told us. "Regardless of how hard you work, sometimes bad luck will come along for a sad ending. I want you to pick up the pieces and move on."

And that was the end of it.

***

Electricity came to rural McNairy County, the Buena Vista community and our farm in the late 1940s. I remember construction crews erecting power lines and hearing people talk about wiring their homes. We could hardly wait

Tom won the Grand Championship Showman Award at the Mid-South Fair with Brampton Beauty Mae.

to get our house wired and turn on the lights. We were glad to set the coal oil lamps aside.

Our house was wired quickly, and as soon as the power was turned on, we had glowing lights at night and a new humming refrigerator. The country was changing rapidly, especially for country folks.

Shortly after we had electricity, Dad talked to Mother about her stove.

"Lena, you have cooked a lot of meals on that wood stove, but it's time for an electric stove."

"Carlos, I'll make do with the wood stove," Mother replied. "We don't need to spend any more money."

But Dad went to Selmer and came back with a new electric stove. And Mother was so proud of it. She no longer had to build a fire in the old wood stove.

"It's the best thing to ever come into my kitchen," she said.

Carlton and I were just as excited; we no longer had to cut the wood for the old wood stove.

***

As the years ticked by, our favorite season was always Christmastime, which we celebrated much differently than families do today. As we picked cotton each fall, we kept an eye out for that perfectly shaped cedar tree. We had several in mind when it was time for our Christmas tree hunt.

Decorating the tree was family fun. Rose and Etta made the star for the top of the tree out of silver paper. We popped popcorn and ran a thread through the kernels to make popcorn chains for around the tree. We had one package of foil icicles, and we saved them from year to year. Mother made artificial snow from starch. My sisters cut out paper ornaments and colored them in Christmas colors. When we finished, we were proud of our handiwork.

Mother made Christmas week special at the dining table with a big four-layer coconut cake. I don't exactly know how she went about it, but it was the best coconut cake you have ever eaten — and we looked forward to it. Dad went hunting and came home with his coat pockets full of quail.

We always had a big fire in the fireplace, and we gathered around for good family conversation, poking fun at each other. We parched peanuts in the stove and kept them in a basket by the fireplace. We popped popcorn over the fireplace with a screen wire popper and used a metal popper if we wanted buttered popcorn. The screen wire popper was great for popcorn balls.

We celebrated Christmas as a family, without gifts under the tree. Mother and Dad bought oranges, apples and stick candy to fill our Christmas bags. Later, even when we could afford gifts, we didn't buy them because we had already set our habits.

I remember my parents would buy me a new pair of Unionalls — the little striped kind that Mother and Dad would have bought anyway. I would look through the pockets hoping I would find a knife. It was important to me because I did all kinds of whittling, creating whistles from sticks that would make funny sounds. I also made slingshots out of forked branches from bushes and an old inner tube. And I kept my eyes open for the perfect slingshot rocks, knowing the right size and shape would improve my accuracy. On the farm, I did not need store-bought toys because I could make own. Making toys was as much fun as playing with them.

So I was truly thankful and proud of my knife if I was fortunate enough to get one. Many times each day, I would feel my little knife with appreciation, but I would always lose it before the next Christmas.

I am convinced our Christmas was as much fun, celebrating Christ's birthday, as it would have been if we had spent hundreds of dollars on presents. I watch my grandchildren tearing into their gifts, one after another, and wonder if they are as proud of them as I was of my little knife. I always enjoyed the way we celebrated Christmas by spending time together around the fireplace and eating popcorn balls and parched peanuts with lively family conversation.

***

As I grew older, my days on the farm were becoming numbered. Soon it was time for my high school graduation. With my parents in the audience, I sat on the stage with my classmates and listened to the class valedictorian give a speech. Then we filed past our principal, who presented our diplomas as a scroll wrapped with a blue ribbon. The class left the auditorium to the well wishes of family and friends.

My family and I crowded in the car and headed home, chatting about the graduation exercise. Everyone was cheerful, but I was uncomfortable. I worried that someone would ask to see my diploma because all I had was a piece of paper wrapped with a blue ribbon. I did not have enough credits to graduate, but the school had been kind enough to allow me to join my class' graduation exercise. To my relief, no one in my family asked to see my blank piece of paper. They had no idea that I had not graduated. And I never told them.

I am still ashamed of myself for not graduating from high school. I don't think I have a good excuse because I certainly had the intelligence.

My family, like many other farm families, focused on getting the work done and making sure bread was on the table. As they saw it, it did not require much education to drive the mules, milk the cows or do rudimentary work. I am sure my parents wanted us to do well in school, or we would not have gone. But the focus was always on taking responsibility to get the work done. I was good at what was emphasized — farm work and hauling logs.

My father certainly was not an academic person. He attended a one-room school through the third grade. My mother had an eighth-grade education and taught school for a while before she married Dad.

My parents thought our lives would be much the same as theirs: living a simple farm life and rearing a good family. They did not expect their children to attend college, and if we did, it would be our responsibility to pay for it. My father expected me to stay on the farm and haul logs for extra money.

"Tom," he told me. "If you will stay with me, I will guarantee you will have more than anyone in your high school class."

My parents operated from their life experience to give us the best life possible. Looking back, I wish they had emphasized good grades as much as honorable work. Decisions have consequences. I have paid a steep price for not having a solid education. I only read one book as a child, and that was in high school. We never had a newspaper on our doorstep. We never read much. Later, I became an avid reader to learn what I needed so I could reach my goals.

My father had strong feelings about certain things. He believed work was an honorable thing to do, and he expected his children to do a lot of it. He would say many times that young boys are like young mules that get mean every time you don't keep them busy. He certainly kept us busy.

He taught us that you could have anything you want in life if you are willing to work for it with a good attitude. He wanted us to see the good of work and to develop a positive attitude toward our work. He wanted us to see work as the best way to live a good life.

My father also taught us that to be successful we also must be honest — even when it hurts. Your word was your bond.

One evening when we were having dinner, Dad told us about Mr. Wilson. My father paid Mr. Wilson $20 too much by mistake, back when people worked for 50 cents a day. Two or three weeks later, Mr. Wilson rode his mule to our house to talk to my father.

"Carlos, you paid me $20 too much," he said.

"Jim, are you sure I gave you $20 too much?"

"Oh yes, Carlos. I counted the money a hundred times. You paid me $20

Back row, from left, Tom, Etta, Carlos, Carlton, Lena, Hoover,
and front row, Roslyn and Alice hugging Ray

too much. Here is your $20. I simply couldn't sleep a wink knowing I had your $20."

When he finished his story, Dad turned to us to make his point.

"This is the kind of honesty I want in this family," he said. "Being honest and sacrificing when you must will serve you well over time."

The lessons I learned on the farm and across the kitchen table were the best part of my education. They gave me confidence and the determination to tackle many projects later in my life — from knocking on doors from 8 a.m. to 8 p.m. selling Bibles so I could pay for college to starting a national business from scratch with borrowed money. My father made work fun for me, and for that, I will always be grateful. Through the years, I never saw myself working. I saw myself on a mission to reach my goals. I was a problem solver, and I don't know if I would have become an entrepreneur without my farm experience.

Growing up in the Hendrix home was priceless.

Chapter 2

First Jobs off the Farm

"If you put your heart and soul into your work, people will take notice."

The year I supposedly graduated from high school was the year I told my father that I would like to be responsible for making the crop. I had plowed the fields and helped plant the crops all my life, so I knew how to make it work. I also knew my father was preoccupied with hauling logs and that he might give in to my request.

Tom, 18, a senior in high school

"Do you think you can be successful farming?" He asked.

"If you will agree for me to make all the decisions," I countered. "And I will tell you upfront that I will not plow as much as you do because in a lot of cases it's unnecessary."

My response gave him pause as to whether I could make a successful crop, but he finally replied.

"It is all yours. But, you had better not let the family down."

In my high school agriculture class, I learned that most farmers plowed too often. The only reason to plow was to control the grass. It did not make the corn grow. We didn't have chemicals for grass control, and we had never heard of no-till. Plowing less enabled me to complete other work while saving fuel.

I liked being in charge, making the decisions to carry out my plans to reduce cost and produce the best crop ever. I worked long hours because I did not have much help. My younger sister and brother were still too young. I hired help only when absolutely necessary. We planted cotton and corn and some truck crops for our own use like peas, potatoes, peanuts and watermelons.

At times, Dad came in from logging and walked through the fields to check up on me.

"Tom, don't you think you should plow this field?"

I explained the plow-less idea again. He accepted my answer because he had promised not to interfere, but he continued to hold me responsible for the outcome. He knew I would put my heart and soul into being successful. The weather that year was decent. The crop turned out well and cost less to produce. I was happy with my first business project. From that point on, making the crop was considered my family responsibility, but with no compensation.

However, I was anxious to earn some money of my own. Other than Dad's cotton-picking bonus, picking cotton for a neighbor or peeling crossties for a local sawmill, I never had an opportunity to earn money. The Hendrix house had no money for the children to spend as they wished.

After finishing the crop project, Dad asked me to help him haul logs. He told me he would pay me $20 a week or $4 a day. Some weeks I got $20, and some weeks I didn't get a paycheck. We worked long hours, almost from sunup until sundown in all kinds of weather. We seldom stopped for breaks. We hauled logs with one extra person, and we would haul 20 or more loads a day.

We had four mules and two heavy-constructed wagons with truck tires pulled by a Ford tractor that took them back and forth from the nearby sawmill. Dad drove the tractor with the logs to the mill, unloaded them quickly and returned for another load. The person we hired snaked the logs up to the wagon with two mules that would pull for a short distance and rest. With help from our bay mule, Belle, I loaded the logs onto the wagon and boomed them tightly for a secure trip.

Belle weighed more than 1,200 pounds, and she was highly trained. We did not need lines to load the wagon — it was all by voice command. She worked on the opposite side of the wagon from where I stood, hooked to a single tree with two chains attached to her collar. I ran a chain over the wagon to hook into a circle chain that held the logs for Belle to pull onto the wagon. Once loaded, I commanded her to back up as I pulled the chain back for another log. We did this all day. Many times, when we had extra-large logs on top of the load, I ran around the wagon to give Belle some extra help by swinging down on the chain to give her better traction. In some cases, Belle pulled with her front feet off the ground while dirt flew from her back feet. Neighbors often came to watch me handle the mule with no lines, and I always made it worth their trip.

We worked fast and loaded the logs by the time Dad returned from the sawmill with his empty wagon. I showed him where I wanted the wagon placed to receive the next load. I pulled the pin from the hitch on the empty wagon and dropped it into the hitch of the loaded wagon when Dad was in position. Then he took off for the sawmill with another load of logs. We raced against time all day to keep that wagon loaded.

My father was always in a hurry with a don't-waste-a-minute type of attitude. One time, as we boomed the loaded logs on the wagon with a heavy chain and big circle hook, we moved too fast.

"Throw the chain over the wagon," Dad commanded.

"Move back so it doesn't hit you on the head," I said.

"Throw the chain!" He bellowed.

I threw the chain.

"Throw the chain under the wagon so I can boom the logs!" I hollered.

Dad did not respond. I walked around the wagon and found him lying on the ground, unconscious, with a big knot from the circle hook on his head. I was worried, but once he came to, I knew he was fine. It was a funny sight, although it took us some time before we both were able to laugh about it.

***

I enjoyed the logging work, but I was determined to make more money. I never dated. I had clean clothes, but they weren't stylish. With no car and no money, girls were out of the picture. A higher paying job could change that.

So I looked for other opportunities. My friend, Ray Tull, went to work in Peoria, Illinois, after high school at Caterpillar making $75 a week. When Ray came back for a visit, I asked him if he thought I could get a job at Caterpillar.

"All you have to do is to turn in your application," Ray said. "They like hard-working Tennessee boys."

Ray also said he was living with the Wilton Isbell family who were from McNairy County. He paid them $12 a week for room and board and a packed lunch for work, and he felt sure we both could live with them. I was excited. It was an opportunity to make real money — the kind of money that could get me a new car. I told Ray I would join him in Peoria the following Sunday.

I told my mother right away that I would be leaving for Peoria and gave her the details about the Caterpillar opportunity and living with Ray and the Isbell family. I hoped she would soften up my father. I was wrong.

"Tom, you can't do this," she said. "Your father will never approve of your going to Peoria, leaving him with the logging."

"Well, I'm leaving with or without his permission," I responded. "It's time for me to start a new life with the freedom to make my own decisions to reach my goals. And very soon, I'll be driving a new automobile."

"Tom, I wish you would get that out of your mind for now."

My mother was the peacemaker in the family, and she didn't want any disagreements between Dad and me. My father and I were close, but he was a determined person. At that time, people thought you weren't a man until you were 21. Times were changing, though. And many younger people — myself included — did not buy into that. With industrialization, we could get a nonfarm job that paid more money and gave us the freedom to go our own way. My father knew he could not compel me to stay with him if I decided to leave, and he knew I was a determined young man.

The following weekend, Dad and I went to Selmer for groceries, which gave me a chance to make some last-minute preparations for my trip to Peoria. We drove our flatbed truck, and before we headed home, I asked Dad to stop by a small department store to pick up something I had purchased. I went inside, returned with a big black suitcase and tossed it in the back of the truck. We started out of town without a word between us.

It was a long while before Dad broke the silence.

"Son, I would about as soon see your casket as that suitcase."

"Dad, I will take care of myself and do my best to be successful."

We didn't say much else for the rest of the trip home. And, I still have the black suitcase. I can't make myself throw away such an important piece of my life history.

We did not harbor ill feelings, just regrets. I did not want to harm my relationship with my father. We were alike in many ways, and we were a good team. I was young, full of energy, strong enough for heavy work and motivated to efficiently mastermind the logging operation. I hated to leave because I was key to his logging operation, but I knew there was never going to be a good time. After I left, he hired two people to replace me, which was frustrating for him. With my take-charge attitude, Dad had no concerns about the loading operation. With the new hires, he had to be more involved with the details of their work, taking the fun out of what was a smooth-running, profitable operation. The new guys worked with their hands better than their minds, creating all kinds of mistakes and inefficiencies. Even the big bay mule didn't cooperate well.

Several people from our area migrated north for jobs that paid much more. I became one of them — fortunate to catch a ride to Peoria with a McNairy County family visiting relatives.

The Isbell family welcomed me with open arms, confirming the boarding fee of $12 a week and offering to provide my lunch for work. The Isbells lived in a poor neighborhood marked by small homes covered with inexpensive brick siding. They lived inside one of the smaller houses in an upstairs apartment with a small living room, two small bedrooms and a small kitchen. Mr. Isbell's brother lived downstairs. Mrs. Isbell was a decent cook and served plenty of food. They were kind, helpful people. Mr. Isbell was a chain smoker.

He had a cigarette in his mouth most of the time, and the smoke made a yellow streak on his mouth and cheek. He died early in life.

The day after I arrived in Peoria, I headed to the Caterpillar plant to find a job. This was quite an experience for a farm boy from West Tennessee. Everything seemed bigger than life. The buildings were tall, and people bustled about. I joined a line of men waiting to fill out applications for work, and before too long, someone called my name for a short interview. I was hired. I learned the details of the job and found out I had to join the union. The dues were deducted from my weekly paycheck. The company also deducted the cost of safety shoes from my paycheck. But I was looking at $75 a week, and that was big money.

My first job assignment at Caterpillar was the burr bench. I shaved off the rough edges from the metal pieces after they were cut into their proper size. My foreman put a lot of emphasis on production, and I had no idea how difficult it would be to meet his expectations. But within a few days, I could finish a shift's worth of work in two hours. The union steward told me to slow down and pace myself so I would finish the work in the allotted time. I found his instructions strange, especially since I was reared to find a way to do my work for the most efficiency. His instructions flew in the face of my competitive nature and took the fun out of the job.

The union steward was not my boss, so I ignored him. I worked at my natural pace and finished each day in two hours. But the union had another crazy rule that prohibited you from sitting down in the workplace, whether you were finished with your task or not. The idea was to look busy. I figured I could have a seat when I finished, but I was wrong. I found myself in a whole new world that was far different than Dad's farm.

The thing that struck me the most was the union's attitude toward work. The union wanted you to do as little as possible for as much as the company would pay. This was completely different from what I had been taught. The union negotiated with the company to keep production numbers low. Maximizing efficiency was never mentioned. Work was no longer an honorable concept that would make you proud. This was not a competition to see who could get the most done. The work ethic I learned on the farm did not apply here.

I did my work my way and simply killed time until the whistle blew to send me home. I watched the people around me slowly plod through their shift with no enthusiasm. I thought about Caterpillar paying me $75 a week for two hours of work per day, passing the extra cost to the consumer. It made no sense.

**

My work experience at Caterpillar was not all negative. I enjoyed getting to know my coworkers, and I liked my superior. I really liked the pay and the amount I was saving — my car was almost in reach. But I thought about the person I might become if I worked there for a lifetime and about how I might move up in the company. I did not see an exciting future. I knew this was a temporary job; working at Caterpillar would not satisfy my appetite.

I noticed a high-rise parking garage downtown with young men parking cars. I asked for a job and was hired to start the next day. I worked the 8 a.m. to 2 p.m. shift before heading to Caterpillar for the 3 p.m. shift. I left Caterpillar at 11 p.m. and headed home for some sleep. At the garage, I earned $1.35 an hour for six days a week, and I made about $50 a week. We also received tips for good service, and I think I made more tips than anyone.

I enjoyed the work. It was fun driving newer cars and testing my driving skills. The job appealed to my competitive nature. We drove the cars as high as six floors up. When we arrived at a parking space, we cracked the side door and backed into the space at a high rate of speed. We knew we would be fired on the spot if we scratched a fender. Then we hopped out and wrote down the parking space number so we could locate the car at the end of the day. Management would not tolerate mistakes. It created confusion and delayed the customer. The standing orders were simple: Don't scratch the car, and keep your facts straight so you can find it again.

After we parked a car, we rode a belt that took us quickly back to the first floor to get another car. It was a busy place, and it was fun to compete against the other boys in the garage to see who could park the most cars and earn the most tips. I was full of enthusiasm and looked forward to going to work. I smiled for customers and helped them any way I could, which resulted in better tips. I learned that a little Southern charm and a good attitude went a long way.

***

With both jobs, I took home $125 or more per week. I saved most of what I earned, and my new car was coming into focus. Ray bought a green 1936 Ford from an older couple who had kept it in storage. The car had not been cranked for several years, but it looked good and seemed reliable. He knew I was eager to get an automobile.

"Tom, let me sell you my Ford," he said.

I bought it on the spot for $300, counting out the bills for Ray.

"I want to road test this new purchase," I told him. "I'm making a visit to Tennessee this weekend. Want to come along?"

After our Friday shift, we set out on the highway. About 25 miles out of Peoria, the oil indicator light flashed red. We stopped and added two quarts. The indicator light flashed again 30 miles later, and we stopped and added more. The car was a lemon. Ray was just as surprised as I was.

The challenge now was to make it home to Tennessee. We bought a five-gallon can of used oil to cut costs and speed up our trip. We drove all night — straight to the house of my brother-in-law, Bob Kennedy. Bob was a used-car salesman, and I wanted to sell him the car before daylight. But he was too smart.

"Does it use any oil?" He asked.

I told him the truth.

I took it to the Ford dealership in Selmer and found a new 1951 Ford, which was exactly what I wanted. I did not know anything about negotiating, so they probably got the best of me. After my trade-in, I had enough money for a down payment, but I needed Dad's signature because of my age. He agreed, but let me know in no uncertain terms that I would lose the car if I missed a payment.

With my new car, finally, it was time for that first date. I figured Mt. Gilead

Baptist Church in our community would be a good place to look. I spotted Ann Mitchell, a beautiful girl with a great personality. She was probably 17. She came from a well-respected, conservative family, and she was reared to go to church regularly. She agreed to a date, but said her father only would approve a double date. I didn't like that idea, so I drove to her house to reason with him.

When I arrived, her father, Marshall Mitchell, invited me into the living room.

"Ann is young," he said. "I think it's best for her to go on double dates for a while."

"I understand your concern for Ann, sir. But you know my family, and you know my father quite well. If you give us your permission, I assure you that Ann will be respected."

"No," Mr. Mitchell said. "It has to be a double date."

"Mr. Mitchell, Ann will return home safely."

He looked me straight in the eye.

"Alright. I will approve, but young man, you had better behave yourself."

I thanked him and assured him he could count on me to keep my word. Ann was ready, so we left the house quickly. We had a great time and went on several dates together. I came home every three weeks or so. Dating was important to me. Three other boys working in Peoria gave me $20 each for a ride home, which paid my expenses with a little profit.

***

My first winter in Peoria brought a record snowfall. It piled high on the sides of streets — a thick blanket of white covering everything. I became tired of snow and anxious for spring weather. All my life, I helped make a crop, turning the soil to plant seed. When spring did arrive, I thought about my farm days and decided I wanted to help someone make a crop rather than park cars as a second job. I told Ray I would put in a good word if he wanted my parking job. He questioned how I would find farm work, but I had a plan.

Farms with vast fields and crops as far as you could see covered the landscape on the outskirts of Peoria. Huge tractors with big equipment tilled the land, and I thought about how much fun it would be to drive them. Early the next morning I left the house and headed for the fields. My plan was to pull over when I saw a tractor plowing a field, hail the driver and tell him I was a farm boy from West Tennessee who wanted to help him make a crop.

"I can work from 8 a.m. until 2 p.m., giving me enough time to reach Cat for the second shift," I said to the first farmer I saw. "I'll work for two weeks, and then you decide if it was worth a paycheck."

"You mean you will work two weeks, and I can decide whether to pay you?" the farmer asked.

"Yes, exactly," I said. "And if I don't earn the pay, you shouldn't pay me."

"If I needed someone, I would hire you."

I thanked him and walked back to my car. The encounter was encouraging. I knew I'd be driving a tractor as soon as I found someone who needed help. It was just a matter of time.

I drove down the highway a couple of miles to another running tractor. I stopped my car, walked across the field and found a farmer with a heavy German accent and a pleasant look on his face. I told him my story.

"Do you see that house up there?" He asked when I was finished.

"Yes, sir."

"Be there at eight in the morning, and I will show you how to operate our equipment."

"I will see you in the morning," I said after thanking him.

I arrived at the farmhouse before 8 a.m. the next morning with my plowing britches on and ready for a day's work. My new boss met me, and we headed to the field for a quick lesson on driving the tractor and using the equipment.

"You understand how to handle everything?" He asked when he was finished with his instructions.

I had a few questions, which he answered.

"I want you back at the house for our noon meal," he ordered. "My wife is a pretty good cook."

"Thank you," I said. "See you at noon."

As he walked away, leaving me with the challenge of learning to operate the huge tractor that prepared the land for planting, I thought, "this is my kind of work." The morning went well, and I felt good, like I could handle my job description. I arrived back at the house on time for lunch. The farmer showed me to the bathroom to wash up. I met his wife. She was a gracious lady who did everything she could to make me feel at home. Her German food was different from my mother's cooking, but after a morning's work, I enjoyed it.

We talked, and I learned that they had three children — all grown. In many ways, our families were the same. But their farm would produce 20 times more than our poor red-dirt farm in McNairy County. They were prosperous with a sizeable herd of cattle requiring a lot of labor. I could not have found a better family. I had more work than I could do anytime I wasn't at Caterpillar.

At the end of the week, the farmer counted my hours and wrote me a generous check. I never mentioned money, and he never asked me how much I wanted in pay. My farm pay was comparable to my parking wages, so I was a happy trooper.

***

Nothing ever remains the same in this life.

Workers were planning to strike at Caterpillar for higher pay and union rule changes. One day when I arrived at work, the worksite was closed and people walked the picket line. These union folks meant business. It was a new experience for me, but I wouldn't participate because I didn't believe in their cause.

I thought about the future. The Korean conflict was ongoing, and I knew my draft number was coming up soon. With my savings, I decided to quit my jobs in Peoria and return home to spend some time with my family before going into service. Also, I needed to catch up on my dating. With my new car and a nice wardrobe of clothes, I was ready.

When I returned home, my parents were surprised, and Dad was between logging jobs. With no pressure to help him, I went to Selmer early the next morning to find a new job.

I talked to the local taxi driver because he would know who might be hiring. He said that I should talk with Mr. Fesmire, store manager at Kroger's.

I walked into Kroger's and met a tall, handsome fellow with dark black hair and a pleasant look on his face. He welcomed me, and I told him the taxi driver said he might need some help. Mr. Fesmire launched a line of questions in rapid fire, but he liked my answers and offered me a job for $40 a week.

My work at Kroger was educational. I worked six days a week, getting to know people and helping them shop. In those days, buying groceries was much different than today. Families came to the store with their grocery list, often written on a scrap piece of paper. They handed me their list, and I walked through the store, picking their items from the shelves. I carried their groceries to the store's counter and added each item's price, totaled with tax, before handing the tape to the customer for payment.

I took the customer's money, gave change and helped carry everything to the vehicle — which sometimes still was a wagon. I became friends with the shoppers, and many times, they would wait for me to personally fill their list. I was full of energy and wanted to be as helpful as I could.

Mr. Fesmire was pleased with his new trainee and asked me to attend a Kroger produce school in Memphis at the famous Peabody Hotel. He said our produce department was losing money with too much waste, and he wanted me to get the training to make the department profitable.

It was exciting to think about staying overnight, for my first time, in a hotel — especially the fancy Peabody. So off to Memphis I went, and I experienced another first when I dined at the hotel restaurant after ordering from a menu. The food was delicious, and I slept, soundly, in my fancy room.

A master communicator taught the produce school, making it fun. I soaked up every word and took good notes. I was determined to learn to display the produce according to the Kroger plan and cut cost and waste for a profitable produce department in Selmer.

When I returned, Mr. Fesmire put me in charge of ordering the store's produce.

"It's your baby," he said. "I expect success from this produce department."

I did my best to make Mr. Fesmire proud of me. Things went well, and he was pleased.

But I did not know anything about the overall store profit. I concentrated on my job and helping our customers. One day, Kroger's district manager came in the store, asked for Mr. Fesmire's store keys and fired him. He was shocked, and so was I. I didn't know why he was fired, but I overheard some of their conversation. The Selmer store was losing money. The district manager stayed a few days until another store manager was brought in to replace Mr. Fesmire.

During his stay, the district manager liked my work and encouraged me to consider becoming a store manager. He wanted me to attend a Kroger training program. I was impressed with his confidence in me, but since my draft number was almost up, I explained to him that I would have to consider the thought later.

My positive Kroger experience taught me that if you put your heart and soul into your work, people will take notice. I worked at Kroger for several months, developing my people skills and getting to know many families in our county.

My experience on the farm and later in the workplace cultivated a strong work ethic, and I always brought a good attitude to the job. I was ready for my next big challenge in life: going to war.

CHAPTER 3

A SIDE TRIP TO KOREA

I never will forget the day I found an envelope addressed to me in our mailbox from the U.S. government. I opened it, tentatively. I was instructed to report for duty in the armed services at the McNairy County Courthouse in Selmer. I gave notice to my manager at Kroger and prepared for my Army service.

When I arrived at the courthouse, 15 to 20 young men were waiting, but I vaguely knew only one or two of them. One person attracted my attention. He was better dressed than most of us, and he seemed to have a confidence about him that showed he had his life together.

On December 2, 1952, we boarded Greyhound buses for the Veteran's Hospital in Memphis, where we were examined for fitness to serve. At the hospital, we were told to strip naked — a new experience for this country boy. But I passed the examination with flying colors, as I expected, and was inducted into the Army.

After a day or so, we boarded a train for Fort Jackson, South Carolina. On the way, I moved over to meet the well-dressed man, who was sitting alone. Estel Mills told me he was a farm boy from Michie, Tennessee, and a graduate of Memphis State University with a degree in math and science.

Estel and I hit it off immediately. As we talked, we learned that we had a lot in common. We were hard workers with solid family backgrounds. Our fathers had similar high expectations for their sons. We liked each other from the start, and we decided that, if possible, we would do our best to stay together.

Army life started in earnest when we arrived at Fort Jackson for processing.

A gruff sergeant stepped onto our bus and started giving orders on what he expected. His voice had finality in it. We were assigned to Fort Leonard Wood, Missouri, for basic training.

I am sure it was more luck than planning, but Estel and I were both assigned to Second Platoon, First Squad, in the same company. During training, Estel marched in front of me, and regardless of the temperatures or how long the hike, it never fazed either of us. When we reached the end of a 20-mile hike, loaded down with a full field pack and Army gear, we always thought we could do the hike over if it was ordered. Being in top physical condition because of farm work was paying big dividends.

Many of the guys, who were from the cities, were not able to make the long hikes and fell out on the way along the side of the road. A truck would pick them up to take them back to the company.

I decided to be a good soldier and learn as much as I could to be safer when we went into action. Basic was 16 weeks of intense survival training.

The time went by quickly, and the training became routine. During the last week, our first sergeant ordered everyone to fall out for company formation to receive our next assignment. The most feared assignment was the Far East, which meant you could go to the front line in the war zone. Some received nicer assignments like Alaska or Hawaii, but I was not so fortunate. When my name was called out, a lump formed in my throat. I was going to the Far East, and it was frightening.

***

Our last days at Fort Leonard Wood were stressful, and we knew we would only get a short leave to go home before shipping out. It became even shorter when someone misbehaved and upset our company commander. He delayed our leave by another three days, from Tuesday to Friday. I felt this was unfair. The company commander's orders also included instructions to turn in all of our military gear on that Friday before we left.

Earlier, when we were training on the far side of our base, I noticed a road without a guard on duty that appeared to lead off the base. I wondered where it went. I had brought my car to Fort Leonard Wood to enjoy some free weekends. The car sat in the parking lot most of the time, but when I had an evening off, it was nice to have it.

I thought about that road after the commander's orders and figured it could take me home. My car was parked on base, and we already had our paperwork for our next assignment. I told two other guys from my part of West Tennessee that I was leaving for home.

Private Tom Hendrix

"What will we do with all of our Army gear we're to turn into the orderly room on Friday?" they asked.

"We will place it on our bed and someone else will take care of it," I said.

Everyone agreed to go for it. We jumped into my car and headed for the road on the far side of the base. Everything worked as planned, and we were able to spend a few more days at home with our families.

My conscience bothered me, though, somewhat ruining my time at home. We left base early, disregarded the company commander's orders and failed to turn our gear in on the Friday before we left. I wondered what the consequence would be for not following orders. We had rolled the dice. We gambled on our superiors giving us a pass because we had our papers in hand. But when we returned for duty, the issue never came up, and we were in the clear.

We spent two or three days in Seattle, giving us time for sightseeing. Four of us rented a car to drive up Mount Rainier. On the way, someone bought a bottle of wine, and I had my first drink of alcohol. As we ascended the mountain, the air grew thinner, and I felt the effects of my first sips of wine. Wow! The views from Mt. Rainier were breathtaking and a new experience, and so was my first drink of wine.

***

Shortly after we left the States on our transport ship, we encountered a terrible storm at sea that seemed to last forever. I sheltered in a berth in the back of the ship. As the huge ship surged through the stormy waves, the motion lifted me out of my berth again and again. And there was a terrible noise when the big propellers cleared the water. Nausea struck everyone on the ship. We spent most of our time heaving over the side rail, sick as dogs.

After crossing the Pacific, we stopped in Japan for a few days. I still remember my first sight of Japan and the ancient city of Tokyo through the thick misty haze of the morning. I realized that this country boy from Tennessee was in a different part of the world. It was an unknown feeling, and it gave me pause.

We had some free time to explore Tokyo. Everything was very different: the language, the food and the city itself with more people than I had ever seen in one place. I bought a few souvenirs for home, which my Mother kept for the rest of her life.

We eventually boarded another ship bound for Korea. The voyage was much smoother. We arrived in the city of Pusan, also spelled Busan, and immediately boarded a train to complete our journey. The sergeant gave everyone a schedule to take his turn to stand guard at the train's doorways with live ammunition, making sure the enemy did not come aboard. I fully realized then that I was headed to a dangerous place. For two nights and a day, we sat on wooden seats with all our gear and no place to sleep. Bombing raids were constant.

When the train reached its destination, we boarded trucks for our ride to camp. For the first time, we could see the flashing lights from the front line. And then I was in the war, with Company C, 185th Combat Engineers. I was assigned to Second Platoon, Second Squad.

Three air raids bombarded our position during the first night. Officers ordered us to fall out of our cots and into our foxholes for 20 or 30 minutes — sometimes longer — until we heard the all clear. I was tired. I hadn't slept in several days, and I didn't wake up for one of the air-raid sirens. When I was found asleep in my cot, I was ordered to report to the company commander.

He gave me a serious dressing down. From then on, I jumped out of my cot and into the foxhole when the air-raid siren sounded.

***

I don't have any battle stories, but I had a front-row seat to watch the war. The combat engineers were the working soldiers, keeping the roads in good repair and building bridges to keep the supplies rolling to the front.

My company maintained several miles of the road into the front line. Some of our work was between the artillery guns and the front line. We watched them fire into the enemy's position with exploding shells. We also saw jets drop their bombs. It was interesting to watch the pilots, who all appeared to have a different personality, maneuver their planes on bombing runs. Some planes came out of their dives upside down, rolling their jets and waving their wings as if they were saying, "I made it without a bullet hole."

At times, the enemy rained artillery fire on our position, and we ran for our trucks to high tail it to safer ground. The soldiers on the front line stayed and fought, but we couldn't build a bridge or repair a road under fire. Most days were uneventful, except for a few snipers in the area, which concerned me more than the artillery. I thought about an enemy soldier, almost a mile away, with my head in his sight, ready to pull the trigger. This made for a stressful day.

We worked seven days a week in all kinds of weather. In the cold and wet winter months, temperatures fell to zero. Every day was the same, Sunday through Saturday. We were relatively happy, though, because we were all in the same situation. No one drove past us on our road with a brand new car and a date while we labored without a day off. We worked hard and kept a good attitude. We kidded each other and had a lot of good laughs.

But we had constant reminders that we were in a war zone. Once, a corporal was relieved of duty and planned to return home in two days. A hand grenade killed him before he could leave; he had a wife and two children expecting him at home soon. It was a tragedy of war — something we saw all too often in Korea.

***

During the summer of 1953, rumors began to swell about an end to the war. It was music to our ears — even as fighting intensified and we faced the prospect of returning to the line. On July 27, our company commander announced the war would end at 9 p.m. We were supposed to sleep outside that night, but no one could. Everyone wanted to hear the last shot. We were anxious and optimistic, but we still faced doubt. It was a strange evening.

The night began with heavy firing as we listened to the roar of big guns increasing on both sides. But, as nine o'clock approached, the shooting began to dwindle to a few sporadic bursts.

Then, it became quiet.

Excitement surrounded us. We threw our hats in the air and opened beers to celebrate the prospect of returning home. The evening was unforgettable. I thought about my father, who witnessed the last shots of World War I. And here I was, witnessing the last shots of this conflict. My father and I lived through two nasty wars, and for us, they were ending the same way.

The next day, we took down our tents and packed everything into the truck except our small single bunk where we would sleep for the night. Our orders were to leave early the next morning and travel to Panmunjom to clear mine fields between the lines. It was called no man's land — our toughest assignment of the war. One mistake could cost you your life.

We used mine sweepers, which would make a buzzing sound when they detected any piece of metal, regardless of the size. The ground in no man's land was full of shrapnel, and the sweepers buzzed constantly. For each chirp, we dug into the ground to make sure it was not a mine. This was a slow go. If we became lax or dismissed a mine for a piece of metal, someone could get blown to pieces.

As soon as we finished clearing the mines, we started building a prisoner exchange camp, which included buildings for both sides to negotiate. North Korean prisoners were incarcerated within a secure compound. We treated and fed the prisoners well — much better than they were used to. Many did not want to return home to a terrible life in North Korea, but they would be tortured or shot if North Korean authorities knew how they felt. The prisoners were friendly to the American soldiers and showed us considerable respect.

One day, we saw North Korean soldiers waving to us to come for a visit. They were about a quarter of a mile from us in no man's land. Because the war was over, we thought it would be safe. We walked to their location and had a cordial visit. They gave us cigarettes and some whiskey, which we did not drink because we didn't know what might be in it. The cigarettes had a terrible taste so we threw them away, too. Their uniforms were very poor in quality, and the visit made us proud to be American soldiers.

I watched the Korean people struggle to eat three bowls of rice a day, wearing ragged clothes while searching for a place to sleep. I promised myself I would never complain after I set foot on American soil. Regardless of my situation, I planned to count my blessings, and I have done my best to keep that promise.

***

From the moment I arrived in Korea, my goal was to make rank as fast as I could. I wanted the advantages of leadership, which brought more freedom. I didn't like being a number, stuck back in the ranks. I decided to use my brains. I worked smarter so I could be seen as a good decision maker, providing leadership with every project. I wanted to stand out from the crowd, and I felt like my day would come if I exercised good judgment.

After we completed the prisoner exchange camp, we returned to our permanent company location. To my surprise, about a week after I was promoted to corporal, my company commander asked me to report to his tent for a visit with him and the first sergeant. I had never spoken with the commander before and wondered if it would be good news or bad.

The commander said Second Platoon needed strong leadership for some Army discipline. He explained that he intended to make some changes.

"I'll waive your time in grade so you can be promoted as quickly as possible," the commander said. "You're going to be platoon sergeant."

I could not believe what I was hearing. The present platoon sergeant was a nice, quiet-spoken African-American — a career soldier. His assistant platoon sergeant was a career soldier. But the platoon had more than its share of soldiers from the stockade who were serving their time in Korea in lieu of stockade camp in the States. They, for the most part, caused the discipline problems. To some extent, they intimidated the sergeant. He was too nice, and they were getting the best of him.

So I became the new platoon sergeant. I told the first sergeant the announcement would cause trouble in Second Platoon. For it to work, he had to give me strong backing. I did not know the problems I would face, but I knew my leadership would be tested on day one. And because I made rank quickly, there would be jealousy.

The first sergeant ordered everyone for company formation, put me in front of my 42-member platoon and introduced

Platoon Sgt. Tom Hendrix

me as their new leader. I gave them a parade rest order to introduce myself. My message was simple.

"Each one of us has a certain amount of time here before we receive our orders for home," I told them. "If we are good soldiers, the time left can be enjoyable. On the other hand, if you insist on resisting orders and causing trouble, I will make your life miserable. Starting today, everyone in this platoon has a chance to wipe the slate clean for a new beginning, and I hope that new beginning is to be a good soldier until you return home."

The next week I met with two of the squad leaders.

"Your leadership must improve starting today," I commanded. "If not, I will have your corporal stripes, and another squad leader will take your place."

Within a week, we promoted R.L. Enterkin to corporal as the new leader of First Squad, demoting the former corporal. R.L. was the perfect person to deal with the stockade attitude. He worked on a dredge boat when he was 16, telling them he was 18. He was a strong leader who could cut through nonsense and command discipline.

After the change, the corporal in charge of Third Squad came to me.

"I cannot afford to lose my rank because I have a wife and a son, and I need the money."

"My message is simple," I said. "Become a good soldier and give some good leadership to your squad, and you will never lose your stripes."

He did just that.

I knew the stockade soldiers would flex their muscles and test my leadership. The company commander set them up perfectly by ordering early morning close-order drills. I had not marched in close-order drills since boot camp, and I had never given drill orders to a platoon. It was a real test for me to learn how to give the commands.

When the first sergeant called for company formation, I gave my platoon the marching order, taking them through the drill commands. They were just as inexperienced as me.

"Forward march!" I called, bringing the platoon to attention and easing the men into the drill.

I told them to straighten their shoulders and chins and stop bobbing their heads. I called some soldiers by name to improve their stance. I was surprised at how well I was doing and was feeling much more comfortable giving the commands. I thought I could be a good drill sergeant with a few more flanking calls.

Then one of the stockade soldiers did the stockade shuffle. He pulled his cap off, slapped the front of his leg with his cap and shuffled forward with a big stockade yell.

I called the platoon to a halt and commanded the soldier to fall out of the platoon.

"The stockade shuffle is stockade stuff — not Army regulation," I yelled. "Anyone who does the shuffle will march around the orderly room with a full field pack and weapons for two hours a day, at attention, for one week after five in the evening."

I sent the soldier to the orderly room to await my instructions. I called the platoon to attention again to resume our close-order drills. We went through the commands rapid fire. But then another stockade soldier did the shuffle. By the end of the march, I sent three soldiers to the orderly room.

That evening, before their march, I addressed the punished soldiers.

"You're prejudiced," one of them said.

I doubled his marching time. In the following days, they continued to test my resolve. But I was firm and to-the-point, making sure they paid the price without delay. I made sure everyone knew I brought a different kind of leadership to Second Platoon. After two weeks, I could see I was getting good results.

The first sergeant and company commander seemed pleased with my approach to Army discipline, and I thought most of the problems were behind me. But one morning, in company formation, I noticed something in a soldier's pocket. His name was Fletcher, and he wasn't generally a troublemaker. I slapped his pocket and found a pint of whiskey. I took the pint and commanded Fletcher to fall out of rank. That evening, I ordered him to dig an eight-by-eight hole with his entrenching tool, while everyone watched, and bury his whiskey at the bottom. Fletcher never forgot the hole he dug, and I made sure everyone could see it to remind the men to be good soldiers.

Despite these discipline issues, we had an outstanding platoon, and the soldiers that received the punishment came to respect my leadership. After a month or two, some of my worst offenders became my friends.

Dishing out punishment bothered me a great deal. I did not enjoy it, but I was determined to have discipline in Second Platoon. And, I knew the stockade guys could soldier like everyone else. I also thought this would be good for them long term. If corrections were not made while they were here, they could end up in prison after their Army discharge.

My leadership plan was not to curse or shout with a mean look on my face, or bluff them into behaving themselves. I kept a happy face that meant business, and I was consistent, making the best of our time until we received orders to return to civilian life.

My company commander and first sergeant were happy with my results. They even sent me troublemakers to straighten out. I detested that, but in the Army, you do what you are asked to do.

***

Our next challenge would take Second Platoon to a location 50 miles away from camp. The company commander wanted us to build a hospital for the South Korean people, who were in desperate need of medical care.

He asked me if I thought I was up to the task. I jumped at the opportunity to get away from close-order drills, spit-shining boots and rifle inspection.

"I'm your man," I told the company commander. "And we'll complete the hospital on schedule if at all possible."

"Company A, Third Platoon, has already started construction," he said. "But they ran into problems with the Quonset hut's alignment and are behind schedule."

The plans for the hospital called for two or three tube-like Quonset huts connected together as a central hallway with 15 or more huts connected to the hallway. The commander and first lieutenant asked me several questions to determine if I had the experience and background for the job.

"Well, I have no experience in construction," I responded. "I'm a farm boy, but I can make up the difference with the experiences of my men."

The hospital was not my sole responsibility. The first lieutenant also would be on the job, making sure the work was being done properly. If we had a construction problem, he would be held responsible before me. But they let me know that doing my job properly was essential for a successful outcome.

My plan was to interview each man under my command to find out their occupation before they joined the Army.

"We are going to use your experience to build this hospital, on time, and you take the credit," I told the soldiers in Second Platoon. "It's your project. Let's make it something we can all be proud of when it's passed off to the Korean people. If a person doesn't get the job done with a good attitude, you will dig a ditch, and we have a lot of digging that needs to be done."

I found serendipity in my interviews. They gave me an opportunity to get to know the people I was to lead, which built respect and made us more successful. In the service, everything is uniform. My interviews emphasized individuality. I did my best to get each person involved in the project to take ownership and create a successful outcome. To my surprise, we had all kinds of talent for building a hospital. We had plumbers, electricians and men experienced with sheet metals — someone for each job. And my men were happy using their minds to do what they had been trained to do in civilian life. I learned that a leader does not have to know everything. Instead, it's better to make good use of the brainpower of the people you lead.

One of our men, Krause, was a master carpenter with a head full of sense. He became my right-hand man, and I frequently turned to him for advice. I told Krause he was in charge of making sure the buildings were in alignment. He accepted the responsibility, and we never had a problem with it.

In the mornings, Second Platoon came together in formation for a progress report — similar to the reports we gave Dad at dinner back home on the farm. The hospital project was educational for everyone. We laid blocks, poured concrete, wired the building for electricity, and installed plumbing and sheet metal. Everything turned out well with the project. We completed on schedule and in alignment.

I learned more than any one — especially what makes a strong, successful leader. I never forgot this lesson, and I used it in my entrepreneurial life.

Making the most out of what we do is the essence of a successful life.

My time in service was a growth experience, and it gave me an opportunity to flex my muscles in leadership.

***

After we completed the hospital and gave it to the South Korean people, we returned to the company base with a great deal of *esprit de corps* for a normal life of soldiering. We formed a special bond of friendship, respect and good discipline. I was proud of the progress that had been made since my first day as platoon sergeant, and we were ready for our next task.

The first sergeant asked me to build an icebox for cooling food in the mess hall. Again, I went to Krause for advice, and we brainstormed the best way to build it. We dug a six-by-eight-foot hole into the mountain, poured the walls full of sawdust for insulation and brought in large blocks of ice. It worked, and everyone seemed to be happy with our new icebox.

Our next project was a well. South Korean civilians did most of the work; they knew more about well digging than we did. The well was at least 15 feet deep and 36 inches in diameter. It was encased with rock laid by the Koreans. As we neared completion, we used a rope to lower rocks down to the bottom to be laid by an elderly South Korean man. The rope broke and almost killed him. I felt badly about the accident because he had been so helpful to us in digging the well.

Up to this point, we had not been able to take a shower for many months. We would wash the best we could from a pan or, in some cases, from our helmet. With our new well, we set up a tent for everyone to take hot showers. Our life was somewhat returning to normal.

Second Platoon was called upon again to help build a road with a rock surface. We used jackhammers to bore 10- to 12-foot holes, two inches in diameter, into the mountain. We packed the holes with dynamite and TNT to shatter the rock and create the road. I stood in a beehive of loud jackhammers, day after day, permanently damaging my hearing. We did not use ear protection, which was a big mistake, and I am still paying the price, even with today's high-tech hearing aids.

I am glad that I could serve my country and come home with only a hearing impairment. I prefer to count my blessings and think about how I benefited from being in the Army. I am a much better person for serving my country for 22 months.

***

During the war, points determined when you could return home. We received four per month, and a soldier needed 36 to leave Korea. Members of our platoon received the same number as the soldiers on the front line — the maximum number allotted for serving in the war zone.

The Army eliminated the points system for early rotation after the ceasefire agreement, which extended my stay in Korea to 17 months. During the last month, I counted the days down on my calendar.

One day, as my time in Korea wound to an end, the first sergeant approached me.

"The company commander would like you to come to the officer's tent this evening for a drink," he said.

"What is the purpose?" I asked.

"I think it's about re-enlisting."

When I arrived that evening, I found the first lieutenant, the first sergeant and the commander. They drank scotch, which I did not care for, but because they served it to me, I drank it as if it was my favorite.

They were convinced that I could be a career soldier because I made rank so quickly. I furnished the leadership for a well-disciplined platoon and successfully completed the hospital on time. The commander told me all the advantages of becoming a career soldier, and as I remember, I was offered a signing bonus. I told the commander I enjoyed my service and benefited greatly from my time in the Army, but I was counting the days to return to my civilian life.

It was an interesting experience, and by the end of the evening, the scotch had a better taste. I returned to my tent and checked off another day on my calendar.

I spent almost 18 months in Korea. On my last day there, we boarded a ship for home. It was smooth sailing — much better than the trip to Japan at the beginning of my tour of duty. The week aboard ship went well. I got to know the guys, and we talked about where they were from and what they intended to do when they were discharged.

After crossing the Pacific, our ship made port in Seattle. My first sight of the United States was thrilling. Soon we were on a train headed for Fort Campbell, Kentucky, for our discharge.

I was so close to home, but we still had to wait a couple of days for our discharge papers. I was anxious to see my family and didn't want to wait. I didn't yet have my Army pay, so I pawned my watch for a few dollars to make a quick trip home. On the way, I took special note of all the changes, especially the new models of cars. I finally arrived at my parents' farm — more than 7,000 miles from Korea.

It was wonderful to be home with my family and to once again eat my Mother's good cooking. We had many great conversations. We talked about my Army experiences, and they told me all about the things that had happened while I was away. It was a short trip, but it was worth it.

I returned to Fort Campbell and received my honorable discharge papers from the Army. When I came home for good, I bought a new 1954 Ford automobile with my Army savings and headed to the store to buy some new clothes. I had to get ready to meet some pretty girls.

I told my father that I was thinking about signing up for a $30 unemployment check that the government offered to veterans.

"Why would you do that?" He quickly asked.

"Everyone can get this check as transition pay," I said.

"Tom, I didn't rear you to stand in a dole line. I reared you to be in the work line. If you have the right attitude toward work, you will always have a job."

I made my trip to Selmer, and I saw him again when I returned home.

"Did you get in that dole line?" He asked.

"No."

"Good, let's go to work."

I came to the conclusion that every person should render enough service to their fellowman to earn enough for a place to sleep and something to eat. If you want a nicer pad, go to work earlier and stay later — and have a good attitude about it.

Poverty is the way a person thinks. If we have a poverty mindset, we will live in poverty. It goes back to the way we view life. Giving families a check is the easy thing to do, but it ignores the real problem. In my opinion, people drawing any kind of poverty check should attend educational classes to change their attitude, helping them see the good of work. They should be taught how to get a job and how to be successful once they get a job. The check should be earned. It's a disservice to them otherwise.

Instead of dependence, people should accept responsibility for their life, and we should be determined to help families in need live a happy, successful life. Is it easy? No. But it is worth the heavy lifting — especially for the welfare of children.

I think people are unemployed for one of three reasons. They don't like the work for what it is, where it is or what it pays. I believe your attitude should be to go to work and work your way to the job of your choice.

So, I started hauling logs, knowing I wasn't going to be hauling logs very long.

CHAPTER 4

THE ROAD TO COLLEGE

*"Being as productive as possible, rendering as much service as possible,
is the best way to live."*

After a few weeks on the farm, I saw Estel Mills — my old friend from boot camp. He said he was going to Chicago to work for a while to decide what he wanted to do long term. I decided to join Estel in Chicago.

He left a few days before me, but he did not leave a way for me to contact him. I headed to Chicago hoping his parents would have his phone number by the time I arrived. But as I drove into the city, I stopped at a small eatery and saw Estel sitting at a table. I couldn't believe my eyes.

"How did you know I was here?" Estel said, looking up.

"Pure luck," I said. "Won't happen again for a million years."

Estel Mills, the well-dressed man

We ate, and Estel took me to his apartment. Then we were off to find a job. Our first stop was the steel mill. The personnel office was closed, but people were waiting outside, hoping to get in to submit their application. We stood with the crowd for a few minutes, and then Estel had a plan.

"I am going around to the side of the building to look for a door to get inside the office," he said.

About 15 minutes later, he popped out the front door and called me to come inside. He had already met the personnel manager, and they talked about how the Tennessee River has the best fishing in the South. It worked. The personnel manager offered us a job. I had only been in town for a couple of hours.

As we discussed the new job on the way back to Estel's apartment, he suggested we check out Fisher Body in Willow Springs to see if we could improve our situation. It was one of the largest plants in the General Motors network — a good place to work at a good rate of pay. I liked the idea. So the next morning, we went to Fisher Body, turned in an application and waited for an interview. Estel's interview was first, and he got a job offer for second shift. I interviewed next and asked for second shift. The personnel manager said he would call me if he had an opening. He didn't like my request, and I left knowing I would not receive a phone call from the company.

I decided to go back to Fisher Body the next morning. I went into the personnel office uninvited, and I walked right up to the personnel manager's desk. He looked up at me with an expression of surprise.

"Yesterday, I was wrong to ask for second shift," I told him. "But, I have driven 550 miles to go to work for Fisher Body, and I would be happy with the toughest job in the plant on any shift. I want to go to work for Fisher Body!"

He looked me over.

"You can have second shift," he said with a slight smile.

I thanked him, and we began processing the details for me to work in the shipping department. It was a good assignment.

We loaded boxcars with trunk lids and pans — a sizeable sheet of molded metal that goes under the seats in the car — on two 80-pound bars in the boxcar, two rows high. A small-framed guy, Will, was hired in with me to be my partner. He was a likeable person with a great attitude. Our job was to load half of the boxcar in four hours, rolling the lids and pans into the car on a dolly before unloading them onto the racks.

Will and I were instructed to watch the other guys and copy their loading techniques. On our first day, the work was cumbersome, and it took the full four hours to load the car. But we learned how to save time. After a few days, I began to experiment with ways to improve our techniques. I dropped a few lids as I tested different approaches. I learned that I could squat down, and with my arm across my knee as leverage, reach for the trunk lid and hoist it into the air. Then I pushed it forward onto the bar in the boxcar, all in one motion. I told Will all he needed to do was keep the lids from turning over on the rack by placing his foot against them. After a short period of time, I had the technique refined, and I could pitch those lids as fast as I could reach for them. It was three or four times as fast as the standard way of loading, which, to me, wasted time and motion.

The people on the loading dock noticed our faster approach. Some of the guys began to copy my technique, but it seemed cumbersome to them, so they stayed with their old ways. They belonged to the union and seemed to have no interest in trying to get more work done. They knew if everyone used my method, there would be a company effort to change production. I could never understand the union's mindset of not wanting to be as productive as possible. I thought they would have a sense of accomplishment and pride, knowing they were doing their best. This attitude of making a living, doing as little as possible, and for as much pay as possible, is not the best way to go about life. It takes the fun out of your work.

One day, Will and I loaded our end of the car in one hour. It was our third week on the job, and it created quite a stir. The first person to raise his head was our union steward.

"After all, you are a union man whether you like it or not," he told me. "You should load your car in four hours. It makes no sense to load the car in such a rush."

I made no comment and went about my work. A company official came to see the techniques we were using and complimented our thoughtful way of quickly loading the car. But the company never changed its production numbers. The union would have called a strike, shutting down the huge plant, before making a change to increase the amount of work to be done.

I enjoyed my work more at Fisher Body than Caterpillar. Both experiences made me believe that the unions should join the company as partners instead of adversaries. I wanted to see how many cars we could build with improved quality, lowering the car's cost to the customer. I wanted my life to be in service to people.

The American work ethic has been successful, but production in some work places can be vastly improved. With the free enterprise system, we would be more competitive around the world, keeping more jobs here in the United States. I believe that being as productive as possible, rendering as much service as possible, is the best way to live.

***

Chicago was a great city, but we were ready to head back to McNairy County after six months of working at Fisher Body.

Estel decided to be an educator and teach math and science. I was not sure what direction to take without a high school diploma. I shared my dilemma with Estel.

"Tom, you need to go to college," he said. "College will set you apart for a more productive life."

The idea was appealing. I knew if I made up my mind, I could get a degree. I went to see my high school principal one Saturday evening. I explained that I was out of the Army and thought it best to get a degree from the University of Tennessee Martin Branch (UTMB).

"That's a good idea," he said. "Come back and finish up your high school work so you can enroll."

I didn't want to go back to high school. I asked him to go to the school with me so I could see my transcript and where I stood on credits. He looked at me with a stern expression.

"I can say, for sure, you lack several credits," he said.

I finally convinced him to go to the school, and he pulled my records.

"Tom, it's much worse than what I thought," he said.

I agreed when he showed me the transcript.

"It's not a pretty picture," he said.

It didn't matter. My plan was to go to college, not back to high school. I even carried a stamped envelope in my pocket to use if I convinced him to increase my credits so I could be a high school graduate. I told him I was not returning to high school after being out for more than three years and that I wanted to go to college to get a degree in agriculture.

"You are the only person who can keep me from going, and if you will mark up those credits, I will make you proud of me," I said.

"Tom, you won't study," he responded. "You won't pass your courses any more than in high school. College is much more difficult."

"But I'm determined to attend the University of Tennessee Martin Branch and get an agriculture degree if you will mark up those credits," I insisted.

He marked up the credits, and I headed to college. I am not saying this was the right thing to do policy-wise, but in my case, I enrolled at UTMB in 1955, and it changed my life forever. I am the first to say that we cannot base our life on exceptions, but some exceptions work out for the better.

***

When we were children, my father talked about college as he sat at the

Tom goes off to the University of Tennessee Martin Branch in a 1954 Ford.

head of our kitchen table.

"If you want to go to college, I will not pay the bill, but your mother and I will be in your cheering section."

He reared us to make our life what we wished. He and Mother believed in us. I have often thought about the importance of that statement to my life. If Dad had paid my way through college, I would not have taken steps to become an entrepreneur. It is a milestone in our life when we fully take the responsibility for our decisions. A parent's teachings are not complete until children understand they are responsible for their decisions, and those decisions have consequences. Decisions determine success — or failure — in life.

CHAPTER 5

WORKING MY WAY THROUGH COLLEGE

"I came to realize that our real security is within. Your job can be taken, but your God-given potential and your successful mindset cannot be taken."

University of Tennessee Martin was about 90 miles from home and certainly a new experience for me. I liked it from day one. At first, I was distracted by the pretty girls on campus, and with my new car, I spent more time on my social life than academics. I never studied in high school and putting my feet under my desk to study in college took some getting used to.

Bruce Gray from Covington and I roomed together with a Presbyterian minister and his wife, who made us feel at home. We had two nice rooms upstairs within walking distance of campus.

At the end of the first quarter, my grades were not good. Cavit Cheshier, a friend from Bethel Springs whom I had shown cows with during high school, was a horticulture professor. I was in one of his classes, and he had access to my grades. One evening, I heard someone coming up the stairs to our room. It was Cavit. He came to give me a piece of his mind.

"Tom, I am not pleased with your grades at all. I think you should move in with me so I can be a good influence on your studies. I have two rooms upstairs, and you can live in the one across the hall from me."

"I'll move into your house, and I'll make good grades from this point on," I said. I kept my word.

I think of the people in my life who were there at the right time to give me a nudge in the right direction and help me become successful. Estel told me to go to college. Cavit told me to be responsible and make good grades. To this day, I still thank them both.

***

After my first year in college, I returned home for the summer and helped my Dad with logging to make some money for college. The next fall, I moved into the newly constructed men's dormitory. Our dorm mother asked me to be president of the dorm. It was an elected position, and if I agreed to run, she thought she could get me the votes. I thought I could come up with some good policies to implement, so I agreed to run for office. I was elected, just as she thought. I served as president for three years.

***

College life during the 1950s in rural West Tennessee was carefree and more reserved than campuses today. We had no co-ed dormitories. Most single students lived in dorms with a dorm mother and a dorm president. Female students were required to sign in and out of the dorm. Freshman were expected to be inside by 10 p.m. and seniors by midnight. If a girl went home for the weekend, she signed out and noted where she was going.

The campus had few cars. School cost $1,000 per year for room and board and tuition. The university had strict policies regulating our conduct. I don't remember crime on campus other than an occasional panty raid, which happened maybe once a year in the smaller dorms as boys ran through girls' rooms stealing undergarments. In some cases, the boys would be punished, and in extreme cases, they were kicked out of school.

Our life was simple and laid back, and we knew everyone on campus. We knew our instructors on a personal basis, and most professors took an individual interest in each of their students. UT Martin had about 500 students on campus in 1955. Today, it has about 8,000 students. The most high-tech thing I found at college was a slide rule used by engineering students. We had no computers and no iPhones in our pockets. If we wanted to make a call, we used a pay phone that cost more than $1 per minute for long distance. We carried a pocket full of quarters, dimes and nickels to feed the hungry machine as we talked. A phone call had to be important.

***

I had to earn money to pay my way through school. My cash benefit from the G.I. Bill for tuition and living expenses to attend the university was $90 per month for nine months. But it wasn't enough to cover expenses — and drive a new car. During my second year at UT, as I walked down the hallway in my dorm, I heard Bobby Smothers from Camden calling loudly to me.

"Tom, come to my room! I want you to interview to sell Bibles this summer."

"I have a job, Bobby. I'll be hauling logs again with my dad."

Bobby laughed.

"Come on, Tom. Talk to us."

I walked into his room and met Dortch Oldham with the Southwestern Company in Nashville. He was recruiting students to sell Bibles during the summer, which enabled them to pay their way through college. Dortch was professional, and he helped me see the opportunity in front of me. I had never sold anything in my life, except our homegrown watermelons, and I practically gave those away.

The idea of selling Bibles, door to door, in a northern state during the summer was far-fetched to me. Another student, Bill Cook from Dyersburg, sold Bibles for three summers. I asked him how much money he made, and he said he earned and saved more than $8,000 in three months knocking on those doors. I couldn't believe it. That was eight times the cost of a year in college. I asked Bobby Smothers the same question, and he said he made about $2,500. Then I turned to Dortch.

"Where do I sign? If these two people can make that much money, I can at least make enough for school."

At the time, I did not realize the significance of signing the contract to sell Bibles door to door. It changed my life forever as I embarked on a new path in a completely different direction toward becoming an entrepreneur. I would never work in the field of agriculture again, other than a hobby farm. Little did I know that Dortch Oldham would become one of the most important people in my life, ranking up there with my father. He became one of my best friends and continued teaching where my father left off.

I went home the following weekend and told Dad that I would not be hauling logs with him next summer. He was disappointed, to say the least.

"How much will they pay you?" He asked.

"They don't pay you anything," I said. "You only get paid if you sell a Bible."

"Do they pay your expenses?"

"No. We also have to pay our way through a week of sales training in Nashville."

"Hauling logs is better than that unknown job," he responded. He thought it was the silliest thing he had ever heard, and I knew I could not convince him otherwise. I left my parents disappointed because they had looked forward to my spending the summer with them and helping Dad make his logging operation more profitable.

***

My first summer was a vivid learning experience. It began with the Southwestern Company's sales school in Nashville, which was an eye opener and taught by the best communicators in the country. Dortch was impressive on stage, but Mort Utley and Max Nunn were the best. I had no idea what to expect when sales school began. Speakers emphasized honesty, fair dealings, treating people with respect and helping the customers see the value of the Bible in their home as a teaching tool for their children. We were taught not to take advantage of people.

I left sales school with a good feeling about Southwestern as an ethical company — a good influence on young people. Its philosophy was in line with my father's teachings from across our kitchen table.

I went to Crawfordsville, Indiana, with my crew leader, Bobby Smothers. I appreciated being with Bobby because he had a proven track record. We came into town and asked preachers for their assistance in finding a home with an extra bedroom where we could stay for the summer. We looked for a family whose children had left home. We needed a vacant bedroom and access to a telephone. Our goal was to pay no more than $30 each per month for the room.

Trust was the key ingredient in getting a room with a good family. If they trusted us and thought we were fine young men, they would open their home to us. We explained our situation in detail so the family would be comfortable with us and to make sure there were no surprises. We found a place to stay with a good family — our first sale of the summer.

We began selling Bibles on a Monday morning, and I will never forget the feelings I had when I knocked on the first door and was turned down. Door after door, when I was able to make my presentation, I was turned down. My first day was a disaster.

My second day wasn't much better, but I did sell a *Comprehensive Analysis,* one of our other books, for $8.95 at about 3 p.m. Southwestern's money policy was to bring $30 or $40 to sales school. From sales school, we went directly to our territory and were within a few dollars of being broke. This way you had to sell Bibles to eat. We carried Bibles in our cars to sell for $29.95. But, in most cases, we would take a down payment of $5 or $10 — sometimes $15, collecting the balance the last two weeks of summer.

I was so happy to make the *Comprehensive Analysis* sale because I was broke. Until then, I didn't even have enough money for a hamburger. I went to lunch and thought about why I was not successful. It was obvious that I did not know how to sell Bibles, even though in my mind I could give my presentation as written and follow the instructions from sales school. After I ate my hamburger, I went back to knocking on those doors. My results still were not good, and I was discouraged.

That evening, I told Bobby I needed help. He agreed to let me observe him to see how he was getting inside the home to make a sale. The next morning, Bobby had the lady at the first door laughing within seconds. He seemed to have more fun than anyone, and he didn't take himself seriously. He told the lady about his newborn son with all the excitement of a new father and asked about her family. Then he got to the point.

"Mrs. Jones, I promised I would be brief, so let's look at my Bible and see if it could be helpful to you and your family. Please sit down."

He sat facing her and made his presentation in a relaxed manner, bringing laughter in a few places. She bought a Bible. The sale seemed to be so easy for Bobby. I analyzed his presentation and how he established rapport. It was a wake-up call for me. I observed three of Bobby's presentations, and he had good results each time. Then, he gave me some advice.

"Tom, I think you are trying too hard. Relax, be yourself, and you will make sales."

I did just that, and my sales were about $500 in the next four days — more than $200 profit for me. The following week my sales were more than $1,000, which was more than $400 profit for me. I began earning more than $50 per day after watching Bobby's skilled presentation. It was more money than I had ever earned in my life. I called my father to share my success after my first week, and he was surprised.

Bobby and I had a great summer and became friends with our host family. We were close in sales volume, and I was the crew's top salesman. Thanks to Bobby's guidance, I was able to relax and meet the customers as if they were my next-door neighbors.

I was determined to be honest and upfront with people. My first statement was always the same.

"If you don't think you will use this Bible, do not buy it. It's only a good buy if you actually think you will use it to teach your family. My presentation will be made to help you see how to use the different features of the Bible and how your family can benefit. Let's see what I have, and you can determine if it would be helpful."

As I gave my presentation, I held the Bible so customers so could read it while I pointed out different features. I looked down at the page, reading the words upside down, which amazed people. I always looked into the customers' eyes to build trust. And, observing the customer closely helped me close a sale. Reading body language is one of the keys in dealing successfully with people. It speaks as loudly as their words. The close is where many sales are made or lost. I stayed on message and pointed out the benefits of the Bible.

For people who could only pay for a portion of the Bible at the time of my visit, I had to get a solid commitment that they would pay the balance at the end of the summer. If they didn't, the Bible wouldn't be delivered. And poor deliveries could ruin your summer financially.

One time, I sold a Bible to an old fellow who was sitting in his swing. He did not have enough money, so he gave me $5 down, which I wasn't happy about. I tried to get a strong commitment.

"Son, I will pay you if I have to sell a hog," he said.

I wrote on my order form, "will pay if he has to sell a hog." He signed the order with the note on the form. I went back to his house at the end of the summer with his Bible, and sure enough, he started giving me a bunch of excuses. But I wouldn't have it.

"Mr. Jones, do you remember telling me that you would pay for your Bible if you had to sell a hog? Well, Mr. Jones, I am ready to load the hog."

He paid me.

It took strong communication sometimes to get people to keep their promises. But I never told a customer that it would ruin his or her credit. In fact, I did the opposite.

"If you don't pay me, no one will ever call on you for the money. You made a promise to me on this Bible because you thought it would be good for your family. I want you to do the right thing and keep the promise you made to me on this Bible. Do what's right for you, and do what's right for me."

One family caught up to me about two miles from their home with their headlights blinking and their horn blowing.

"I started thinking about what you said, and I don't think I could live with myself if I did not keep my promise to you," the fellow said. "Here is your money for my Bible."

"Thank you," I said as I shook his hand and handed him his Bible.

I seldom had a Bible that I did not deliver.

***

I sold a lot of Bibles, met a lot of nice people and had many interesting experiences. One household stood out, though. When I knocked on the door, a lady and her beautiful daughter met me. She was a knockout. She eyed me, and I was certainly fascinated with her good looks. She had just graduated from high school. Her mother said she was busy and asked me to show the Bible to her daughter. I thought that was fantastic.

Just before I finished my presentation, I popped the Bible shut, loudly, which startled her.

"I want a date for Friday night," I told her. "I will pick you up at 6:30."

"My mother will not let me go with you," she said after a pause.

"Let's call her in, and I will ask her," I replied.

Her mother came into the room, and I told her I had an unusual request. "I would like a date with your daughter Friday night."

"We don't know you," she said.

"I'm a UT student working my way through college selling Bibles. I would like a date with your daughter, and you can trust me to be a nice young man."

"Well, would you like to go?" She asked her daughter.

"Yes, I would."

Her mother gave us the okay. It was a fun date, and we had a good evening together.

***

I discovered that selling Bibles was a rich experience in how to do business with people. Every time I knocked on a door, I learned a lesson in human nature — a lesson in communication that is not taught at universities. I dealt with all kinds of people, making adjustments in my communication as I spoke with them on their turf.

The work could be fun and enjoyable, especially in the home of a good family after rapport and trust were established. Knocking on doors for 12 hours each day, however, and not knowing who would answer was challenging. I had to expect anything. I encountered drunk, unreasonable people who were having a bad moment and third-shift workers awakened from sleep as I spoke with their wives. Sometimes, these people came into the room in a rage. I learned how to handle it. I did not take it personally and remained focused on selling.

This made the work more rewarding as I encountered the full spectrum of human nature. The only way we could be successful was to become master communicators — astute observers of human nature, reading body language for positive signs to close the sale.

During my first summer, I learned more, grew more as a human being, gained more confidence and made more money than I had ever made in my life. I sold Bibles hoping I could pay my way through school, but that was not the real benefit. The value was in the education, learning about human nature and how to deal with all kinds of people.

When I became an entrepreneur, working with truck drivers, factory workers, accountants, office workers and a national sales force, selling Bibles was more beneficial than my college studies. Both were fantastic. One filled me with information. The other gave me real-world experiences and taught me what works and what doesn't. I was in more than 2,000 homes and observed families dealing with their children, which helped me later as a parent. I gained so much confidence that I felt I could fly over our nation, parachute down to any city and earn more than enough money to live a good life in service to people.

I came to realize that our real security is within. Your job can be taken, but your God-given potential and your successful mindset cannot be taken. I see this kind of thinking as a pass to freedom. This is financial freedom. The objective is not to make a living but to go for the higher reward — a mission of service, reaching your personal goals and living the life you dreamed.

Selling Bibles changed the way I viewed life. It raised my sights, and it taught me that I could set high goals and reach them.

***

After that summer, I returned to campus with about $2,500 — more than enough to cover my college expenses. Some of our professors only made $4,500 a year.

I bought a new 1957 Ford automobile and went to a clothing store to prepare for the new school year. I was one of the few people who could drive a new car, pay my way through school and have my closet stocked with up-to-date clothes that made me a well-dressed man. I can still see, in my mind's eye, my father in his blue serge suit with Mother's perfectly ironed white shirt taking up the collection in our little Buena Vista Church — a perfect example of a well-dressed man.

I spent a lot on the car and the clothes, so I decided to go to St. Louis to buy three cars and sell them for extra money. I went with my brother-in-law, Bob Kennedy, and purchased two 1950 Plymouths and an Oldsmobile.

I drove the blue 1950 Plymouth to the barbershop in Selmer for a haircut. George Huggins, who owned the drug store on the corner of Main Street, showed interest in it. I finished up with my haircut, went outside and told him I needed $300 for the car. George drove the car to check it out, liked it and paid me for it. He said it was exactly what he had been looking for in a second car. I was excited because I spent $150 on each Plymouth, and I had just made my money back.

The next week, I sold the other Plymouth for $300. This gave me enough money to clear the three cars with money left over. But the Oldsmobile became a problem. I wanted $350 for it, and no one was interested. I cut the price and sold it for $250, making a $50 profit with my gas expense. I made about $300 profit on my trip to St Louis, and it was a good learning experience. After selling the Oldsmobile, I realized I wasn't an expert on used car buying, but my profit would more than pay my tuition for the quarter.

I realized the importance of working from the neck up and taking risks.

***

When I returned to college, I sold flowers and shower shoes, but my main focus was signing up a large crew to sell Bibles with me the following summer.

Dortch came to campus and said he thought I should recruit about six people. He promised to come back to sign them if I could get them to agree to attend a meeting with him. I did not tell Dortch then, but my goal was a much larger crew, and I did not think I needed him to sign them.

I went to work to find the most capable people on campus — high-energy students who needed money to pay their way through school. I looked for people who had an outstanding personality and confidence, and people I could teach. I would not sign a person if I didn't think I could make him successful. If he didn't earn enough money, he couldn't pay his way in school, and I did not want to be a part of that.

I made a list of 15 to 20 people to interview after observing them in different settings. I asked for a meeting and told them I needed 30 minutes. I went into their dorm rooms and asked to lock the door so we would not be interrupted. Then, I presented the door-to-door, Bible-selling story without any sugarcoating. I wanted them to know upfront that it was a tough job. Not everyone had the ability and toughness of mind to knock on doors 12 hours a day, six days a week for three months. I gave them the details of the job with the financial benefits, but I talked more about the educational benefits of becoming a master communicator and developing empathy for people. I told them the earnings of different people — the good and the bad. Again, I did not sugarcoat anything. I did not want them to sign a contract unless they were dedicated to the idea of paying the price for success.

I motivated students and furnished leadership to make sure they made the money to pay their way through school. But many of them ran into resistance from their parents — just as I had. Many times, I would visit with their parents to help them see the picture in a more positive light. I did my best to help them understand that the experience of meeting doctors, lawyers, preachers, teachers, factory workers and farmers would change their sons forever. They would develop communicative skills they would carry throughout life, making them more successful in whatever they chose to do.

I told the students that their parents would be their first sale. "If you can't make that sale, you might not be able to sell Bibles."

Right away, I signed 12 students. Dortch called, asking if I had anyone for him to talk to.

"Yes, and I'm ready for your visit," I said.

Dortch asked how many guys I had for him to speak with and I told him I had more than six. I did not tell him that they had already been signed, and I only wanted him to meet them.

When Dortch came to campus, I told him how I had made my list to qualify the students before signing them. I was not interested in easy signings. I was interested in people being successful. He could not believe I found 12 people.

As we met with each person, Dortch was more than impressed with the guys and their attitudes. I explained that I let them know upfront that it was a tough business and required dedication and sacrifices.

"I did not want them to sign a contract unless they would dedicate themselves to paying the price for success," I said.

"This is a big crew for your first year," he said. "It is quite a responsibility."

Dortch didn't know it, but I planned to sign even more people.

About that time, Bill Cook came to visit and said that he wanted me to sign him a crew of 12 or 15 people, and we could work our crews together. Bill graduated the previous year, and he was a big name on campus. He earned $8,500 his last summer, and he drove a new Century Buick, which was one of the nicest cars on the road at that time.

My incentive for working our crews together was a portion of Bill's override commission. He thought Dortch would go along with the idea. My override was seven percent on my crew's sales, and Bill's was 12 percent because he had been selling for several years. I would get six percent on Bill's crew.

The word was out on campus that I was looking for students to work the following summer. Talk was very positive because I signed some outstanding people, and they talked up the benefits of the job. I also taught a class about the fundamentals of Bible sales. Some professors sat in on the class. Dr. John M. Gibbens, an economics professor, observed a class for about 15 minutes.

The next day he asked me how I was able to generate so much enthusiasm. He wanted to have some of that in his classroom.

"Do you believe that knowing economics will help your students?" I asked.

"Of course!" He replied.

"Then you should show that you mean it," I said. "Enthusiasm comes from the way we feel, and if you feel strongly about something, you can't help but be enthusiastic."

Dr. Gibbens and other professors talked about the money students were earning for their college expenses and the educational value of the sales experience. They asked me to join them for coffee to talk about my business. I saw this as an opportunity to spread the word further.

One evening as I walked down the hallway, Dr. Grady Taylor, a biology professor and one of my favorite teachers, said he wanted to talk to me about selling Bibles. We set up a time for me to visit with him and his wife at their home. Dr. Taylor was a confident man in his early 40s. He was handsome and slender, taller than six feet with dark, wavy hair. I was surprised by his request.

I went to his home and met his lovely wife. I began the interview by asking why he was giving thought to selling Bibles. He explained that he had been in school for many years. He obtained his Ph.D. and married while in college. He just bought a beautiful home, and his university pay wasn't adequate to give them the standard of living they wanted. I asked him if he had thought through what it would be like to compete with students and work 12 hours a day knocking on doors with numerous turn downs. He would also be away from his family much of the time.

Dr. Taylor was a great human being whom I respected, but I could not visualize him in the sales field with his students. It was a tough decision, but I told him that I did not think he should sign up to sell Bibles. I have often thought about what it would have been like if I had signed Dr. Taylor and taught him to successfully sell Bibles. If he had been my top salesman, it would have made recruiting on campus much easier.

***

Bill and I continued to sign our crew until we had 26 people. Dortch returned to campus to meet everyone, still surprised at the number we recruited. He expressed his appreciation to me for the job I had done. But, he reiterated the responsibility. I had to help the young men be successful. I told Dortch I planned to have one of the best crews in the Southwestern Company.

When the Nashville sales school ended, Bill and I asked our crew to divide into pairs and select a conveniently located town in their territory. Generally, only one person would be assigned to a county. For the most part, the students had already discussed and decided who would be spending the summer together. Our crew worked a good part of Indiana and some counties in Illinois. We then gave them instructions on how to find a good, supportive family with whom to spend the summer.

Southwestern's practice was for crew leaders to meet each Sunday afternoon, in a park or other suitable location, to encourage their crew and help them reach their sales goal. That was what Bobby Smothers, my crew leader, did the previous summer. We mostly talked about who sold the most Bibles. To me, too much attention was given to the top salesman and not enough attention was given to teaching Bible sales. We had no organized sales training, and I disagreed with their approach.

I was determined to change that practice with my crew. My idea was to go to the local university in my sales territory and reserve a classroom where we could meet from 1 to 4 p.m. each Sunday for training. The young men wanted to be successful, but there was too much to learn in the Nashville sales school. They needed and wanted help with the problems that arose each week in the field. In a classroom setting, we could share our experiences in an organized way and talk about what worked and what didn't.

Bill was not positive about my teaching the fundamentals in a classroom setting. He was No. 2 in sales for Southwestern out of up to 775 student salesmen and one of the most driven young men I had ever seen. He set goals and paid the price to reach his goals. But up to this point, Bill had not been very successful with his crews because he concentrated on his personal sales goals.

He would meet in the park on Sunday afternoons and brag about the top salesman, but his other crewmembers had to fend for themselves. I was convinced, however, that we had been missing an opportunity.

When I arrived in my territory, I called on the local university president. He looked over his glasses at me as I explained how I wanted to reserve a classroom on Sundays during the summer where I could have meetings with my crew. He was not impressed with my request and said the university closed its classrooms on the weekends. His attitude irritated me greatly — a university president who was not interested in college students working their way through school.

I let him know I could not believe what I was hearing. I put a guilt trip on him. He relented and said he would support my request if I could get the custodian to unlock the room and clean and lock it back after our meeting. I stood up, shook his hand and asked where I could find the custodian.

The custodian could not have been a nicer guy. He said he would be delighted to make the arrangements. I gave him a few dollars each Sunday for his efforts.

We sent word to our crew about our upcoming Sunday meetings. Bill and I were in the center of our territory, and most of the guys were within 100 or 150 miles. They could team up, saving money on fuel. Someone asked about attending church on Sundays. Bill told them that they were there that summer to sell Bibles and they could go to church when they went home. He took the job very seriously. But I thought differently. I told them that I was glad to hear the question and emphasized that I wanted them to continue their church habits. Find a church on your way to the meeting, I told them, stop for service and then continue on. I don't know how many took my advice, but I did not want to stand in their way of going to church.

Every person came to our first meeting, which impressed us. It was unusual to have a crew of 26 men with no one quitting the first week. They survived, which was a good sign they were off to a good start.

The comprehensive sales meetings were upbeat and solved problems. It was important that we enable students to increase sales and provide inspiration for another week of knocking on doors. We always spoke about maintaining a healthy body — getting at least eight hours of sleep and eating a balanced diet with plenty of water. We cautioned to not live off hamburgers and fries. Our meetings were the lifeblood of our successful summer, and we looked forward to them.

We asked the company's top salesmen to give a presentation to our group, following the sales script taught in Nashville. I called Ted Welch — the company's No. 1 salesman and one of Bill's fierce competitors. He came to one of our meetings to demonstrate the importance of eye contact and mannerisms to garner trust and goodwill. It was a long drive for Ted, and I was grateful for his sacrifice. He did a super job and received a standing ovation. Ted spoke about saving time and not wasting a minute with idle conversation. Every word had a purpose. He was an inspiration to the group, and I am sure he increased our sales.

***

Furnishing leadership to young men was a wonderful learning experience for me, and I think I learned more than anyone that summer. Bill and I had our individual strengths. I could not match Bill's sales. He would not work with the men in the field, so it was my responsibility. And if some men did not get extra help, they might quit. I felt a serious obligation because they had placed trust in me when they signed up, and I had promised that, if they would do their part, I would do my part to help them be successful. It was a promise I would keep. I was reminded how helpful Bobby had been for me the previous summer.

I turned my attention to Johnny Fowler and his roommate, Wallace. Johnny was an engineering student who had just gotten married, and he needed to make some money. Johnny was struggling, and I went to ride with him. He was to observe as I made presentations. When I arrived at their room, they opened their refrigerator to show me that they were down to a few pieces of cheese and bologna. Johnny sat on his bed as I laid out the plan for the next day. I could see his eyes were full of emotion. He desperately wanted to learn how to be successful earning enough money to get back in school.

The next morning, we went to make our first call. As we drove into the yard, we noticed a man and his wife coming from the barn. They were about 65 years old. Their children had left home. They had been milking before we arrived, and the lady wore a bonnet that reminded me of my mother. I greeted them as they approached us. We sat on the ledge of their well. They were not excited about the idea at first, but I gave them the presentation, and they bought the Bible.

We headed back to our car, and Johnny was impressed.

"Tom, I could not have sold that couple a Bible," he said. "This is amazing."

I was happy I made a sale on our first call together. Having two sales people makes everything twice as difficult — especially getting in the door. We made two or three more sales, and Johnny realized that his problem was not his territory. It was his approach. He was much like me when I first began selling. He was most grateful.

I then rode with Wallace and made some sales. They got the hang of it, began to believe in themselves and had a successful summer.

Johnny eventually graduated with his engineering degree and later accepted a position as the director of Pickwick Electric in Selmer. I went by to see him one day.

"Tom, I would not be behind this desk if you had not signed me up to sell Bibles," he said.

"Why do you say that?"

"I learned how to communicate with people with a confidence I did not have previously. I am a different person because I sold Bibles." Johnny went on to become president of a bank in Union City and have a successful career.

***

As our summer continued, few people dropped out. The organized meetings saved the day. They went so well, boosting individual sales, that Dortch sent guys from other crews to learn from us. It was an honor, but I had about all I could manage. Bill and I were busy answering questions from our men when other people would raise their hands with more questions. We tried to be helpful to everyone, but it was challenging.

Our group reached some impressive numbers by the end of the summer. Dortch said we had the top crew in the company. We were not, however, recognized or given a traditional plaque. In those days, they had not established an incentive program for successful crew leaders, which was a mistake. Dortch did introduce me at the crew leaders' meeting during sales school the next year in Nashville. I believe it was the first year for training crew leaders, and Dortch asked me to share my experiences. I talked about securing the meeting room, our well-planned meetings and how they increased sales and decreased turnover.

***

At the end of that summer, I suffered a close call. Bill and I rented a big upstairs room from a family with a gas heating system. One evening, Bill and I called an end to a long day. He decided to go out, and I decided to take a shower before going to bed. When Bill returned, he found me unconscious in the shower with the water still running. Bill pulled me out of the room and called an ambulance.

I was rushed to the hospital and treated for gas inhalation. I regained consciousness in the hospital and did not recall anything about the incident.

The attending physician praised Bill's quick action. My arrival at the hospital was just in time. Five or 10 minutes later, I would have died. The gas system in the home had sprung a leak, and the fumes could have killed us both.

***

I developed and ran a successful business. I worked with my Bible crew successfully through the summer. I knew I wanted to be an entrepreneur, and building this business was perfect training. I made a considerable amount of money that summer from override commissions and my personal sales commission.

My crew returned to campus celebrating a successful summer. They were able to pay their way through school and had the freedom to buy things they would not have had otherwise. Their success and positive talk on campus made it easier for me to sign another capable crew of Bible salesmen for the following summer.

My third year selling and second year as a crew leader was similar to my previous year. I signed more people, and it was much easier as a sales manager. I was a better teacher with stronger leadership, helping my crew become more successful. Russell Caldwell was my top salesman. Russell and I roomed together our senior year and have been best of friends since. He started an office supply business from scratch after college and became a prominent businessman in West Tennessee.

***

I returned to campus that year with a new Bonneville Pontiac, paid for with earnings from Bible sales. During the school year, I made extra money selling flowers to the guys when they had a date to a dance. It was customary to present your date with a beautiful corsage for the evening, and generally, an orchid or carnation was ideal. I made $150 to $200 from my flower sales on each dance. We had three or four dances each year, which gave me extra spending money.

I also imported shower shoes from Japan that were not sold here in stores. Because no one had any, I had the market cornered. I bought them for 30 or 40 cents a pair and sold them for $2. I sold almost every person in the dorms a pair of shower shoes. We were accustomed to walking barefoot down the hallways to take a shower. My shower shoes were a perfect way to protect against cut glass and athlete's foot. These shower shoes would hit the market years later as flip-flops.

On-campus sales were good for my cash flow. Opportunities to use your head instead of your back were plentiful. We had students working their way through school at 50 cents per hour on the UT farm. I could make $15 or $20 an hour selling shower shoes.

My professors did not understand why I would not interview for a job during my senior year. I told them I wasn't interested. Three insurance companies came to campus to recruit me into the business. Harold Winstead, from Dresden, Tennessee, visited several times. He told me I could make the $1 million round table with my Southwestern background in selling. I think he was right, but it was not my mission. I turned him down.

Tom, his last year in college

Selling Bibles enabled me to be my own man. It gave me the courage and faith to believe in myself, set goals and reach them.

***

I majored in agriculture, but my heart was in other places. I spent a great deal of my time reading autobiographies of successful people. As I read, I was amazed to learn that the common thread was that they felt strongly about their mission and were willing to give their lives to accomplishing it. They were good, decent people with courage, faith and belief in themselves. They believed service to their fellowman was their highest calling. As I continued to read, I convinced myself that I should become a person on a mission.

The successful people I read about valued and respected their time. The only thing we have in this life is time. Everyone has a different amount of time before we end our life's journey. If we give time to something, we are giving a part of our life. This means our mission must be important — something we feel strongly enough about that we are willing to give a good part of our life.

I began to understand that selecting your mission is not to be taken lightly. And by the end of the year, I was willing to drive my stake down. My mission was entrepreneurship.

I saw that a successful business, in service to people, could provide many families a paycheck. It could enable them to send their kids to school, pay doctor bills, take vacations and do other things while living a good life. Being an entrepreneur was my calling. I had a successful mindset, and I was willing to take risks to build and expand businesses. I thought it would be a fruitful career and an exciting life.

My financial success would be measured by how much our company did for others. I knew there would be sacrifices, but I knew I could succeed.

Many of my Bible-selling friends shared the same passion.

At the sales school in Nashville, about ten of us would go out to dinner and talk about what life could be like after selling Bibles. At our dinner meeting my last year, Royce Reynolds — the top salesman in the company for two years — rose from his chair.

"I have decided on my mission," he said. "I'm going to General Motors to teach their dealers how to sell cars."

"Royce, have you ever sold a car?" someone asked.

"No, but that doesn't interfere with my mission. As I teach dealers how to sell cars, I will be looking for one of the more successful dealers — someone with the money to be financially free, whose wife wants him to retire to Florida to get some sand between his toes. I will become his partner in the dealership, and he can go to Florida with his wife. That's my mission!"

Our summer work gave us confidence. Royce went to college to get a good job. Selling Bibles changed him into a man with a mission to become one of the most outstanding businessmen of our time. Royce knew the fundamentals of selling as well as anyone. He also had the stage presence to dramatize ideas for excellent communication to any group for any product. He was a teacher of salesmanship.

I saw Royce about a year or two later in Birmingham, sitting behind a desk in a plush office at one of the largest General Motors dealerships in the country. His partner was in a Florida vacation home.

"Royce, it looks to me your mission worked out as you planned," I said.

"Exactly," he said. "My partner is one of the finest men you could ever hope to meet, and I am so fortunate to be his partner in this well-run dealership."

"What are you reaching for and striving for now?" I asked him.

He smiled. "You may think my goal is money," he said. "It's much simpler. I want to be a businessman under construction — to create and expand the business in service to people. With these goals, I should always have plenty of money."

Royce wasn't the only one of us with that philosophy.

Ted Welch and Jim Ayers, two boys from Parsons, Tennessee, who worked their way through college selling Bibles, have made a huge difference in the lives of thousands of people.

Ted became the commissioner of Finance and Administration and chief operating officer for the state of Tennessee from 1971 to 1974 under Governor Winfield Dunn. He was state finance chairman during Lamar Alexander's first bid for Governor. He also was finance chairman of the Tennessee Republican Party and finance chairman of the Republican National Committee.

In 1985, I was in Washington for the President's Dinner, which Ted chaired. President Ronald Reagan stepped to the podium after Ted's introduction and put his arm around Ted's shoulders.

"Ted Welch is the greatest political fundraiser the country has ever produced," the president said. As I watched Ted with President Reagan, I thought that this Bible peddler had done well.

Jim Ayers built a chain of nursing homes throughout the country and sold them. He is now one of the most successful bankers in the United States. He is the sole owner of FirstBank, which is headquartered in Lexington, Tennessee, with more than 50 locations across the Southeast. In 1999, he launched the Ayers Foundation Scholars Program, which has made higher education possible for qualifying, graduating seniors in Decatur County, Tennessee. He has since expanded that offer to students in other counties.

Another friend, Spencer Hays, came from humble beginnings and worked his way through Texas Christian University selling Bibles. As a 14-year veteran of summer sales, he became president of Southwestern in 1972. A few years later, he and other investors organized a buyout and formed Southwestern/Great American, which later became Southwestern Advantage. Spencer is the executive chairman of the board. He founded the Tom James Company — one of the largest manufacturers and retailers of custom clothing. In 2013, he was listed in *Tennessee Trivia* as being worth around $800 million.

With all of his success, Spencer still invested long hours pursuing his mission. One Saturday, I stopped by his office. He greeted me with a big smile, full of enthusiasm.

"You're in your office early on a Saturday morning," I said. "What drives you as a businessman?"

"Tom, I was born into a poor family and reared by my mother and grandmother. I remember running down the street barefoot, and the neighbors would say, 'there goes that Hays kid.' I may well be running from that picture in my mind, doing my best to leave it in the distance."

The day Spencer signed the Southwestern contract to sell Bibles and pay his way through college, he had no idea it would change his life forever. He has inspired thousands of young people to become promising entrepreneurs of tomorrow, to build and expand businesses.

Young men, who signed up to sell Bibles to work their way through school, were transformed. We developed bigger-than-life missions and the confidence to live our dreams.

***

Dortch Oldham and my Southwestern experience changed my life. He was a great teacher and a perfect role model. He taught Sunday school during most of his professional life in a large Presbyterian church in Nashville. He was a dedicated Christian with a value system from which he never strayed in his business life.

Most of his Bible boys, like me, did not know anything about selling other than what we were taught at Southwestern. Dortch made sure he filled our empty vessels with good stuff to make a positive difference in our lives.

He taught us to never, ever give up. He also was interested in each of us personally.

"If I can get the boy right, the company will be right," he would say.

He focused on elevating people to have the confidence to dream big and the courage to make those dreams come true. He wanted us to understand that honesty pays.

"Don't dig in the dirt," he told us. "Never sell a Bible dishonestly. Sell as if your customer is your best friend. You are not a beggar. Don't tell the customer you're working your way through college unless they ask. If you want to beg, get yourself a tin cup and go to the street. Help the families see the value of having a Bible in their homes to teach their kids how to live a good life."

Dortch also was a good listener. I called him once to dump my bucket. I shared all the problems I had: keeping my crew positive, working with crew members and demonstrating how to make sales to keep them from quitting.

"Tom, if you didn't have problems as you've described, you wouldn't have a job," he said, quietly. "Be thankful that you have problems to solve and the opportunity to help those young men get back in school with money in their pockets to pay their bills. You are doing important work. Be thankful."

He always knew what to say as a leader to keep his boys going in the right direction. He had enough maturity and wisdom to know he was making a difference in young men's lives. He was in the business of molding us for a successful future.

After his Bible boys earned their college degrees and went their different paths, he did his best to stay in touch and express words of encouragement to celebrate their success.

Years later in 2008, after Sherry and I developed our furniture business, I spoke with Dortch by phone. He asked how my business was going and said he had heard so much about our unusual showroom. He really wanted to see it. He planned to drive 150 miles from Nashville with his wife, Sis. He said he could make it if he took his time.

"I have a better idea, Dortch," I said. "Just the other day, I was talking to another one of your Bible boys, Russell Caldwell, and we discussed getting together at my store. So, I'm calling Russell to set a date, and we will pick you and Sis up in our motor home to make the trip to Selmer. Sherry and Russell's wife, Patricia, will come along. We will have coffee on the way, and I want you to sit in the co-pilot's seat. It reclines, and you will have a comfortable trip. I will have you home by 5 p.m."

We came in through the front door, and he saw the showroom, which depicted a small-town Main Street with glittering lights and oak trees. My daughter, Susan, met and embraced him. He began to cry. He was proud of what his Bible boy had created, and his emotions got the best of him. To me, that is love in action. We gave them the grand tour and had lunch at Henco's Whistle Stop Café.

Dortch and Sis were grateful for the day's outing. I was happy they were able to see the store and that we could visit. Dortch died February 26, 2009, after an incredible life far removed from its humble beginnings. He was 89.

He earned millions of dollars, becoming one of the great success stories in Tennessee. His greatest success, however, was helping young men acquire the mindset to live their dream.

Dortch served in World War II, was a candidate for Governor of Tennessee in 1974 and was named by President Reagan as the highest-ranking U.S. official at the Knoxville World's Fair. He came out of retirement to be president of Nashville's Chamber of Commerce. He was instrumental in bringing American Airlines to Nashville, and he did much more.

Dortch was a role model who shaped my life and my business philosophy to do my best to elevate people as I built my business. Because of him, I knew that if you get the employee right, you would get the business right.

There is no way to count how many businesses have been created in this country as a result of Dortch's Bible boys. He helped create more millionaires, in service to other people, than anyone can imagine. We would be much better off if we had more men like him.

I had the privilege to speak on behalf of UT Martin to a group of Bible boys at Belle Meade Country Club in Nashville. The purpose was to endow the Dortch Oldham Center for Economic Education and Entrepreneurship for $1 million. I reminded them how this good man had changed all of our lives for the better, and it was our time to be generous.

"We should open our wallets in honor of Dortch, in appreciation for his contributions in the lives of the people here tonight," I said,

Charlie Cox stood up and pledged $400,000. Originally from McKenzie, Charlie had no family and was forced to live with several different families as he grew up. When he graduated high school, service clubs in McKenzie raised money to help pay Charlie's college expenses for his first year at UT Martin. Charlie met Dortch and sold Bibles. Charlie invested in the stock market as he worked his way through college. He said he never made an important decision without Dortch's counsel. He had never had a father until he met Dortch, and that was why he enthusiastically gave his money.

When UT Martin dedicated the Dortch Oldham Chair of Economics, Charlie and I were asked to speak. When Charlie stood at the podium, he became too emotional and could not speak. His love for Dortch was overwhelming.

***

Lamar Alexander invited a group of us to the Governor's mansion for a presentation. When it was over, Governor Alexander stood at the door and thanked us for coming. He looked around and remarked that we should have a Bible sales meeting.

"There's a full house!" He said.

In the doorway stood Bill Cook, Jim McCarthy, Ted Welch and myself. All of us were Bible boys. And none of us would be in the Governor's mansion if it weren't for Dortch Oldham.

CHAPTER 6
STARTING A NEW LIFE

"We never know our strengths until we are tested."

I often say that my college years were the most fun of my life. I enjoyed dating different girls on campus, but I was determined to keep from getting serious with any one girl until my last year in school.

But in the spring of 1959 — a very important year in my life — everything changed. I found that perfect person. Her name was Sherry Lynne Smith.

Sherry dated my roommate. He told me she had class and was a sweet person from a wonderful family.

The yearbook staff held an annual beauty review on campus, and the queen and her court were featured in the yearbook. Sherry was chosen to be in the queen's court. To me, she was the most beautiful girl on the stage. I thought to myself: "I believe my roommate is right; she does have class."

A few weeks later they ended their courtship. One evening, my best friend, Robert Patrick, and I were at the girl's dorm. Robert suggested we get a date and go to dinner and a movie in Jackson.

"Robert, I don't have a date," I said.

I looked up. Sherry walked down the stairs with two other girls, and I changed my tune.

"Robert, I may have a date," I said as the girls approached, and I turned my attention to Sherry. She was surprised, but agreed to go. When I returned to my dorm, she called me on the phone to cancel. Her parents had come for an unexpected visit. They drove about 100 miles, and she needed to spend time with them. I said I would take a rain check.

The following week, Sherry and I had our first date at one of my favorite restaurants in Fulton, Kentucky, the Brown Derby. It was a nice place with white tablecloths and great food — a beautiful setting. We had a great evening. I was smitten.

Sherry did not have a pretentious bone in her body; she was genuine. I said to myself that she was my kind of girl. She was 18, and I was 27, but the

Sherry Smith and Tom Hendrix at a college dance

age difference did not seem to matter because she was mature thinking and a smart young woman. We dated consistently until the end of the school year.

Then it was time for me to attend Southwestern's sales school in Nashville. Sherry and I exchanged letters throughout the summer, and I certainly missed being with her. I returned home a few days before the fall semester began, and I looked forward to seeing her. By our second date, however, I sensed something had changed. While I was away for the summer, a former boyfriend had come back into the picture.

We enrolled in school the next week. We would see each other, as friends, but there were uneasy feelings between us. We were sorting things out in our minds, and I think it bothered us that we were not dating. Some of her friends even told us we needed to get back together. About two or three months passed before I picked up the phone and gave Sherry a call.

"Sherry, I would like to buy you a milkshake at Zippo's, and I can be there in 30 minutes," I said, and a short pause followed.

"Great!" She finally said.

That evening at the Zippo stand, we began dating again in earnest. We talked and got to know each other on a different level. I wanted to delve into her mind as much as possible to see how she viewed life. I was determined to find a person with whom I could be happy. I needed someone who was special in many ways, because I knew our lives would not be smooth sailing. The more we got to know each other, the more I felt she was the one for me. I thought we could have a happy life together regardless of the problems we encountered.

Just before we finished the winter quarter of 1959, I called Sherry and asked her to go to the Zippo for a Coke. We drove south on Highway 45 about three miles to a roadside park. I backed my car up to a fence and asked Sherry to marry me, to take a journey with me. She said "yes!" We were engaged.

We decided to tell her parents at Christmas. I bought an engagement ring in Jackson and prepared to ask her father for her hand in marriage. Sherry's school quarter ended, and she went home to be with her family.

She knew her parents wanted her to finish college, and she knew they would be apprehensive about her marrying when she was only 19. Our age difference didn't seem to matter that much to them since her paternal grand-parents' ages were similar when they married. It was more a matter of Sherry getting her degree before she married. Sherry was nervous about their reaction and delayed discussing our decision. They knew we had been dating steady, but they didn't know our relationship was that serious.

***

I finished my senior year at the end of the winter quarter. College life was over. On my way home, I stopped at a Milan restaurant and saw a man who had attended UT Martin. He asked me what I planned to do after graduation. I told him that I wanted my own business, but wasn't sure what it would be.

"Mr. Worbois, sitting at the other table, has a warehouse full of stack stools that he wants to sell and will sell them below cost," he said.

I asked a few questions, and he told me that he would ask Mr. Worbois to join us. I met Mr. Worbois, and he suggested that we go to his warehouse and see the stools. They were neat little stack stools with black metal tubular legs and available in four colors. He was going out of business and said he would sell them below cost at $1.25 each. I was impressed with them, es-pecially the price. I bought four, in different colors, to make up my mind about selling them. I also wanted to get other people's reaction to buying one for $4.95. Everyone I showed them to reacted well.

I telephoned Mr. Worbois and said that I could sell his stools. I called three of my Bible boys and asked if they'd like to make some Christmas money. They agreed to meet me in Milan to try our hand at selling the stools.

The next morning, we had a sales meeting. Our plan was to take the seat out of the car, empty the trunk and load as many stools as possible, leaving just a small place to sit and drive. The boxes were four inches by 16 inches. My Bonneville Pontiac, with the seat out, could hold more than 70 boxed stools. I had a Tennessee road map and divided the roads around Milan into four territories, using highways as boundaries. We planned to stop at every retail business, including service stations, unstack the stools and sell as many as possible. They were perfect Christmas gifts.

We sold them to retailers for $2.95 so they could sell them to customers for $4.95. We sold a lot. Some people would buy six, 12 or 24 stools. Occasionally, I would sell 48. We sold for six days up until Christmas, and I sold two carloads each day. I earned about $1,000 in six days with $1.70 profit per stool and my 45-cent commission on the other guys' sales. Selling the stools was fun and much easier than Bibles.

***

I went to see Sherry before Christmas, and we helped decorate the Christmas tree. Sherry's mother, Johnnye, stood on a footstool, placing ornaments.

"Mrs. Smith, I would like for you to get down off the stool and have a seat here by Mr. Smith," I told her. "Sherry and I have something important we want to talk with you about."

"Go ahead," she said. "I'm listening."

"No, you need to get down off that stool for what I have to say," I responded.

She heard the seriousness in my voice, and she sat down. Mr. Smith watched as I reached for Sherry's hand.

"I'm asking for your daughter's hand in marriage," I said.

Her parents were shocked. They had many questions and emphasized how they wanted Sherry to finish school. As we talked, they could tell we were serious, and they gave us their support and blessings.

That was one of the happiest days in my life. Sherry and I were getting married! We went to Jackson for dinner at a nice restaurant, and I gave Sherry her

December 1959: Engaged

engagement ring. Our friends, Robert Patrick and Jacqueline Haley, joined us later to celebrate.

Sherry's parents requested that we plan our wedding for the end of the summer. Sherry, who worked summers at Harvey's Department Store in Nashville, wanted to be home to help with the preparations. We set the date for August 28, 1960.

***

I went to Nashville to visit my mentor and good friend, Dortch Oldham, to tell him about our marriage plans. Dortch had met Sherry, and he was excited for us.

"Tom, what are your career plans?" He asked.

"I want to create a national business with a national sales force, but I have no idea how to go about it," I said. "I am looking for ideas that I can turn into a national effort."

"That could take some time," Dortch said.

"I've turned down several job offers," I said.

Dortch reached for a pad on his desk and listed 13 companies.

"Tom, I think you can go with any company, and I will arrange for you to interview. Why don't you go to work with one of these companies and continue to brainstorm ideas on your national sales force?"

I looked at the list of companies.

"How do I get started? What is your number one recommendation?"

"I would start with National Cash Register," he responded.

"Why is NCR at the top of your list?"

"It's a progressive company with a dominant share of the market," he said. "It has an excellent reputation. With your sales ability, you will do quite well."

In 1960, IBM had not yet brought its computer system to the business community. NCR was the dominant player with the most advanced business systems. They sold cash registers, calculators and other business products. Of course, things would change a few years later.

I told Dortch I wanted an interview with NCR. He called Mr. Klutz and made a 1 p.m. appointment.

The reason Dortch could list 13 companies was Southwestern's great reputation, and people knew his Bible boys were seasoned salesmen. Companies called him regularly for a chance to interview the young men he recommended.

When I went to the NCR interview, I liked Mr. Klutz immediately. We hit it off, and he said he wanted me to come to work with NCR. He needed me to go through a battery of tests and fill out a lot of paperwork. It was long and laborious and took the remainder of the day. When I was done, Mr. Klutz told me that I had passed with flying colors.

"We have not talked about money," I said.

"Tom, you will start as a trainee at trainee pay. Then you will move to our starting pay."

Trainee pay wasn't enough for me to live on, so I told him I'd give it some thought.

Mr. Klutz called me a few nights later and asked what pay I could live with. He told me to come in the next day so we could work it out.

The training was interesting and educational. I spent every minute learning as much as I could. When the NCR salesmen came into the office, I asked as many questions as possible.

I learned about their attitude, their earnings at different commission levels, and how they viewed the business. I was not impressed with their responses.

As I spoke with these people, I pictured my future. I did not like what I saw.

I shared my concerns with Sherry. If I stayed with NCR and lived in Nashville, we discussed how she could continue her college education there. My decision would affect that possibility.

At the beginning of my third week, I went to see Mr. Klutz. (In the two weeks I worked at NCR, I never learned his first name.)

"This is not what I want to do," I told him.

"What happened?" He asked.

"I interviewed your salesmen, and I cannot picture myself in their shoes in the future," I responded.

"What are you going to do?"

"Start my own business."

"Young man, you are too energetic for your own good!"

I thanked him for hiring me and explained I was truly sorry for it to end so quickly. I shook his hand and left as his friend.

On my way out of town, I stopped by to see Cavit Cheshier, my friend and college professor at UTM, and his wife, Mary Evelyn, to tell them I was leaving NCR to go into business for myself. Cavit couldn't believe I was leaving NCR so soon. He thought I was making a big mistake parting ways with a national company with a great reputation. He had been impressed I got a job with NCR and thought I would spend a lifetime with them.

It was customary in the 1950s and 1960s to find a respected company for a lifetime career and a gold watch at the retirement party. To think I would dismiss that opportunity to start a business with a new idea on borrowed money did not make any sense to Cavit and Mary Evelyn. But I told them I had strong feelings about being in business for myself.

"Where are you going to get the money?" Cavit asked.

"I'm not sure."

"If you reconsider, do you think NCR would take you back?" He asked.

"That's out of the question. I'm going to pursue my dream with my own business, and I know it won't be easy because I don't have any money."

We turned our focus to dinner. It was a delicious meal with great conversation. When we finished, I left for Bethel Springs to share the news with Mother and Dad. They also thought it was a mistake to leave NCR.

Sherry's parents were disappointed, too. They wanted her to finish college.

And I needed to figure out what to do next. I thought about those stack stools and questioned whether I could develop a plan to sell them to department stores and furniture stores. Could the stools be manufactured efficiently for a quality product? What would be the capital outlay? Could I borrow the money with a partner? I had more questions than answers.

I called Russell Caldwell and Jimmy Joe Freeman, my Southwestern colleagues, to discuss going in business with me. We met in Adamsville, and I presented the idea of the three of us borrowing $10,000 each to manufacture and sell the stack stools. They were an attractive product, and I thought we could sell them for a profit.

We discussed the importance of a business plan based on facts to be sure the idea made economic sense. We certainly did not want to start a company only on emotion and good intentions. It also was important to spend the time necessary to gather the facts before we thought about borrowing money.

Russell and Jim agreed the idea was worthy enough to develop a business plan, and they said they could borrow the necessary money if they thought the plan would succeed in the marketplace. We went to work on the plan. Jimmy's father, Artill, provided expertise about manufacturing the stools. We priced out the materials, labor, rent, overhead and selling cost. I went to the Small Business Administration office in Nashville for an SBA loan. It was a new experience for me, because I knew nothing about SBA's lending policies.

I asked the loan office for suggestions to make my business plan better, because I didn't have all the answers. I explained my Bible-selling experience, and they were familiar with Southwestern and its reputation.

I went through our business plan, and they asked many questions. Some I could answer, and some I couldn't. But I wanted to be brutally honest. I was there to present as many facts as I could. They liked the idea enough to plan a visit to Adamsville to see where we would manufacture the stools. We set a time for 11 a.m. the following Wednesday.

Russell had second thoughts. He was interested in starting an office supply business. Jim and I were the only remaining partners. After looking over our situation in Adamsville, SBA agreed to loan $20,000 to match our investment.

I drove to the Home Banking Company in Finger, Tennessee, to see its president, Mr. Rudolph Barber. I dated Mr. Rudolph's daughter after high school, and I knew him quite well. He knew my father very well. I presented my plan for a $10,000 loan. Mr. Rudolph said he would make the loan if my father would guarantee it.

My father agreed to sign the note, which jeopardized the farm he had worked 20 years to pay for. Asking my father to sign the note was one of the biggest mistakes of my business life.

Jim and Artill could borrow only $7,500. SBA loaned us $20,000, and we launched our business as Mid-South Products Sales Corporation. A short time later, we changed the name to Nasco because we thought it sounded better.

Artill began setting up the plant to produce stools. I helped him on weekends and during my free time because getting a quality stool produced was important to launching our company.

Drawing on my Bible experience, Jim and I decided to recruit and hire about 20 college students to sell our stools door to door during the summer. We went to north Alabama to hire them. School was to be out within three weeks, and students were looking for summer jobs, so our timing was perfect. I felt sure I could teach them how to sell stools successfully, and based on my previous experience, I knew home owners would be more likely to buy a stool than a Bible.

We told the students to attend three days of intensive sales training the first week out of school. We wrote a simple but effective stool presentation to cover the advantages of purchasing them. We knew it would work if the presentation was given properly with a happy face, which was a must in the business.

The students arrived at a hotel in Savannah, eager to learn how to sell stools to pay their college expenses. As I taught the sales school, I focused on making the job fun. I told them to make Mrs. Jones laugh as often as possible, but stay on message to make sure she understood how handy the stools would be around the house.

The stools were $4.95 — a great price for making many sales each day. Their profit per stool was $1.75. I told them that some days, after some practice, the better salesmen could sell 50 stools in a day. They could earn up to $2,000 in a summer, which was more than enough to pay their college expenses. They would meet many families each day and learn how to improve their communicative skills. It was an experience never to be forgotten.

We adjourned the sales school and everyone went to the factory in Adamsville to load their cars with stools. But when we arrived at the plant, Artill said the stools were not ready. I had called him each day to make sure the stools would be ready, and he assured me the students would be able to pick them up after their training. It was an embarrassing situation. After a very successful sales school, a motivated group of young men was ready for a great start only to find out there were no stools.

Artill had done his best to manufacture them, and I am sure he did not deliberately lie to me, but I wished many times that he had prepared me for the fact that the stools might not be ready. If he had, we could have told the young men to pick up their stools a few days later.

Artill said they could come back the next week. It was only a delay of one week, but after promising them the stools, we immediately lost credibility. They were upset and rightly so. We could not recover from this mistake, and we knew our hard work was flushing down the drain.

The situation made me realize I had a rocky road ahead. I had to maintain a positive mental attitude, which would require much soul searching.

***

I went back on the road selling stools to furniture stores, small and large department stores, and anyone else who would buy them. My sales ranged from 24 to 200 stools on 30-day terms. I didn't sell to everyone, but my credit checks were surely lacking to be able to collect the money as promised. Because I did not have the stools with me, I could not sell them for cash.

In essence, I was selling myself out of business with each order. After a month, we realized we had a collection problem. Because the stools were not a part of the retailer's major lines, store owners had no pressure to pay the invoice. If they did pay it, it was 60 to 90 days later. Our operating money dwindled. The businesses knew we had no practical way to collect a small account because it was not enough money to sue them. I created an account receivable problem that paralyzed our company.

The straw that broke the camel's back was a Chicago stool company. It produced a plastic molded stack stool at an unbelievably low price and could sell them retail at about our manufacturing cost.

Our business model would not work financially. There had to be another way. I laid awake at night trying to think of another market to better control our price. Our business had a rocky start with manufacturing problems, and Jim and I had problems relating to job descriptions. We agreed we would do the selling, and Artill would be responsible for manufacturing. But Jim would not make a sales call. He always had a reason to not make the call. It caused me to doubt our partnership. His father was there early and late doing everything he could to make the business successful. I could not have asked for a fairer, more diligent person. Artill was a gem. But Jimmy was in over his head, and I realized I had relied too much on friendship and not enough on good business judgment. I racked my brain daily to figure out how to get out of this trap. The partnership must come to an end.

It was my mistake to select a person without the depth of experience to pioneer a new company. I should have known better. I never blamed Jimmy as much as myself. I misjudged him. It was immaturity, on my part, to look no further than our friendship and his investment dollars.

***

Sherry and I moved closer to our wedding date. We talked about where we were going to live. Our lives were changing. I made sure she knew about my negative business situation and limited my spending to the bare necessities. She listened, but did not seem alarmed. We talked about financial problems that

Jimmy and Artill Freeman and Tom with stack stools.

could happen when starting a business with borrowed money. We prepared ourselves for a rocky start. My attitude was to do my best to make the most of each day.

Sherry's parents asked about my business. I told them that most new businesses struggle in the beginning, and that was as much information that I had for them. I did not want to alarm them. They would be highly concerned if they thought their young daughter was marrying a person in financial trouble with an unsure future. They were conservative, and they avoided risks whenever possible. I thought the less they knew of my new business, the better.

As our wedding day approached, I rented a small house in Adamsville. It had two bedrooms, a living room, a bath and a kitchen. I borrowed $400, and we bought an inexpensive bedroom and dinette suite and a used refrigerator and stove. My sister, Roslyn, gave us a sofa and chair she had discarded. One sofa cushion had a sizeable hole. We placed a magazine over the hole, but it only called attention to the problem. Sherry and her mother made drapes for the living room and bedroom windows. Sherry's father built a bookcase, and they gave us a television at Christmas. With our many wedding gifts, we had the basics to begin housekeeping.

Sherry and her mother planned a nice wedding on a lean budget. Sherry's cousin, Betty Burton Laster, loaned her a wedding dress, which fulfilled the traditional, "something borrowed." Sherry's mother custom-made her mother-of-the-bride dress and a junior bridesmaid dress for Sherry's nine-year-old sister, Jonetta, her only sibling. Sherry's generous aunts loaned many items for the wedding and reception. They prepared a rehearsal party for us at the home of Sherry's Aunt Nell and Uncle James Lawson England in Decaturville. Our close-knit family came together to make our wedding day special for us.

The wedding began at 4 p.m. at the First Methodist Church in Decaturville. Reverend John Horton, a longtime friend of mine, officiated. John and I first met when he pastored our Buena Vista Church and attended Lambuth College in Jackson. He enjoyed bird hunting with my father and my mother's good food. We became close and are still friends today.

Sherry suggested we memorize our marriage vows and repeat them to each other. It made us a little nervous, but speaking the vows directly to each other, looking into each other's eyes, was special and emotional. The part, 'til death do us part,' was poignant. We married for keeps.

Our groomsmen, bridesmaids, vocalist and pianist were friends and members of our family. We decorated the church with baskets of white gladiolas, greenery and white satin bows. We had a nice reception in the recreation hall among family and friends, cut our wedding cake and drank some punch. After receiving loving best wishes and the traditional rice was thrown, we set off for our honeymoon in Gatlinburg and a new life together.

We spent our wedding night in Nashville at a Holiday Inn on James Robertson Parkway within sight of the capital. When we checked into the hotel, I told the desk clerk that we had just married, and she gave us a black ashtray designed as a skillet as a memento. We thought it was an interesting gift, but we appreciated it. I asked a porter to buy a bottle of pink champagne, thinking it would be romantic. Sherry only had a few sips because she had never tasted any kind of alcoholic beverage. I had the champagne all to myself.

Our honeymoon in the Great Smoky Mountains was perfect. We spent the last two days in Asheville, North Carolina, where we toured the Biltmore Estate. On our return through Chattanooga, we toured Ruby Falls deep inside

Lookout Mountain. It was a memorable week.

I borrowed $100 for our honeymoon from Artill Freeman. As we drove back into Adamsville, we spent $5 on groceries for our next week as newlyweds, using part of $20 that Sherry's parents had given her.

Married and a glass of punch

Life is a bit like getting into an automobile at night and turning on the headlights. They don't shine all the way home. They shine to the bottom of the hill. When you get to the bottom of the hill, they shine to the top of the next hill. Through faith, we believe the road will take us home. It's the same with life. Our light, simply, doesn't shine all the way.

After graduation from college, we see our first job and not much further. God must have known what He was doing when He made sure we could not see all of life in the beginning. We see it one piece at a time so we can completely concentrate on that project, gaining some experience and broadening our vision to see a bit farther.

Sherry and I had talked about the steep hills in life on the horizon, but we were ready for the challenges. We knew that one day the sun would shine brightly, and we could look back at our journey with pride.

Full of hope, I prepared to return to my new business. If it came to starting over, we could do it. I reiterated to Sherry that our challenge was not earning a considerable amount of money for a nice lifestyle, but to build a national business from borrowed money with little experience. I felt that I could become the person to build the business. I truly believed success was an inside job. I would become a student of life, learning from its experiences. We were going to live an unusual and exciting life if we could keep the faith and believe in ourselves to cushion the bumps in the road. We would grow daily in the direction of our ultimate goal. I knew that a lot of good could come from a gutsy approach, and I resolved to decline high-paying job offers as we climbed our mountain.

***

In the first year of the new business, we drew little in salary. In my case, I drew $50 per week. I traveled two or three days each week, making sales calls. To save money, I stayed in tourist homes for $4 a night and Junior Holiday Inns for $5.

Quarterly payments to the bank in Finger were required on my loan of $10,000. My weekly salary barely paid for our rent, electricity and groceries. I had to come up with some creative ways each quarter to make extra money to pay the bank and keep other bills up to date. I had no choice. I could never live with myself if the bank called the loan and put my father's farm in jeopardy. To generate cash flow, I called Southwestern and ordered some Bibles to sell for extra money, and I looked for creative ways to earn extra cash.

Brooks Roudebush in Adamsville manufactured tom-walkers, which worked like stilts. He showed them to me one day and asked if I could sell them. I thought about it, and I figured they probably would sell if I could get all the kids in Memphis to use them. We could have a tom-walker contest day with prizes for the best walkers and create lots of conversation. The contests could raise money for a worthy community cause, and the community would rally around the event. I wanted to create something similar to the hula-hoop craze. It was another venture to catch up on my bank payment.

I picked up samples from Brooks and headed to Memphis to call on Trent Wood at the WMCT television station. Trent's show, "Looney Zoo," was the most popular kid's program in Memphis at that time. Trent was fascinated with the idea.

I knew that in order to sell tom-walkers to many different groups, I had to sell the sizzle and stretch the mental picture for everyone to see it well. The idea must come alive in their minds and stir their imagination.

I told Trent my plan was to enlist Coca-Cola or Pepsi to sponsor the idea with their logo on the walkers. I also would solicit every Jaycee Club in Memphis and outlying towns, such as Collierville and Bartlett, to sponsor the idea. The Jaycees would select a charity as beneficiary. Trent's role would be to promote the event. I planned to kick off the fundraiser while walking around on 10-foot tom-walkers on Trent's show. I paused to see Trent's reaction.

"If you can sell Coca-Cola or Pepsi, come back to see me," he said.

I thanked him and left for the Pepsi office. I found the right person to speak with, and lo and behold, he bought into the idea of sponsoring the program. I think one reason that he agreed was he didn't want Coca-Cola's name on the walkers.

Trent was impressed.

"Do you think the Jaycees will participate?" He asked.

"Yes, if you will join us," I said. "Talk up the idea on your TV shows."

I felt good about the promotion. Trent thought it would be successful, and he agreed to help.

I called Jaycee presidents for appointments. My first was with the president of the Bartlett Jaycees, Ed Gillock. Ed was an attorney who later became a Tennessee state senator. I presented my idea to Ed, and he asked if I would show it to his club. They were meeting that night at seven. I said yes.

Ed was originally from Savannah in Hardin County. Because he was from a neighboring county from where I grew up, we had some common interests, and he knew many people that I knew. These were advantages as I made my first presentation to the club. Ed gave me a strong introduction.

My presentation went well as I laid out the program's concept, and the club voted to proceed. Club members were asked to call on every local merchant to sell a small quantity of tom-walkers until they reached a saturation point. I agreed to contact the department stores. We wanted tom-walkers to be in places throughout the city — everywhere you looked.

The Jaycees went to schools and set up tom-walker contests in shopping malls. I walked around on tom-walkers on camera for the evening news. The idea snowballed, growing bigger by the minute. I procured participation from all the Jaycee Clubs in Memphis and surrounding towns. They also contacted local merchants and visited schools.

Everything went as planned. For two weeks, Trent teased his audience with the statement: "Tom-walker is coming to town." And then it was time for my performance. I walked on the stage of Trent's "Looney Zoo" show on my bigger-than-life tom-walkers. It broke the place up with laughter.

We provided several pairs of the regular size for the audience so they could try their hand at walking on them. Trent tried, too. He put on a show for everyone! He was a good sport. The show went well, and I was pleased with the program's progress.

I frequently phoned the Jaycee presidents, making sure they were doing their part as promised. In return, they worried that I wouldn't be able to furnish the tom-walkers. I assured them they would be delivered as promised. We sold a ton of tom-walkers, but it did not become a new hula-hoop craze. Whoever pulled that one off was a dynamic promoter. I should have taken lessons from him. However, I earned some much-needed money to make two payments to the bank, and I had a rich experience with thousands of Memphians, young and old.

***

In a couple of months, to stay afloat and keep the bank from pulling my loan, I went to the Tri-Cities in Alabama — Florence, Muscle Shoals and Tuscumbia. I sold my stack stools door to door. I enlisted the Jaycees in Florence and Muscle Shoals as sponsors in a fundraising project for a worthy cause. I gave the Jaycees a dollar from each sale. They publicized the project, paving my way into the community, and furnished a delivery vehicle — a hearse painted red with "Jaycees" lettered on the sides. It grabbed attention, and it was fun to drive.

I made sales in a high percentage of the homes I visited by saying the stools were handy and could be used almost anywhere. We manufactured more stools than we could sell, so this was an effort to turn them into cash. I paid the company's manufacturing cost plus a small profit. I sold the stools for $4.95, and that gave me $3 per stool to pay my debts. I worked from 8 a.m. until after sundown. It was summertime, which gave me a lot of selling time. I earned up to $150 each day. I worked for several weeks to catch up on my bills, making $500 to $600 per week. In today's dollars that would be $1,500 to $1,800. It was good pay in 1960 when schoolteachers, for example, earned between $2,000 and $3,000 a year. Minimum wage was $1.

***

I chose my entrepreneurial mission and was determined to see it through. Sherry and I talked about the price to be paid, and we were willing to pay it.

I often called that period of my life my most successful because I was doing what few people would do. My problems were a test to see how much grit I had. I came to realize that it's not what's happening that makes you unhappy. It's what you think about it. We are in charge of our happiness by controlling our attitude.

It was nine years before Sherry and I could afford to live in a decent home. We lived in basement apartments or upstairs for lower rent. Regardless of our home, we were happy to be together and pursue our dream. Sherry never griped about not being able to pay our bills on time.

Years later, when Henco reached financial success, many people were happy for us, but they never had the opportunity to witness the best part. We paid the price for our financial blessings, and I will always treasure our time of struggle. They were our most successful years — in personal growth. We never know our strengths until we are tested. I drew strength recalling the biographies I read during my last year in college about people who were tested dramatically before they found success.

Chapter 7

Building a National Company

"Risk takers must have a deep resolve and thick skin
to pursue their dream."

When Sherry and I discussed our life together, I was upfront about my dream of building a national company, even though I had few tools in my tool chest to accomplish the task. I emphasized that I would build the company without money or a business degree. My strengths were a good understanding of human nature, the ability to sell any product if it was a good value, teaching salesmanship, helping people see my vision and leading people. I felt sure of my abilities to create a national sales force, but it would take time and patience, and we would have many disappointments.

I had my life to give to my mission, and I would not give up on reaching my goal. The challenge was to build a company from scratch with borrowed money.

Sherry was a special person to agree, without complaining, to struggle through hardships, knowing we could earn more money than we needed from different job offers. We chose to live a life of sacrifice to achieve our goal. At times, it was quite embarrassing for her when our creditors called or knocked on our door asking for money to pay our late car payment. But she stood by me, and we stayed the course.

***

During the time we were struggling with our fledging business, we had a visit from Jack McConnico, who owned and operated our local newspaper, the *Adamsville News*. He grew up in Brownsville, Tennessee, and attended Rhodes College and West Point. He had worked at Sears in Memphis as head of the creative department. He developed new ideas and expanded the business. One of Jack's ideas was opening catalog stores across the country. Sears insisted Jack move to Chicago, but Jack was determined not to rear his family there, so he left Sears. He recognized an opportunity with the newspaper in Adamsville, and his views on local issues benefited the community. Jack had prolific curiosity and strong philosophies. His first visit to our business was mainly out of curiosity and his journalistic profession of reporting the local news. A new business was a news story.

Jack questioned me about Nasco, and I saw immediately that he was a wise and thoughtful person. Further into our conversation, I shared some of the problems we faced. He continued to draw me out about our situation, and I am sure he saw a desperate young man looking for answers. The more we talked, the more I could appreciate Jack's experience and wisdom. I wanted to get to know him better, so I invited him to have dinner with us. He accepted with a big smile.

During dinner, Jack asked me to describe my ideal company.

"What are your goals?" He asked. "What are your goals for your employees? How can you best serve them?"

I shared my experiences of working with Dortch Oldham and how I had been inspired to be all I could be as a person. I explained how Dortch wanted us to be able to pay our college expenses, but he was more interested in us finding success in life. He wanted to elevate us.

"Jack, I would like that kind of company for my employees," I told him.

"Your success as a businessman will be measured by the quality and quantity of service you render," he responded. "You must shine your spotlight on service in order to build a successful national company."

My dinner with Jack was interesting, thought provoking and motivational. My immediate problem was getting out of the trap in which I found myself.

Jack said he didn't have an answer, but he told me if I kept a positive attitude and didn't give up, the resolution would come.

After that evening, I was more motivated to search for a new market for our stools. It helped me refocus my energy on building my dream company. I never let the ideas Jack and I discussed fade away. I pondered our conversation and could clearly see the company we would have one day. Building the dream was worth getting up early for and working late.

Sherry and I insisted that Jack be our dinner guest as often as possible. Our time together was a win-win. We relished his wisdom, and he seemed to enjoy a home-cooked meal.

***

One day, I got an idea about school fundraising. I could control the price for a profit, and, most importantly, I could collect the school accounts. The only thing I knew about the prospect was that schools sold products to raise money for various projects. So I decided to give the schools an old college try. I called on North Side High School in Jackson, Tennessee, to pioneer my new idea. I thought it best to call on a school where they did not know me for a more objective test.

School fundraising programs were not conducted in Bethel Springs when I grew up. I did not have any experience or any idea of how it was done. I didn't know what the objections might be. I was ill prepared, but I had sales experience, and I was determined to make a sale on my very first call.

I went into the principal's office at North Side and unstacked my stools, displaying all four colors. I told him I wanted to work with a school group that needed money.

"Young man, do you think we're a furniture dealer?" The principal asked.

I could see I had my work cut out for me. I pointed out how handy the stack stools were in the home, with all their different uses. I told him they were a great value at $4.95, and the school could make $2 per stool.

"Who can I talk to?" I asked.

He called the home economics teacher. We met in her office, and I went through the program. She asked several questions and then agreed to proceed. She also agreed to let me talk with her students to kick off the program. Our goal was to raise $500 for the Home Economics Department.

I walked out of that school with the hope of saving our company. I called on schools that week and set dates to start programs in 10 or more of them.

I came back to Adamsville and visited Brooks Roudebush whom I considered a jack-of-all-trades. I asked him if we could silk screen a basketball on the stools' white vinyl covers. I thought the North Side students would like it because they had a winning basketball team. The next morning, he had a basketball screened on the stool. It looked pretty crude, but I was happy to see it. We also silk screened "North Side High School" in a circle around the basketball. In my mind, my situation was improving by the minute.

When I went back to North Side to start the program, the kids went crazy over my crude basketball on the stool's cover. I printed colored brochures with pictures of the stools for the students to use as their order form. They contacted their family, friends and neighbors to sell one or more stools to help them raise money for their Home Economics Department. When the program was completed, they earned $456 — close to their goal. In today's dollars, that would be about $1,500. The students were happy. I was happier, but I was still deep in the woods with Nasco.

***

Of the other schools I signed, some did well and some didn't.

But our company still was going broke. I thought I could save it if I could get the right people involved. I also needed Jimmy to sign over his stock. The handwriting was on the wall. We were going to lose the $7,500 Artill had borrowed and my $10,000, but the big problem was the $20,000 SBA loan.

It took a while to convince Artill and Jimmy that we were going broke. It could take years to pay off the loan, and we faced bankruptcy — something that was tough to bear. They offered no ideas as to how we could save Nasco.

I came to the conclusion that I might be able to convince Dortch Oldham of the merits of the fundraising idea, and with his help, the company would survive. I told Jimmy and Artill that I would visit with Dortch at his home in Nashville and do my best to convince him to invest in the business. But they had to agree to relinquish their stock and cut their losses. We felt that if I could convince Dortch to invest, it was unlikely that the company would go broke.

Artill and Jimmy finally agreed to sign their stock over to the company for one dollar if I could persuade Dortch to invest. With their commitment and no time to waste, I went to Dortch's home before he was to leave for Sunday school and knocked on his front door.

Dortch was certainly surprised to see me so early on a Sunday morning. I explained to him, upfront, that we had a big problem with our company. I gave him the financial facts and told him the company was going broke. Dortch asked questions in rapid fire. As time passed, he explained to his wife, Sis, that she and their sons should leave for Sunday school and church without him. They left us to continue our conversation.

It was a long day. Dortch did not want to get involved in a company on the verge of going broke. I told Dortch that we could build a successful business, developing the fundraising idea that I had tested. I was very convincing. At about 5 p.m., Dortch said he would consider investing $5,000 if the stock could be re-divided and if Bill Cook and Tate Rogers would agree to join the effort. They did, and we put a plan together.

Dortch had controlling interest, and I was left with 20 percent of the stock. Dortch's lawyer drew up the transfer papers on the premise that Jimmy and Artill would sign over their stock to the company for one dollar. The new team would assume the company's debt, accounts payable and SBA loan. Jimmy and I were responsible for our personal loans. This was much better than the company going broke — it was the reason I knocked on Dortch's door.

Dortch came to Adamsville to close the deal, and we met in our local bank's boardroom to sign the contract. Everything progressed well until Jimmy laid a $5,000 note in front of me to sign. It was his price for his signature to sign over his stock. I could not believe he went back on his word. He was ready to bluff me into signing his note. I glanced at Dortch, and he didn't look very positive at that moment. I could not afford for him to walk away, and I was not prepared to stiff-arm Jimmy by not signing his double-crossing note. I signed his note and looked at him.

"I will never pay you because you double crossed me at the last minute," I told him.

Jimmy never asked for payment on the note. He didn't want to face me, so he sold the note for collection to Reggie Churchwell at a discount.

***

Sherry and I only had one car, and I was traveling several days during the week. Sherry was thankful we lived close to downtown where she could walk to local businesses. Jack McConnico offered Sherry a part-time job. She also discovered an opening for a part-time librarian. She took both jobs to help pay our bills.

We struggled to survive financially and make quarterly payments to the bank. But one day, the bank called my loan, which jeopardized my father's farm. I knew I had to convince the banker to work with me, which was a tough sale. He agreed to give me 30 more days.

"Where are you going to get the money?" He asked.

"I don't know, but I will get the money."

I left the banker's office, took a very deep breath and thought: "That was a close call."

As I drove home, I pondered what to do. I passed a memorial garden, which triggered an idea of going into the "underground business" of selling memorial plots.

I put my fledgling Nasco business on hold through the summer months until schools re-opened in the fall. I called Robert Shackelford Sr., who owned our local funeral home. He did not know me. I asked if he knew of a successful memorial garden operated by honest people — people with integrity.

"Yes," he said. "I know Ed and Dayton Phillips in Nashville, and I have their telephone number."

"Bob, you seem to know these people well," I said after taking down the number. "Can you tell me more about them?"

"They are successful business people who believe in ethical dealings," he said. "They are good people."

With Bob Shackelford's recommendation, I headed to Nashville. I had less than a dollar in my pocket. I didn't telephone ahead to set-up an interview, and I was fortunate that the Phillips brothers were in their office. I thought it best to explain my situation up front. It made for an interesting interview. I told them that I was developing a new business and that my banker was about to call my loan. And I could work only three months.

"I am here to make as much money as I possibly can to resolve my financial problem," I said. "I will put in long hours and then get back to my business."

They doubted whether I could be successful in that short period of time. I assumed they were wondering who I was and what I was up to.

"Is Bob Shackelford a friend of yours?" Ed asked.

"Bob doesn't know me other than the conversation we had on the phone," I said. "I called him to make sure you were respectable people before making the drive to Nashville. Bob, in fact, bragged on you and said you were people of integrity."

To give them confidence in me, I told them that Dortch Oldham and Ted Welch, both prominent and respected businessmen in Nashville, were personal friends. I gave them Dortch and Ted's telephone numbers. Sharing the names of these two outstanding businessmen certainly helped my situation.

They questioned me about being able to learn the business in three months. I told them that the key to my success was the quality of their service. They offered me a job with straight commission with a percentage on what I sold. No salary. They had several memorial gardens across the country. I told them that I would go anywhere.

They decided I should go to Texas. They had a new memorial garden there, and it was showing a lot of success.

"What's wrong with the garden in Murfreesboro?" I asked.

"We have hired three people, and they have all failed," Ed said. "We have not sold the right people. It does not have a good reputation, which makes it more difficult to sell."

At that point, I convinced them that I could be successful in Murfreesboro. I told them to make a list of influential people, and I would sell them. They gave me names of college professors, walking-horse farm owners and other business people. It was a great beginning. We shook hands, and thank goodness, they bought my lunch!

I returned home to Adamsville relieved, anticipating a great summer selling cemetery plots. I told Sherry about my meeting and that we would be moving to Murfreesboro as soon as we could find an inexpensive, decent place to live. Within two weeks, we moved into a small upstairs apartment across from Middle Tennessee State University's main campus. We didn't have much furniture, so it was an easy move with the generous support of Sherry's parents.

I surprised the Phillips brothers with my sales, and I sent every nickel possible to the banker, who probably thought I was selling something illegal. Everything was going well until the GMAC guys came to repossess my car. I had not been making the car payments on time, because I was trying to satisfy the bank.

When they arrived, I was at the garden's sales office, and Ed came out to see what was happening. I asked him if I could sell while riding a bicycle because I didn't have to actually deliver the memorial plots.

"You can't sell on a bicycle!" He said. "How much money do you need to satisfy GMAC?"

We were told $450. Ed went back into his office and came out with a check for the payment. That was a lot of money in the 1960s, and I was appreciative. It was another close call, but it gave me even more determination to make good on my promise. The next week was outstanding, and I repaid Ed.

Selling cemetery plots was tough, but the art of it came naturally. I followed the Phillips' sales script for two weeks before going my own way. I told customers up front that I wanted to show them our services at the memorial garden, and it would take only about 20 minutes. Then I told them they could decide if our services suited their family's need. I closed the presentation for a high percentage of sales. I didn't show them anything morbid — no families under black umbrellas on a rainy day in the cemetery. People liked my straightforward approach, which was absent of emotion, as they selected a plot for the family. The plots, for a family of four, sold for $2,000. With a down payment, they could pay over time. The memorial garden gave me an opportunity to make a considerable amount of money and resolve my problem with the bank.

One day, I called on a retired military officer, who lived on a small farm near Murfreesboro. The gentleman was hauling hay with his horses hooked to a wagon. I walked out into the field and approached him about the memorial garden. He looked down at me and said he didn't have time for me. I was wearing an inexpensive suit, which I had bought the day before. I walked over to a nearby fence post, took off my suit coat and tie, hung them over the post and jumped up onto the wagon. I figured he would listen to my presentation if I helped him with his hay.

He looked at me like I was crazy.

"I've had a lot of practice hauling hay, and this is an opportunity to renew my skills," I said. "Let's go!"

"Gitty-up," he said to the horses, and we began loading his bales of hay onto the wagon.

It was a hot day, but we didn't stop until all the hay was in the barn. We unhitched the horses and went into the house for my presentation. His wife was a delightful person, and we gathered around their kitchen table.

"Since we are hot from hauling hay, please give us two tall boys," the man said to his wife.

She set us up with two tall boys, and I began my presentation. As he drank, he became relaxed and dozed off to sleep.

"I don't know how many spaces we would need," his wife said when I finished my presentation.

"Wake him up and ask him," I said.

She did, and he asked her how many kids they had. Luckily, they had four children, and I sold a six-plot order. My hay hauling paid off!

After three months passed, I told the Phillips brothers that Sherry and I would be leaving.

"You came here broke, behind on your car payment, and you have done a remarkable job," Ed said. "We have an offer to make to you. We would like for you to be the general sales manager, over all our cemeteries, and teach the how of this business."

The offer came with a salary and a commission on all sales. Sherry and I could have bought the new home we wanted and maybe put a Cadillac in the garage. This was the only time Sherry asked me if we should seriously consider the offer. The money would have been great, but that was not my goal. I was determined to build a national sales force of my own with a service I could be proud to render.

About this time, my cousin, John P. Hendrix, came for a visit after hearing about my financial problems. He was a sales manager for Farm Bureau Insurance. He told me he had one of the most financially lucrative agencies opening in Middle Tennessee, and he wanted me to consider it. The business had been built over several years and would enable me to start with a high income. I could grow it from there. I told John how appreciative I was, but that I had another mission to fulfill.

"Tom, I don't think you understand," he said. "It is much better than you realize."

My biggest temptation was accepting the money that Sherry and I desperately needed to afford a good life, to be successful in the eyes of our family and friends. If money had been our goal, we would have abandoned our mission.

Risk takers must have a deep resolve and thick skin to pursue their dream. Sherry must have wondered many times whether our hardships were worth it, but she never wavered in her support. That made me more determined to build a fine home one day and show my appreciation for her sacrifice.

***

Nasco relocated to Ashland City near Nashville, which was closer to the homes of Dortch, Bill and Tate. After selling cemetery plots for three months, Sherry and I moved to Ashland City. We rented a small, comfortable one-bedroom basement apartment. We were happy to be together after long days of work with our struggling company.

Bill, Tate and I hit the road, calling on schools. We sold our stack stools with silk-screened school emblems. Another one of our Bible-selling buddies, Bill Roark, came to us looking for a sales opportunity. Bill had been a top Southwestern salesman. He could sell with the best, and we were happy to have him with us. We gave him the Mississippi territory, and he went to work.

We were constantly improving our sales presentation as we worked. We met on weekends to share what we had learned to prepare for the upcoming week.

Utilizing Nasco's silk-screening department, we screened emblems of school logos, university mascots, civic clubs, antique cars and anything else we could think of to make the stools more attractive to students and the general public. We were always in search of something that would make the products sizzle.

Rip Reagan was band director of Emma Sansom High School in Gadsden, Alabama. It was one of the most famous bands in the South, and almost all band directors knew Rip. He wrote us a tune called the "Cool School Stool" song, and we had 45-rpm records made. It was a fun song that dramatized making stool sales, and it made people happy. It was perfect to make the fundraising program fun for students. (Words to "Cool School Stool" are on Page 372.)

The students asked radio stations to play the song every 30 minutes. In some towns, with two or more stations, the community heard the song many times a day. Everyone talked and laughed about the cool school stools that band students were selling to raise money. We could drive from town to town and listen to the song and hear the radio talk about the band students.

One weekend, as we came together to share our week's experiences, we decided we should stand on the stool and dance the twist to the music of the cool school stool song as we kicked off the program. The twist was popular at the time. As we danced standing on top of the stool, students broke into a big applause. It was a blast! The band directors and school sponsors thought it was as funny as the students did.

In one of the schools, the superintendent heard all the commotion and came into the band hall. He walked into the room with a stern face, but within seconds, he was laughing as much as the kids when I finished my presentation. He told me the presentation was a masterpiece. He was right — it was the best presentation of my career. It had everything to capture the imagination of people and motivate them to buy.

***

Fundraising in schools at that time was geared more to selling products than to helping schools raise money for needed school projects. Students mostly sold vegetable and flower seeds in the spring and Hershey candy throughout the year. Schools had to buy these products first before they sold them to the community. If the school sold everything, it would have the money it needed. To do that, each student had to sell a certain amount. A few students did that, but many didn't. They brought their unsold product back to the school after the sale period ended. Often the school would re-issue the candy or seeds to the good salesmen. But by this time they had lost their enthusiasm. Schools were left with unsold merchandise. They could return unopened cases within a certain timeframe, but most schools had too much product in the back room and not enough money in the bank.

To say the least, fundraising was not very successful in schools in 1961. We were determined to change attitudes, limiting a program to a three-day sales campaign with no leftover merchandise.

Our program was a completely different concept. Students collected orders from neighbors, and schools purchased the exact amount they needed from us. It was also the most exciting fundraising program the schools had ever seen.

The schools liked not having leftover merchandise and the three-day selling period with less school interruption. We learned that if the kids were properly motivated, they could sell more in three days than they could in three weeks.

We sold our fundraising program to more and more schools, reaching out to different parts of the country. After the first year in school fundraising, our sales were more than $500,000. We met for a strategy meeting to plan for the next year. Our priority was to find a more suitable, consumable fundraising product. We had doubts about our ability to repeat the stool program because the stools would last a long time. It was not a consumable item. We wanted to run successful programs with products that people would buy year after year. We knew the idea would come to us, but no one had anything in mind that we felt was worthy.

Dortch was happy with our first year's progress, and he could tell we were excited. I became general sales manager of Nasco with the responsibility of building a national sales force. Nasco's operations were relocated to Springfield, Tennessee, north of Nashville.

***

Our school fundraising effort had a major flaw: We did not have a sales program for the summer. So we turned to college students again. Bill and I knew how to hire students, and I knew from experience that we could teach them how to sell the stack stools successfully door to door.

We agreed we should go for it, and we decided to recruit 30 to 40 college students from Troy University in Alabama. We quickly put together the recruiting information, including brochures, stools, applications and contracts. When we arrived in Troy, we went through the proper channels to start our recruiting and hiring sessions. Students responded positively, and we began signing contracts for summer work. We signed 38 students in two weeks.

We set up a three-day sales school in Clarksville, Tennessee, which went extremely well. We had a successful summer, and Bill and I were proud to have a greater average income per student than the Southwestern Bible boys.

However, we created a firestorm for Dortch. Southwestern recruited 1,500 or more students, and they saw Bill and me as a real threat to their efforts. They did not want our competition. Bill and I had plans to recruit 75 to 90 students the following year. Dortch had bought Southwestern and owned controlling interest in Nasco. But he had no idea we would be so successful so quickly. By now, it was obvious that we could have hundreds of stack stool salesmen on the streets, recruited from universities and in competition with Southwestern.

Dortch told us no more door to door selling. "Find another way to create summer sales," he said.

*****

Later that year, Bill Roberts came to see us with the idea we had been looking for. He showed us a household cleaner he had been selling to Western Auto Stores across the country. Bill had done well, but his profit was meager because Western Auto asked for all kinds of promotional money to sell the product.

Bill showed us how to produce REX All-Purpose Cleaner. I went on the road with him to sell it, and I became convinced he had a good product that could be sold in schools for repeat programs. But Bill wanted too much money for his secret formula, and we thought we could find a formula just as good from another company. We continued to negotiate until Bill sold his company to us for a good price. Even though the equipment included in the sale was crude, it gave us a start in bottling the cleaner.

Bill had been selling pint bottles to Western Auto for $2. When we saw the low cost of ingredients, we decided to bottle a quart size. Using the same formula, the schools could sell a quart and double the value for the customer. We wanted to give people their money's worth to repeat the program each year. It was a trouble-free program for the schools and a good value to the school's supporters. And repeat business would be easier to get.

Because I was given the responsibility of general sales manager, I went on the road to call on schools to pioneer the new program. I wanted to develop a sales plan that could be taught successfully and build a national sales force.

I picked the state of North Carolina to be my testing ground. I started making calls, presenting our REX All-Purpose Cleaner as a fundraising program, and discovered problems. Schools were accustomed to selling flower and vegetable seeds for 50 cents a pack and Hershey candy bars for $1. It was 1962; they doubted people would pay $2 for a fundraising product. Our cool school stools were a fun item with a lot of pizzazz. Soap didn't have the sizzle. School after school turned me down. I knew I needed a "wow factor" that would grab their attention.

I stopped by a carpet store to test its cleaning power by rubbing black shoe polish into sample pieces of carpet. The store manager was helpful and gave me several pieces. He was amazed at how well it worked. In my presentation at schools, I massaged black shoe polish into an area of white carpet with small brushes. I then massaged a few drops of REX All-Purpose Cleaner into the black stain. The cleaner removed the black shoe polish perfectly, demonstrating its fantastic cleaning power.

It was the sizzle I needed, and I was ready to make some sales.

***

Preparing to hire and train a national sales force was a daunting task. With the completion of each presentation I made to school sponsors, I analyzed my language to make sure it made sense. It was extremely important for the program to be successful the first year.

My first priority was to determine where to recruit perspective salesman — people who could learn the business and who would be comfortable calling on principals, superintendents and sponsors. We needed people who could be effective making presentations at parent-teacher associations and band booster groups.

We previously worked with employment agencies and recruiting companies, but found it was difficult to locate the right kind of person to do this sort of specialized work. Agencies would send the people they represented whether they were qualified or not. I insisted on reviewing the resumes before prospects were sent to an interview to make sure I met the right people.

We had to be willing to say no, because hiring people who could not be successful was a waste of time and energy. Getting the right person was im-

Tom, in forefront, at left, poses with his first sales team at Nasco.

portant. We needed to train them to be successful, but I also wanted the job to be good for the salesman's family. When it was all said and done, I wanted them to tell me it was the best thing that had happened to them. I did my best to get the wives involved in supporting their husbands to increase the family's income — a team effort was important for success.

My objective was to design a simple program that we could teach to a new salesman. Developing a common-sense presentation was my next step. I wanted it to be seen as a win-win for everyone: easy for the students and a good learning experience, more money for the schools in less time, a good value for customers within their grocery budgets and a program that Nasco could repeat year after year.

I spent several days writing and re-writing the presentation to counteract the reasons people came up with to not buy the product. For each objection, I would re-write the presentation to better communicate the thought, which would hopefully eliminate the objection during the next presentation. I continued to test the language for a greater close ratio, communicating each thought as clearly as possible. Clear language, delivered properly was the secret. And honesty was a must for repeat business. I knew I could not build trust with clever or tricky language. Nothing outperforms the truth!

After numerous presentations with my tested script, long hours of selling, and black-shoe-polish-on-white-carpet demonstrations, I had achieved an outstanding close ratio. The program also was getting good results in the community. Most groups reached their profit goal. I could see repeat business and a national sales force.

***

At the end of our first year of selling REX All-Purpose Cleaner as a fundraising item, we had more than 20 people who could sign and conduct successful fundraising programs — with most repeating. Our sales were more than $1 million.

We placed the salesmen on a draw against commission. The draw needed to cover the families' expenses, and we needed enough sales to cover the draw. Nasco did not have the cash flow to pay draws without the sales commission to support them. I walked a tight rope while pioneering a new product in the marketplace. But the sales force was successful enough to generate a positive attitude in our sales meetings. We had many success stories, which were encouraging to people who were having a difficult time making their draw.

I was just out of college in a new business with much to learn. My philosophy was: "You become the person to do the work at hand, and success is an inside job." I was a businessman under construction. I had asked for this pioneering life, developing new ideas that could become a national effort.

But our product line was not complete with cool school stools and REX All-Purpose Cleaner. Schools were closed during the summer, and we still needed to figure out how to make it through those months.

Rip Reagan came to our rescue a second time with the idea of selling ads on the backs of stadium cushions. The ads would pay for the cushions with money left over. Then the cushions would be sold with school emblems at ballgames for $2. Five hundred cushions generated about $1,200 profit for a civic or school group. In 2014 dollars, that would be $3,600 or more.

The cushion idea seemed workable. I went to Texas to pioneer the program with Jaycee Clubs.

Many times, I suggested to service-club presidents that we call on two or three merchants to demonstrate how they would buy the ads. I could sell two or three ads to prove the program would raise $1,200 for their club. If the Jaycee president was excited about the program and made a commitment to me, he would be responsible for selling the ads for the money to order the cushions. I would get a commitment from him that he would complete the ad sales in one week and mail in the ad copy.

If I did not sell the Jaycee president, I would call on the Lions Club or Rotary Club. The first week I signed 25 groups. My goal was at least 30 percent return on completing their ad sales, knowing not all would follow through as promised. In some cases, if I doubted the civic group's resolve to follow through, I offered to take them down the street to show them how to sell ads.

Selling a few ads would increase the chances they would complete the ad sales. This was another time my experiences selling Bibles paid big dividends. Having the confidence to make a sale under all kinds of conditions was my strong suit.

My goal was to produce at least 100 cushion kits as a test for percentage returns. After the second week, we created a professional kit with all the information necessary for Jaycee groups to complete ad sales, along with instructions on how to sell the cushions successfully. In the beginning, I didn't have much to work with — except for my ability to sell.

***

Pioneering new ideas and concepts in the marketplace takes an extra measure of confidence and creativity. You are constantly changing your message to better communicate your service. Selling is simply communicating clearly the benefit of your service. The words you use are important, and the way the words are delivered is just as important. It's not what you say, it's what you communicate. Our best salesmen had strong feelings about their service. That made them enthusiastic, and nothing was accomplished without enthusiasm.

I believed my idea of having ad-sales kits for service clubs and other groups was better than Nasco salesmen selling the ads because it was less complicated to teach the program to the sales force. Selling ads ourselves would limit our cushion sales to one or two groups per week. With the kit idea — at 25 kits per week with a 30 percent return — we could sell six or seven groups per week, increasing everyone's profit.

This extra sales commission would strengthen our sales force and reduce turnover. Many sales people would not sell ads every day. Plus, a stranger faces a lot more pushback when selling ads than the Jaycees calling on fellow businessmen to support a worthwhile cause.

But a problem was brewing in Nasco. Bill Cook did not like the kit idea, and my ad sales were going much slower than planned. I called Jaycees every evening to find out the status of their ad sales. They would tell me they were just about finished. But Nasco couldn't put talk in the bank.

I knew the kit idea would be a success, but Bill talked to Dortch daily, spreading doubt about the program. I came home and met with Bill. He was ready to pull the plug and had already convinced Dortch we should not pursue the program. Bill thought we should sell the ads for the group. I disagreed. I suggested Bill call the groups to listen to their response. I told him that if he did, he would agree that we would get at least a 30 percent return on the cushion kits left with the service clubs.

Frustrated, I went home after our meeting and told Sherry we were going on a vacation to Florida. I knew nothing would happen at the company until I returned. I didn't tell Bill I was leaving.

When I returned, I walked into Bill's office, and he was more positive. Our sales force, through the summer months, sold more than 500,000 cushions, earning more per week than during the school year. Salesmen liked the cushion idea, and the cushions stabilized our sales force for a year-round income.

**

In developing Nasco, I realized wealth is built from great ideas. Stadium cushions were a great idea at the time, giving us an outstanding profit center. And cushion seats enabled our fundraising salesmen to earn a considerable amount of money through the summer.

But Bill and I could not agree on how to build the company. It was not that I was right and Bill was wrong. We just saw things differently.

My philosophy was to only hire people who could learn the business and earn a decent income to support a family. We promised a decent income when we interviewed them, and I believed it was important to live up to that promise. This meant we needed to be patient and hire the right person — a person with the talent we could train for success.

Bill wanted capable people, but he could not say no when hiring people. Bill was more inclined to say we need 30 or 50 people and believed success was in the number of people hired. My philosophy meant we would build a company at a slower pace. But in the long run, we would have fewer turnovers, and our service to the schools would be better. We would spend less time hiring and re-training. I liked Dortch's philosophy: "If you get the employees right, the company will be right." We were in the business of elevating families. If your objective is to dedicate your life in service to people, start with your employees. If your service is right for the employees, they will get the service right for the customer. This is a win-win.

The divide between Bill and me was getting to be an unmanageable problem. We argued often.

We were close and even vacationed together, but Nasco was taking a toll on our friendship. And then, during our second year of cushion sales, a straw broke the camel's back. The decision was made to hire another sales force to sell cushions through the summer with a goal of 800,000 cushions. Jim Mc-Carthy would be in charge, which meant I would pioneer another idea for summer sales. But I told Bill I would never build another sales force for Nasco.

Dortch knew we disagreed about how to build the company. But he was implementing a plan with Southwestern that required a big change in the direction of that company, which was growing rapidly. He was busy, and he left Nasco for Bill and me to manage. Nasco was growing rapidly, and Dortch was happy with the company's progress.

I went to my office and closed the door to do some soul searching. I thought about my first meeting with Jack McConnico and my vision: a company that would dedicate itself in service, starting with the employees. Get it right for the employee; they will get it right for the customer. The success of the company will be measured by the quality of service rendered. I questioned whether I could partner with Bill to reach my goal. I realized that if I stayed at Nasco, I would have to give up my vision.

I decided it was time to resign. I could not sacrifice what I believed to stay with the company. My beliefs were not for sale.

"Tom, we can work this out," Bill said. "You can't resign from Nasco."

But, I had heard that before. I told him my decision was final, and I went home to break the news to Sherry. We were leaving Nasco and selling our new home. She took the news in stride.

"If you think it's best, I am with you," she said.

I have never been so proud of her.

I went back to Nasco to work out an agreement with Bill to sell Nasco products if I could buy them at a good price. We negotiated the price with the idea that no one would interfere with my selling. All I wanted was a territory and products to sell. I told Bill I wanted to put out cushion kits that summer in Missouri. I planned to call on every town in the state of Missouri with a population of 1,000 or more.

I did just that, working long hours, five days a week with service clubs. Each weekend I headed to the airport for a flight home to be with Sherry.

Selling was an easy thing for me to do, and it lacked the pressure of managing a sales force. I was living a simpler life. My summer went well, and I kept my note current with my bank while accruing $2,000 to start a new company.

I went to see Bobby Smothers. He and his wife, Wanda, had expressed an interest in our home. I gave Bobby a price for the house, and he said he would buy it if he could work out the financing. My next stop was my local banker. He was astonished to learn I had resigned from Nasco. People saw Bill and me as good friends with a fast-growing and admired company. After the banker got over the shock, I asked to borrow $1,500 to start over. He loaned the money and told me he would help in anyway he could.

I shook his hand and left to keep my appointment with my doctor, who diagnosed me with a bad case of ulcers.

It was a difficult decision to leave Nasco because the company was on the financial road to success. Sherry and I knew Nasco could make us financially independent. Nasco had attracted some outstanding people who were eager to build a national company. In my time with the company, we outgrew four building locations and were established in a 250,000-square-foot-building with plenty of room to expand. Nasco was one of the fastest-growing companies in the country and began to make a solid profit.

Leaving Nasco was painful for Sherry and me. We paid a high price to help build it, living in basements and upstairs apartments to cut expenses so we could pay our bills. We created debt, and we were still paying off loans. We finally had a nice income. I had a corner office with a secretary. As far as the community was concerned, I was an up-and-coming business executive.

We owned a new home in a nice neighborhood with nice furniture and had a new 200D Mercedes Benz in the driveway. We knew we were poised to become successful financially. In many ways, our dream had come true. If our goal was to earn a a lot of money, we were well set for the future.

But I was determined to build a national company that I could be proud of. I was willing to start over and get back on the road, selling.

***

Sherry and I were glad to see Nasco expand into a national effort. It became a diverse company with several profit centers. Its corporate offices were located in downtown Nashville in the high rise beside the AT&T "Batman" building. Bill was recognized as one of the outstanding businessmen of the Nashville community. When I went to visit him in his fancy office, I couldn't help but think: "I was the founder of this beautiful company."

As we looked back to the day I resigned, we were so glad we had what it took to be true to our beliefs, which many times requires gutsy decisions. If you are a young person reading this book, I want you to fully realize that you should never, ever give up on your dream. Success is a mindset!

CHAPTER 8

TRANSITIONS AND BEGINNINGS

"Smoking is as destructive as putting a handful of sand
in the motor of your car."

Our lives were about to change. I had just resigned from Nasco. We were about to move to Selmer to start a new company. It was 1967, and Montreal, Canada, was hosting the World's Fair. We didn't want to miss it.

I told my parents it could be an exciting trip, but Mother said it would be too much for them to handle. I didn't really expect them to accept my invitation, but to my surprise, they called me a week later with a new opinion. They wanted to go.

"We have never been much farther than Memphis," Mother said.

My parents were about 70 years old. This would be a trip to remember.

We started making plans. I drove a 200 Mercedes-Benz diesel, which got more than 30 miles a gallon. Diesel fuel in 1967 cost about 30 cents per gallon. We could drive 1,000 miles for $10, which greatly helped our finances.

Because the trip was long and we spent many hours in the car, Sherry decided we should stop along the way at roadside parks for picnic lunches. It was good for our budget, and it gave us some much needed exercise and sunshine. The weather was nice, and the picnics became a highlight of the trip.

We traveled east to Washington, D.C., and toured various historic sights. The Capitol and every monument or building we passed were eye-openers for my parents. Then we drove north to New York City and arrived at about two in the afternoon. Sherry and I had been to downtown New York before, and we thought it would be a great experience for them.

"We are going downtown to Wall Street," I told my dad.

"With all this traffic, I would take the simplest way possible out of this place," he said. "I have never seen so much traffic!"

Sherry navigated. We headed to the heart of the city and Wall Street. Witnessing the towering skyscrapers and heavy traffic on the streets was exciting. It was quite different from rural Bethel Springs.

Motels were another new experience for my parents. When we checked in, we made sure they knew how to call our room if they needed us. Mother called me our first night. She was concerned about the toilet.

"Your dad has pulled the paper strip off the commode seat," she said. "I told him we should ask before tearing it off. It might be there for a reason we don't know about. But, he tore it off anyway!"

We had to laugh. Dad had little concern about the sanitizing strip across the seat — it was in his way and needed to go.

We arrived in Montreal and planned a three-day tour of the fair. Mother had periodic back pain, so I rented a wheelchair. She fought against renting it, but it was a blessing as we spent hours visiting the exhibitions.

After the fair, we traveled home through Pennsylvania, Ohio, Indiana and Kentucky for different scenery. My parents enjoyed seeing the farms with unbelievably large fields and huge tractors turning the soil to plant crops. They also enjoyed the countryside and its timber. It was an experience they never forgot, and they talked about the trip for the rest of their lives.

They had worked so hard on the farm. They certainly deserved the trip, and Sherry and I were glad we could be a part of making it happen for them. It was a token of appreciation for the good they had brought to our lives. And even though we could not afford it, it was a great trip — and the last one Sherry and I would take as a family of two.

***

We had been married almost seven years, and we wanted to start our family. When we returned home from Montreal, Sherry made an appointment with our doctor, who confirmed that she was pregnant.

Our lives were changing. We sold our home in Springfield, and got ready to move to Selmer. Soon, we would be parents. This was life at its best.

As we loaded our furniture into a rented U-Haul, Bill Cook paid a visit.

"Let's have dinner together before you leave," he said.

"Well, John and Beverly McConnico have already invited us to dinner," I said. "But why don't you join us? I'll call John and ask him to set another plate." The son of Jack McConnico, John was one of the first salesmen I hired at Nasco. He has excellent communicative skills and is a wonderful human being.

We had a beautiful evening together, and I realized Bill and I would be friends for a lifetime, in spite of heated arguments and my resignation from the company. I always knew that if I needed help, I could call Bill. Bill even told his people not to criticize me after I left because I was his friend.

***

Sherry and I had discussed where we should locate our new company. She suggested Jackson, Tennessee. It was close to both of our parents, and it had a convenient regional airport. But I wanted to build our company in my home county. I knew that building a sizeable company in a small town would have some disadvantages, but I thought the positives would outweigh the negatives. As I have often said, I am glad we returned to my home county to build a company and follow my dream there. So many young people leave their small hometowns looking for opportunities elsewhere.

We rented a small brick house on Hillhurst Drive and moved in mid summer 1967. It was a great neighborhood and convenient to local businesses. Since I was traveling extensively throughout the week, location was important — especially because we were soon to be a family of three.

The move went well, even though I was concerned about Sherry over-exerting herself in the early weeks of her pregnancy. As soon as we settled in, we announced our expected baby to our families. They were ecstatic. It was the first grandchild for Sherry's parents, and my parents had been wondering if I shouldn't be staying home more so they could cradle another grandchild in their arms.

With the extra money from cushion sales, we had enough to start anew. I was much wiser, and hopefully, I would make fewer mistakes in building a new company. I planned to write a sales manual based on my philosophy to elevate people and built on what Dortch Oldham taught me when I sold Bibles.

"If you could get the employees right, the company will be right."

My objective was to only hire people I felt certain could learn the business and be successful.

When schools returned to session after summer, I sold Nasco's REX All-Purpose Cleaner. Selling to schools came easy for me. I chose Mississippi as my first territory, and I called on notable band directors. I sold a high percentage of the bands. They ran their programs successfully and reached their financial goals. I felt I could get repeat business from them the following year.

I earned a considerable amount of money, and Sherry and I made progress paying off our past debt from Nasco.

**

During this time, I made one of the smartest decisions of my life. My ulcers were doing much better, but I still had a bad habit of smoking cigarettes, which I picked up in the army. Cigarettes were easy to get, and free packs were commonly distributed to servicemen in the war zone.

A little boy in our neighborhood rode by one day on his bicycle, and I wanted to test myself. I asked him if I could ride his bike around the block. I rode down the hill fine. But the trip up the hill gave me a lot of trouble. I returned the bike to the child and thanked him.

I sat breathlessly on a nearby concrete ledge over a culvert. And I decided to quit smoking. It was 5 p.m. I gave myself 30 days from that moment to quit. I was mad at myself for not being able to ride a bike up a hill. The next 30 days gave me plenty of time to think my decision through to make sure I would never smoke another cigarette in my life.

I knew smoking was ruining my health, sapping my energy. Smoking is as destructive as putting a handful of sand in the motor of your car.

I found myself in Dallas, Texas, on that 30th day. At 5 p.m., I had a full pack of Winstons in my pocket. I laid the cigarettes on the console of my car and made the long drive home. I wanted them within easy reach. When I got home, I put the pack by our telephone.

Sherry knew I was not smoking.

"I'm just going to throw this pack in the trash," Sherry said.

"No," I said. "Leave it there. I want it within easy reach."

I had been smoking two packs per day during the long hours I was working. After I quit, I gained considerable energy quickly. Looking back, I cannot believe I was a heavy smoker because no rational person can justify the habit. I believe we should be stronger than our strongest habit. That's why I quit.

***

Our first child was due in February 1968. I traveled extensively then. But on one snowy Wednesday morning, I was home. It was Feb. 21, and I planned to take the car into the station for service. Sherry felt uncomfortable and asked me to wait.

I figured I could get back in plenty of time if I had to. So I left. At 10 a.m., as I was waiting for the car to get finished, Sherry called the station.

"You had better get home now!" She yelled.

The hospital was in Jackson. We loaded her bag and drove her old car to my parent's home to trade cars with my father. But we couldn't get into their driveway because of the snowy, icy conditions. Sherry had to walk with me across the highway and down their slippery driveway to reach my dad's car.

We worried the road conditions would be bad on the 45-minute drive north to Jackson, but thankfully, we had no further delays. We arrived at the hospital around noon. Our beautiful, healthy daughter, Susan Lynne, was born at 1:21 p.m. We had little time to spare!

We were two blessed people; we were parents.

***

Not long after Susan's birth, I bought a fancy, well-outfitted motorcycle to

*Daughter, Susan Lynne, at left, was born Feb. 21, 1968,
and daughter, Leigh Anne, was born May 30, 1970.*

ride in parades with our local Shrine Club. The parade crowds liked it when the Shriners exhibited their skills on their fancy motorcycles.

My father saw me unload my motorcycle and wasn't pleased. He could not believe I had bought it.

"That's exactly what you need as a married man with a young daughter," he said. "That is a dangerous machine."

"Dad, they are safe if you use good judgment," I responded.

I did not know anything about riding motorcycles. I rode around the block and slipped on loose gravel while making a turn. The machine dumped me on the pavement, and I skinned my arms and legs. Dad watched it all.

"I can see how safe it is to ride with good judgment," he quipped.

I brushed myself off and took note of Dad's advice.

Later, I rode with five other Shriners from McNairy County in parades across West Tennessee. It was a lot of fun. During the parade season, our club was booked about every weekend. On one trip, as I was riding the motorcycle across the levy from Savannah to Adamsville, a car pulled in front of me and made an abrupt stop while I was trying to pass it. I almost hit the back of it, but I was able to stop about a foot from the bumper.

I decided that day my father had given me good advice. I sold the motorcycle. Owning one was fun, and it caused me to mature a little more.

***

John McConnico, surprised me with a visit one day. He was on an important mission for Bill Cook. Bill had asked John to convince me to return to Nasco.

"I can't return to Nasco, John," I said. "I'm going to stay in Selmer and build my fundraising company based on my business philosophy."

"You know, Bill doesn't want you to build a company that competes with Nasco," John said.

"Take this message back to Bill," I said, leaning into John. "Tom Hendrix will build a successful fundraising company. It will compete with Nasco. He can send his best salesmen to Mississippi, including himself, if he sees fit. But there is no turning back."

After that exchange, John and I had a nice visit. He left for Springfield with my message to Bill.

Bill called a little later and said that he wanted to come for a visit himself. I was certainly glad for him to visit because we were still good friends, but he would not reveal the purpose of the trip over the phone.

When he arrived, Sherry and I were happy to see him. We talked for a bit, and then Bill got down to business.

"I think you should come back to Nasco, but since the answer is no, I am here to buy your stock," he said.

He started with a ridiculously low offer, and I told him my stock was not for sale. We haggled most of the evening, and he was tenacious.

"I am in a position to write you a check for $20,000," he finally said.

As it turned out, two or three days before Bill's visit, our landlord had called to tell us he and his family were returning to Selmer and gave us three months to move. Sherry had been looking for another house, but had not found a suitable one.

Bill had the check in his pocket. When I accepted it, Sherry and I had the money to pay off all the old Nasco debts and build our new home.

Bill and I promised not to let our competitive spirit interfere with our friendship. And to this day, Bill and I remain the best of friends. I once walked into my office and found an Allen Edmonds shoebox on my desk. It had a note from Bill: "Tom, I was in the shoe store and thought of you. I remember you liked Allen Edmonds shoes. I hope they fit. Come see me. Bill."

When Bill left after purchasing my stock in Nasco, I turned to Sherry. "Let's build a house," I said. "Go find a floor plan we would like."

"Are you sure we should build now?" She asked.

"Yes," I said. "And find a nice one. If anyone deserves a nice home, it's you."

"What about the company?" She asked.

"I will work that out, too."

I was a confident young businessman, and I felt sure about building the most successful fundraising company in the United States. I couldn't wait for it to unfold according to my methodical plan.

We found our favorite house plan — a ranch-style home with 3,500 square feet of living space on one level. We called a contractor to give us a bid on building the home. I went to our local building supply business to get a quote on the materials.

We were motivated to have a nice home as a place to interview educators as prospective salesmen for our new fundraising company.

Our contractor said he could get to work immediately. The next step was to find a suitable lot. Bill McCullar had inherited a tract of land with beautiful white oak trees, which he named Mollie Drive. It was close to the elementary school, supermarket and other community conveniences. We thought it was a perfect location for our new home.

We visited with Bill and found the lot we liked, but it was not a viable location according to the neighborhood's development plan. We offered to buy a larger lot if Bill would reconfigure the street so I could conveniently drive into the garage. We thought the change would help him develop the property. Bill didn't think he could grant our request, so I asked him to think about it.

The Hendrix home on Mollie Drive

The next day, he said we had a deal. We later bought two more lots, which made a nice setting for our house with plenty of room for the children to play.

***

We moved into our new home on Mollie Drive in August 1969.

Susan moved into a "big girl" bed, and we prepared the baby bed for the next addition to our family expected the following spring. We were excited! Sherry was feeling well and continued to support our business while being a mom. Her due date grew closer, and we enjoyed our spacious home.

***

On a sad note, I received a phone call in late May 1970 and was shocked to learn that my father was being hospitalized as a result of a heart attack. He was 74 years old.

I was reminded of a conversation we had a couple of months earlier. We had driven to Selmer, and when we stopped at the traffic light across from the funeral home, he said, "I hope I go straight to the funeral home, not stopping at the hospital or nursing home. I hope my death comes quickly." I thought it was strange that he was talking so openly about his death.

When I received the call, I rushed to the hospital.

I could tell right away that Dad was in serious trouble. I felt helpless. He passed away a short time later on May 23, 1970.

My father and I were close. I admired his work ethic, leadership, love for his family, dedication, integrity, forthrightness, boldness and fierce determination. The life lessons I learned from him sitting at our kitchen table, working in the fields and hauling logs affected my life in so many positive ways. His lessons and spirit will be with me for my lifetime and will be instilled in our next generation.

The question remained. How would I handle his death? It was in the forefront of my mind as the family made arrangements for his funeral service. After all, at 74 years of age, he had lived a long, productive life. He watched his children settle into careers and productive lives, and several grandchildren showered him with affection. He also experienced heartaches in his journey. The answer to my question then came to me. He would want me to celebrate his full life in a positive way. Ultimately, I filled my mind with all the happy memories of my father. I even remembered the time I threw the circle hook chain over the wagon and knocked him unconscious.

One consolation I had was that he almost got his wish to go straight to the funeral home. I did regret that he could not be a part of my unfolding business life. He placed a lot of faith in me, and I would have liked for him to have seen Henco thrive.

My philosophy is that death must be accepted. It is part of God's plan, a generous event. But, I still miss my father.

***

With the loving memories of my father fresh in our minds, our family looked ahead to brighter days. We were approaching the due date of our second child. We did not know if our baby was a boy or girl. Nelda, the daughter of my sister, Etta Kennedy, and her husband, Bob, were planning a June wedding. We agreed to host a bridal tea at our home at the end of May, which was about two weeks before Sherry's due date.

Sherry went to her weekly appointment with her obstetrician. He said she should plan on the baby's arrival that weekend.

"Oh, not this weekend," she said. "We have Nelda's bridal tea at our house! Maybe our baby will arrive next week."

She awakened me that night at midnight.

"I'm in labor," she said. "We better get to the hospital."

We woke Susan and headed to the home of my sister, Roslyn, which was near my parents. They volunteered to look after Susan and our dog while we were at the hospital.

About 8 a.m. the next morning on Saturday, May 30, our precious daughter, Leigh Anne, was born. She was healthy and beautiful. We were richly blessed with two daughters whom we anticipated would be best friends forever.

Nelda's bridal tea was held in our home on Sunday afternoon as scheduled. Sherry wasn't there, but I tried to be a good host in her place. Everyone had a great afternoon, and the circumstances surrounding Sherry's absence became a memory for our niece's wedding album and Leigh Anne's baby book.

The path in our life's journey can have hills and valleys and take us in many directions. The past three years were filled with growth, joy and sadness. Beginnings and transitions were ahead, and we looked forward to the adventure.

CHAPTER 9

SUNDAY SCHOOL

"Remaining a student, as long as we live, is the best way to live."

While we were in the midst of growing our new business and raising our young family, the Reverend Matthew Tomlin, the new pastor at Selmer's First Baptist Church, asked me to consider teaching a Sunday school class of high school and college students.

Sherry and I were both raised in the Methodist Church, but we found ourselves attending First Baptist when Susan and Leigh Anne were young. Matt and his wife, Carolyn, had just moved to Selmer. She was Leigh Anne's kindergarten teacher. They were young, with two children, and we liked them from the start. Matt's prolific mind and Carolyn's vivaciousness brought new life to the church. Matt searched for ways to make changes when it was deemed necessary.

So, I told Matt I would consider teaching Sunday school, but I first needed to attend the class and assess the situation. I shared with him that I had never taught a Sunday school class, and for that matter, had never made a serious study of the Bible.

"That's fine," he said. "If you accept the responsibility, I think you will be an outstanding teacher."

"Why do you want me to teach the class?" I asked.

"Tom, this group is important in so many ways. They are at the age of deciding what they believe. If Sunday school is not relevant to them, we can lose them. They can drop out of church at a time we can do the most for them."

As soon as I stepped into the Sunday school room, I could see what Matt was saying. For one thing, the young people were sitting on uncomfortable, metal chairs in rows in a typical classroom setting. As I sat in on the day's lesson, I listened to the teacher lecture on how to live a good life as outlined in the Bible. There was no discussion from the students. The whole situation was formal.

Afterward, I told Matt I would accept the challenge of making the Sunday school lessons more relevant to young minds. It would take me some time to determine my style of teaching, but I did want to create a relaxed seating arrangement to provoke more open discussions. Matt gave me a green light.

I knew at times I would be out of town for work, so I asked Jimmy and Peggy Daniel to be my backup to teach the class. I had known them for several years. At that time, Peggy was teaching at the elementary school, and she had been Susan's kindergarten teacher a few years earlier. Jimmy was an engineer with the phone company, and they were active in the community. Both were capable teachers and were happy to work with me. They began attending the class every Sunday. They related to the students as well or better than I did. We were determined not to have dull classes. We set high standards for the students to expect an exciting class.

After I told the students they could repaint the classroom in a color favored by the majority, Matt came to me.

"Tom, suggesting they paint the room in their favorite color may be moving too fast with these kids," he said.

"Why don't you visit with them and help them decide on an appropriate, joyful color for the room?" I said. "I want them to take ownership of their Sunday school class and feel like they are a part of it."

I went to the furniture store and bought a couple of sofas, loveseats and comfortable chairs. We arranged them around a large round coffee table where we would have juice, coffee, donuts and muffins.

When the students walked into the classroom the first Sunday, their excitement was obvious. They could see it was a new day for their Sunday school class.

I introduced myself to the group and explained how I wanted each Sunday's lessons to be practical and interesting.

"Christ came to Earth and spent three years teaching common-sense ideas about how we can live a fun, productive and happy life," I began. "He wants us to live our lives with a smile on our faces as we become more like Him, rendering service to our fellowman. He taught a sermon of love and forgiveness. These are common-sense ideas. It makes sense to love your neighbors. When you express love, you get a good result. When you hate, you create all kinds of problems. When you forgive, it gives everyone a chance to start over for a better result. He came to make new beginnings. We are here to make sense out of what Christ had to say. It will be a class where we exchange our views on how we see things from our experiences. We will learn from each other, and everyone must participate."

I told them this was my first experience teaching Sunday school, and that I would learn as much as they would or more.

"Let's learn and grow toward God together. I think Christ would want this to be a fun class. So let's make it so! Christ's teachings are for everyday living. I think we should use our experiences to discuss Christian principles. We should not leave them here in the classroom. Let's take what we learn home with us and make it a part of our decision making, a part of our life."

My overview was meant to set the stage for an interesting class. It was a class for these young people to decide on their beliefs — beliefs that would be a part of their decision-making process to create a happy, fruitful life.

"I will not play games," I said, in closing. "I will tell you as I see it. I want you to join me in using common sense as we think through each lesson."

Later, we decided to invite other young people to our class. The plan was to make a list of people and ask them to join us for three Sundays. If they didn't think the class was the most interesting place to be on a Sunday morning, they could go elsewhere.

"What about our black friends?" asked one young man. At the time, churches in the South were segregated.

"We don't care whether our guests are black or white," I responded. "If they are sincerely interested in deciding what they believe, this is the place to be."

"What will they think about it upstairs?" Another youngster asked.

"I think Christ is color blind. This is not an effort to integrate the membership, but we will not shy away from doing what is right by all people. Our door should be open to anyone who is truly interested in learning about Christ's teachings."

At that time, to my knowledge, there was not one black person in a white congregation in West Tennessee. Even the civic clubs were segregated. In this regard, times have changed for the better, and for the most part, we have moved past skin-color prejudice.

Another class member brought up the controversial subject of alcohol.

"What do you think about drinking?" He asked

"You should not be drinking alcoholic beverages at your age," I replied. "That is a decision you can make later as you get to the proper age."

"But what do you think about it?" They pressed.

They knew I belonged to the country club. I assumed they were pretty sure I was a social drinker. I had already told them I would do my best to be upfront with them. So, I shared my beliefs on alcohol with all honesty.

"First, I believe alcohol is an inanimate object," I said. "It can be found in our medications, and its use can be beneficial at times. For example, in the early days of surgery when anesthesia wasn't available, the patient might ask for whiskey to dull the pain."

"We could set a fifth of Jack Daniel whiskey on this table, and as an inanimate object, it would sit on this table forever if no one touched it. It is harmless on the table. It's the misuse of alcohol that gets us into trouble."

"I have been in the Army, served in Korea, attended college and, yes, I belong to the country club. I am a light social drinker. That is not to say you should drink alcohol when you are older. You can make your decision according to your beliefs. But I can tell you this, for sure. Never, ever misuse alcohol.

If you misuse alcohol, it will be a destructive force in your life. Christ warned us against the misuse of alcohol, and for good reasons."

***

My biggest challenge was the Old Testament, and for the students, it was more than a challenge. My practice was to ask them what they found in the lesson that they understood well enough to use the following week in school.

"How can you incorporate the lesson into your decision making?"

After they had their input, I highlighted what the Sunday school writer had to say, and I asked for their input again.

"Does it make sense to you? Can you put it into practice?"

We would have more discussion to make sense out of the lesson so we could apply it in our daily lives.

Later, it was easier to apply the lessons from the New Testament in our lives. As I began a class, I asked if they made any decisions based on the Christian principles we discussed the week before. Hands shot up, and they described their situations.

"Did you get a good result?" I asked.

"Yes!" They answered.

"Remember, in this class, we take what Christ said home with us for good results and a better life," I told them.

I have a problem taking the Bible from a literal point of view, and I know this statement gets some people up in the air. My effort was to study the Bible with a common-sense point of view so I could use it in everyday life. I think at the end of the day, what counts is how much we can get into action for a more Christ-like life, which gives us a happy and productive life.

The Sunday school superintendent attended our class to monitor our conversation. He attempted to set us straight from time to time.

Before long, Matt told me that some of the deacons would visit our class to observe us. I said we would be delighted to have them, but I would not alter my style of teaching to suit them.

Three deacons came with Matt to check us out the following Sunday. We welcomed them to our class, and I directed them to seats we reserved for their visit. My only request was that they not interrupt our class.

The class had a lively discussion that day. When it was over, our pastor came across the room and shook my hand.

"Great class," he said. "You have their interest."

As time went on, they accepted our new way of teaching, and we gained a lot of support — especially from the superintendent and parents.

As the young people drove home with their parents after class, I am sure their parents asked about the day's lesson. It must have created lively conversation in the family car. At Christmas, many of the parents wrote "thank you" notes to me. They said they could see a difference in their son or daughter, who never wanted to miss a class.

***

Teaching Sunday school and observing our young people was gratifying. I watched as they decided what they believed about the teachings of Christ and the Old Testament. They reached an understanding and began to make decisions based on what they had learned. They were young people under construction to be more Christ-like.

As a teacher, you wonder if you have made an impact on a student's life. Does it stick to his ribs? A letter from one of my former students, Steve Smith, was gratifying.

He wrote: "What I have always remembered and actually used in my adult life was your teachings about God's laws — laws of nature and physical and moral laws. You would say, 'you can trust God because you can trust His laws. God's laws will never let you down.' Each Sunday, you would challenge the group to take what we had learned and use it during the coming week. Using God's laws in our life taught us all to make better decisions. My time in your Sunday school class taught me to observe the universe, to see how things work and how to use that knowledge to help others. Later I used the principles of God's laws to teach my own children how to make good decisions."

I was honored that I had an impact on the lives of young people, but I also was aware the impact on my life. You can make a contribution to your church in many ways. For me, teaching a Sunday school class was one of the best. The time I spent preparing my Sunday school lessons was time well spent; it was preparing me to be a better husband, father and leader.

The class prompted me to read the New Testament each January. Also, it prompted me to brainstorm with my friend and mentor Jack McConnico about his insights on the Bible. Through these experiences, I firmed up my own beliefs. I am still learning, though, because as we experience more, we continually refine our beliefs. Remaining a student, as long as we live, is the best way to live.

Sherry and I later joined the First United Methodist Church, which was a good decision for our family. But our experience with the Baptist church was positive and gave us a broader view of our church life.

CHAPTER 10

THE BIRTH OF HENCO

*"Success is an inside job — a successful mindset with the determination
to carry out the mission to achieve the goal."*

The year before we built our new home, I formed my own company. I was off to a good start, and sales were going well. It was the spring of 1968 and time to start the next chapter in my business life.

Most of the money from the sale of my Nasco stock went to pay off the Nasco bank note and the down payment on our new house. I only needed a small investment to start the new company — just enough to buy my first order of bottles. Ours was a shoestring operation.

My operating expenses were low, and I wanted to start the company with low capital outlay. My concentration during the first year was to detail the company plan in writing. I didn't want to hire salesmen until I had a plan in place.

I went to First National Bank to visit with its president, Charlie Foresythe, and requested a $3,500 loan. When Charlie turned me down, I went to the Selmer Bank and Trust and met with Montie Smith, who had been with the bank a number of years. I shared my financial statement, which listed everything we owned, but it wasn't impressive. He looked it over and said that the only way he would make the loan was if my father signed the note.

I quickly told him I would not ask my father to sign the note. Montie thought my idea to manufacture, bottle and sell an all-purpose cleaner through schools was crazy. If I had asked for a loan to open a service station, he would have been more likely to approve it.

After the second rejection, I looked elsewhere.

John Harrison was an important businessman in Selmer with a successful furniture company. He also was a neighbor and good friend. We had numerous conversations about our businesses. John would ask how I planned to build a national company from scratch, and I would share my thoughts. John was always fascinated with the picture I painted.

I told him about my problems getting a loan, and he came to me a few days later.

"Tom, I want to be your business partner with $50,000 in cash," he said.

"John, I could hug your neck. If I were to have a partner, it would be John Harrison, but friend, a partnership is not in my plan."

He told me he would be a silent partner, and I could make all the business decisions. I still told him no.

John was one of Selmer Bank and Trust's most important customers. The following week, he found himself at the bank while the directors were waiting to begin their monthly meeting. As they were having coffee in the lounge, he spoke to them about my loan.

"I can't believe you turned down Tom Hendrix's $3,500 loan," he said. "His new company could provide a sizable payroll for our town, and he is a capable hometown boy."

"Have we turned him down?" They asked.

"Yes, you have not made the loan to him," John said.

The directors continued their meeting and discussed my loan application. I am sure Montie told them it was not a safe loan without my father's signature, but the next week, he called me back to the bank for another conversation.

When I arrived, Montie passed a yellow pad across the desk.

"List every piece of equity you have," he said.

I listed everything again, including furniture and an old 1960 Dodge that had not been cranked in several months.

"I am going to make the loan, even though you don't qualify," he said.

I thanked him and left after signing the paperwork. I don't think Montie was too sure about his new customer. Building a company on borrowed money is a bit of a problem, and it's not for the faint-hearted. But, it is our free enterprise system at its best. In what other country can a young man have a dream of building a national business and pioneering a product line with a concept to revolutionize an industry? If we don't let fear paralyze us, we can dream big.

The following week I called Montie again.

"Mr. Montie, I appreciate the $3,500 loan, but now I need a pickup truck to haul my cleaner," I said.

"Son, I have about all I can handle with you," he said.

I went back to First National Bank and talked with Charlie Foresythe again. I kidded him about not loaning me $3,500. I hoped he would have it in his heart to finance my pickup because I bought it at $100 over cost without a down payment. He agreed.

Things were falling in place — our new house was underway, and loans were secured to finance our new company and a pickup truck. Sherry and I had struggled for seven years with Nasco, and then we began anew to build a company based on our deep-seated beliefs to create something good for every person who joined the mission. We were excited. We had faith that the sun would shine one day, and we could look back and say that we did it our way.

***

I think everyone, from time to time, will let negative thinking overshadow their work and their goals. In my case, struggling to start a new company was overwhelming at times. I pulled into roadside parks to contemplate my situation and refocus on my goals. I played what-if games with myself on my yellow pad, projecting sales and profits. I ran the numbers on sales forces of 50 to 200 salesmen, selling variable amounts of products, raising money for schools and earning a percentage for the company.

After two or three pages on my yellow pad, I projected millions of dollars with a dynamic sales force, encouraging team members to reach their full potential as we revolutionized fundraising in America. Our service attitude would begin with our employees. If we got our service right for our employees, they would be more motivated to get the service right for the schools.

Entrepreneurs find themselves in a lonely world at times, with no one to turn to but themselves and maybe a prayer for extra strength. It is difficult for other people to identify with your situation — even good friends. They simply cannot stand in your shoes to understand the pressures you feel. In spite of the difficult times, I am convinced entrepreneurship is one of the most exciting ways to live. We are always thinking through our problems, looking for solutions. It is a life of constantly educating yourself to do more and solve that next problem. Boredom, for sure, isn't an issue. We are too busy becoming the person to accomplish the mission.

Success is an inside job — a successful mindset with the determination to carry out the mission to achieve the goal. Entrepreneurs blaze trails with many disappointments, turndowns and discouraging results, but in spite of all the problems, our resolve is strengthened to climb the mountain. We feed off plowing new ground, taking risks to reach our goal.

Sherry and I faced some strong headwinds in the early days as we built our fast-growing company, but we followed a written plan with multiple objectives.

The first was for me to write all the sales manuals from my day-to-day selling experiences. Then we needed to develop a summertime business to ensure our future salesmen had year-round income to support their families. We also needed to develop a product line that would fill the fundraising needs for schools and could be sold year after year.

Our goal was to create a comprehensive company plan that would allow employees to grow to their full potentials through servant leadership. There would be no room for bosses. It was important that our new company reflect our service philosophy and that it begin with our employees. Our service should be a positive experience for everyone involved.

To upgrade school fundraising in America, we needed to develop programs that raised more money in less time and had less school interruption. Students needed to sell for a period of two or three days instead of two or three weeks. The programs needed to give people in the community a good value for their money, and they needed to provide a good learning experience for students. We wanted to teach children how to communicate with honesty so they could see business as a service and cast aside greed. Running a well-organized fundraising program could be a positive and practical experience for students with valuable lessons.

To achieve these objectives, I knew we needed to hire well-qualified people with proper training and strong feelings about carrying out our mission. To become national in scope, we had to find a new source to hire qualified people to call on schools, and we had to team up with a large bank to loan us money.

My biggest challenge was maintaining a good cash flow to pay my bills, which required me to spend a lot of time on the road in sales, while growing a surplus to build the company brick by brick. Sherry and I no longer were supported by a professional organization. If something needed to be done, it was our responsibility.

Sherry supported me from our home kitchen. She was in charge of accounts payable and receivable, typing and whatever else was needed. She was totally involved in starting the new company.

Back then, we had no cell phones, fax machines, computers or email services. Our office had a typewriter, adding machine and telephone. To make a phone call when I traveled, I had to find a telephone booth and feed it with nickels, dimes and quarters.

***

I traveled to Atlanta to purchase bottles for the all-purpose cleaner. I stopped several times to brainstorm a name for the cleaner, as well as the company. I ran through several possible ideas and researched them to find out if they had already been copyrighted, but I could not make a decision.

Then it hit me.

I stopped at a telephone booth, called Sherry and suggested that we divide my last name. I told her we should use the first part, "Hen," for the company name (Henco) and the last part, "DRIX," for the cleaner name. We debated the possibilities and decided that we would go with my suggestions. Both names served us well through the years.

On Monday morning, I drove to a printing company in Savannah, Tennessee, to design and print brochures for our fundraising programs. We wanted the brochure to be fun for students and bring a smile to their customers' faces.

As we designed the brochure, we realized we also needed a company logo. That's when I saw A.D. Caldwell, a local high school art teacher, doodling at a nearby desk in the printer's office.

"Can you sketch a corporate logo for my brochure?" I asked.

"What do you have in mind?"

"Do five sketches, and I will select one as my

DRIX, an all-purpose cleaner in a blue bottle, is the only product Henco sold for the first few years.

logo," I responded. "When Henco is national in scope and a highly successful company, you can say, 'I did the Henco logo!' So make it a good one — one we can be proud of for years."

He sketched five ideas within a few minutes, and I picked one with three connecting ovals and Henco lettered across the center. I thought it was perfectly balanced and would serve us well. As I remember, A.D. charged me $5.

I returned to Selmer and contacted Howard Maness, a longtime friend who was driving a school bus. I spoke with him about working part-time bottling the cleaner. Howard agreed to help. My father also pitched in to help any way he could.

Henco's humble beginning was in a rental building in Bethel Springs.

I rented an old building in Bethel Springs for $20 per month. We cleaned it out and built a platform for a 55-gallon barrel to mix the cleaner's formula. We put the barrel on top of the platform and a small electric motor on top of the barrel. Connected to the motor was a long steel rod that was attached to a small boat propeller. This was our mixer for the liquid cleaner formula.

I stopped by the drug store and picked up the largest surgical hose I could find to use for filling the bottles. We bored a hole in the bottom of the barrel and connected the hose. Howard moved the hose from bottle to bottle, filling the cleaner. He filled a new bottle every six seconds or so.

Locals in Bethel Springs heard about the new soap manufacturer coming to town and wondered if it could be Procter and Gamble. They could not believe their eyes. They sat, chewed their tobacco and watched Howard work.

"Tom said this thing would become a national company started in Bethel Springs, and I am the start-up guy!" Howard told the crowd.

I would have liked to have been a fly on the wall to hear their responses.

Shortly after we started filling the bottles with cleaner, I thought we should speed up the process. I went back to the drug store and bought another surgical hose. I went back to the building and found several townspeople sitting around watching Howard fill bottles.

"I am here to double production," I told him.

"I am moving this hose as fast as I can," he said.

We bored another hole in the barrel for the second hose.

"I don't think that will work," he said. "I can't handle two hoses."

"It will be simple," I replied. "Start filling bottle No. 1 and when it is half full, start filling bottle No. 2."

I showed Howard how it would be simple to manage. I left for about an hour, and when I returned, he had bubbles seeping out of his shoelaces.

"This is not as easy as you thought!" He exclaimed.

His friends, the townspeople, were amused with his new job and had fun watching him.

***

Little League baseball was going strong that summer, and teams needed money to improve their baseball fields and equipment. I decided to call on them, which was another new experience for me. But I knew that if I could make Little League fundraising successful during summer, my company would be a year-round business.

I made as many Little League calls as I could. Because they practiced in late afternoons and evenings, I worked 16 hours per day. I was a bit clumsy in the beginning, not knowing anything about their organizational structure. I used my white carpet and black shoe polish in my demonstration to convince them the all-purpose cleaner had the cleaning power for just about anything in the home. And because a household cleaner was a part of their grocery budget, it made sense to coaches.

The Little League boys could collect names of most people in their community and sell at least one bottle. The league earned 80 cents for every bottle sold. I sold a high percentage of the Little Leagues I contacted. I hit the road, calling on Little Leagues for five days a week, leaving most of the work of setting up the company for weekends.

When school began in August, I continued to do extremely well. I had outstanding sales with the best band directors in Mississippi. My close ratio was good, and word of mouth was spreading from school to school. My reputation was building my business.

***

I went to see Jim T. Hamilton. He and his family were longtime Selmer residents, and he had recently begun practicing law. He also had just been elected Selmer's mayor. Jim T.'s sparsely furnished office was up a flight of stairs over a storefront on Main Street. I asked him if he had any law books we could read about incorporating a national fundraising company that would possibly do all kinds of projects in the future. I wanted flexibility.

We had a big laugh, and we incorporated Henco on September 25, 1968.

***

Nasco was my competition, and after about eight months, Nasco salesman Lewis Mohundro came to my home to see me. He wanted a job at Henco. I was not home at the time, but Sherry was impressed with Lewis' sincerity, and she promised him that we would visit soon.

When I returned home for the weekend, Sherry told me about Lewis. I explained that I was not ready to hire anyone, but I called him to set up a meeting anyway. Lewis arrived a little later, driving an old car.

"I can't make a living in competition with you," he told me. "It is partially the Nasco program, but also, I want you to teach me how to sell."

He pulled his front pant pockets inside out. He said he was broke, and his car needed repairs.

"My wife and family want me to work in a factory, but I want more."

I liked Lewis for being so upfront and honest with me about his situation. I explained I didn't have plans to hire anyone at the moment, but he continued to try to convince me.

"All I want is a chance to prove myself, and I will put in the long hours if you will hire me now," he said.

I asked him several questions. I learned that he was a high school graduate with a young wife and two small children. Nasco was his first sales position. Previously, he had been an hourly employee in manufacturing.

"Who can I call that you've worked for outside of Nasco and manufacturing?" I asked.

"I worked for Jack McConnico in Memphis," he said.

"If I call Jack, do you think he will remember you?"

"Yes," he said.

"Lewis, give me a few words that best describe you."

"I am honest and hardworking with a desire to be successful."

I called Jack.

"I have a young man here, Lewis Mohundro, who would like me to hire him as a salesman. He has described himself as honest and hardworking with a desire to be successful. Does that accurately describe him?"

"Yes, he is a good kid," Jack said.

I turned to Lewis to complete the interview.

"I will give thought to hiring you, but you must call Bill Cook," I told him. "He must agree to your leaving Nasco to join Henco. Also, you must tell Bill that I did not recruit you. You came to me for an interview."

Lewis called Bill, and Bill agreed to not stand in his way. I did not have a restrictive contract like a no-compete agreement with Nasco, but I did promise Bill that I would not raid his sales force. Bill knew I could hire most of his people if I wanted.

With Sherry's urging and Jack's recommendation, I hired Lewis. I was determined to successfully teach him the business because I certainly didn't want my first Henco salesman to fail. Lewis joined Henco in August 1969.

Before schools adjourned for the summer, I signed the top Arkansas bands to run the DRIX cleaner program in the fall. I assigned Lewis to manage them. I asked him to memorize the student presentation and give it to me flawlessly. I wanted him to be as good an actor as John Wayne when he delivered his lines to students.

"When you are ready, put on your best suit and tie and give your student presentation to me," I told him. "We may even ask Sherry to sit in."

A short time later, Lewis gave his presentation to Sherry and me. It was flawless, and we were proud of him. He had a good personality and a great deal of confidence. I assumed he practiced his lines before the mirror numerous times, and I gave him some advice.

"If anyone suspects your lines are memorized, you don't know your presentation," I cautioned. "When you watch John Wayne on the screen, you don't think John has done a good job memorizing his lines. Instead, you live the story with him. It must be the same with the fundraising presentation."

I made a quick trip through Arkansas to introduce Lewis to the band directors. I asked them to agree to Lewis conducting their program instead of me. If they didn't, I would conduct their program as promised. We made the rounds, and all the band directors agreed except the director in the town of Helena. Lewis forwarded the results on each program he ran, including the amount of sales and the band's profit, to Helena's band director. After the results of two or three schools had been sent, the band director agreed for him to conduct his program, and it was a success.

Lewis was a unique salesman. He was younger than salesmen I would have normally hired, which required more of my time in teaching the business, and he was not a college graduate. But he was excited when I hired him, and he was eager to learn the Henco way of doing things, which was much different than the Nasco plan. He also was happy with the personal attention I gave him. I visited with him and his wife, Sandy, to help them make a detailed budget to determine his company draw against his commission. He could make professional money with his commission if he mastered the business. I set their draw to pay their bills so they could live without fighting their creditors. We did not want Lewis to be distracted as he learned the Henco plan.

When Lewis was not running programs in Arkansas, he rode with me to learn my philosophy of selling to build a long-term business. It was all about rendering the best fundraising service in the country. Our success would rise or fall based on our quality of service. We needed to be completely honest with band directors and sponsors and live up to our presentation.

Lewis knew that if he did not run successful programs in Arkansas, he would lose his job. Keeping our commitment to the band directors was serious business.

But Lewis' fall business was excellent. He earned much more than his draw. He came to see me after two months in the business, and his old car was smoking. The motor was shot. I suggested he follow me downtown to the Ford dealership and surprised him by saying he was getting a new car. We selected a Ford that would serve him well as he traveled his territory. The dealer gave us a price with his trade in, and I said I would sign the note. Lewis could not believe what was happening. He drove off in the first new car he had ever owned. It motivated him to work long hours to show his appreciation for our confidence in him.

At the end of the first year, he had earned a considerable amount of money and asked me what I thought about his buying a new Thunderbird.

I suggested that he should consider saving his money for a rainy day.

"Get in the car with me," he said.

We drove into an area with low-income housing, and he showed me a house with brick siding — the place he grew up.

"Before you get excited about this 'big' home, you should know we only lived in one-half of the house. We ate mostly beans and cornbread. Once, I saw a Thunderbird in an automobile showroom and told myself I would drive a Thunderbird one day. This is the first time I have earned the money to make my dream come true."

I was touched.

"Buy the Thunderbird," I said.

Lewis was a great employee. A couple years later, I promoted him to area manager. But one day in December 1973, Lewis died in a car accident as he drove home in his Thunderbird. He was 27.

Two or three months before the accident, I asked him if he had any insurance. He said no. We contacted the local Farm Bureau agent, H.J. Maxedon, and he visited with Lewis and Sandy. They bought a sizable term policy, and we adjusted Lewis' draw to pay for it. Lewis also purchased Henco stock. It pleased me to see the progress Lewis had made financially and to know his wife and children were able to live comfortably as they made their transition after his death.

Lewis was special to me, and I often have thought about what his life could have been as he grew to his full potential. He was Henco's first salesman. He also was a high school graduate who came from a poor background, but he grew as a person and gained success. His death was terrible news.

***

One of the objectives I outlined when I started Henco was to find a place to recruit outstanding, well-educated people to whom I could teach the Henco sales plan. Before he died, Lewis had suggested that I contact Bob Brooks, the band director at Malvern High School in Arkansas. Bob traveled to Selmer for an interview. I was impressed with him and hired him to join Henco at the end of the summer. We spent a few days traveling together, calling on schools, and I taught him the Henco way of salesmanship.

Hiring Bob helped us solve one of Henco's toughest problems — developing a source of good people to hire. It was easy to teach Bob how to work with the schools and sell fundraising programs. He had conducted successful programs himself as a school band director. He understood the needs of large band programs, and he was very much at home speaking to other band directors. He understood how to do business in a school. He had a master's degree in education and understood the importance of learning the Henco program.

We sought top band directors to hire — people with well-known reputations and the determination to win band contests. They were teachable. Schools were their turf. They knew other band directors in their state, and they were a perfect fit for our organization.

These young men had already paid the price to build the top bands in their state, and they were hungry for financial success to solve some of their family's financial problems. Henco was just the place to help them climb their financial mountain. We made it a team effort to achieve their goals.

Until that point in my career, I had hired and re-trained salesmen. In so many cases, they had bad sales habits. They resisted giving a fundraising presentation with our tested language. They had a tendency to revert to just talking, leaving out many of the program's details, which caused misunderstandings and jeopardized the program's success. People who had never been in sales before were more apt to accept and learn what was taught. This attitude was refreshing to me.

Bob Brooks earned $8,000 a year at Malvern High School as the senior band director. He earned $25,000 his first year with Henco. Gene Hébert, band director at Nederland High School in Texas, earned $12,000 a year before joining Henco. He earned $65,000 his first year with Henco in 1975. These kinds of earnings gave them the financial freedom to do a great deal for their families.

We learned that the top band directors could have well more than 100 students in their senior marching band. Most had master's degrees and earned

$10,000 to $12,000 a year during the early 1970s.

During their first year in the business, Henco salesmen would learn the business while at least doubling their previous earnings. The second year, in most cases, they would double their earnings with a sizeable bonus over their weekly draw. Their wives were able to stay home with their children, if they wanted, and they could begin to furnish their home or save for the future. They were a delight to work with, and it was wonderful to observe their progress.

They were appreciative for the Henco opportunity, especially our professional training and the Henco education on how to live a more productive life.

With our band-director strategy in place, Henco was poised to grow in leaps and bounds. Our sales manual was written from my direct selling experiences. And we found the place to hire well-educated people to teach our business so they could provide a professional fundraising service to schools.

It was a wake-up call. I knew if we hired the most outstanding band directors across the country, we could build a 200-man sales force much more quickly. I said goodbye to employment agencies and the bad habits of existing salesmen. We were compelled to build a national company based on strong beliefs that reflected our values. It was imperative to visualize, as clearly as possible, the company under construction. So we initiated clear policies to create harmony with as few surprises as possible.

***

Two women from Selmer Elementary School's parent organization came to see me to help them raise money for two air conditioners. I asked them why, and they told me that classrooms reached nearly 90 degrees in August and made the children miserable.

"The environment is certainly not conducive to a good education, and we want to change that," they said. "These children are reared in an air-conditioned home and ride to school in an air-conditioned car. To ask them to pay attention and learn in a classroom that is 90 degrees is unfair."

"How many 90-degree classrooms do you have in the elementary school?"

"Thirteen, but the principal will not go along with a school-wide fundraising program."

I visited with the principal about air conditioning the classrooms and told him we could raise the money in one weekend.

"I will not involve the total school in a fundraising program," he said, frankly. "If the county wanted the classrooms air conditioned, they should spend the money to do so."

I noticed his office was air conditioned.

"I assume one of the first things you do when you walk into this office in the morning is to flip on the air conditioner," I said. "I want you to hear me out so you can flip this switch in each classroom to improve the quality of education."

I proceeded to give him a convincing presentation.

"Do you really think we could raise enough money in one weekend to air condition the school?" He asked when I finished.

"Yes," I said. "Beyond a doubt, if you will provide good leadership. We will send a note home with the students saying: 'With your help by signing your name for a bottle of all-purpose cleaner, the Selmer Elementary School will be air conditioned for a quality education.' We will make the program fun for the kids with mystery houses in each neighborhood worth $5. The next day in class, teachers will ask who found a mystery house. Winners will get a $5 bill. I will write a check for 20 mystery houses and a $20 top prize. They will canvas their neighborhoods, looking for mystery houses. Let's you and I decide today that this school will be air conditioned for a quality education."

He agreed.

The week before the program began, the county newspaper published a nice article that pictured the principal endorsing the effort. The program was conducted in one weekend and was successful, raising more than $3,000 to purchase 13 window units to cool classrooms for about 300 students. Teachers and parents were equally excited as they observed the positive reaction of students.

I stopped by to see the principal on the first day the air-conditioning units were in full operation, and he was delighted to see me.

"This is the best thing we have done this year to improve education for the students," he said.

School fundraising done in a professional way can benefit many people.

When my daughters attended that elementary school, the air conditioners were still running. And they kept running for many years to enhance the environment for better education.

As a result, upgrading school fundraising in America became Henco's mission. In speech after speech to Henco sales people and other in-house employees, I always dramatized the good we were doing in schools across the country.

"Whether you sweep the floor, call on schools or keep the books, you are part of our mission to upgrade school fundraising in America — it's our mission of service," I would say.

The mystery house idea also stuck, and we used it as an incentive for students in future fundraising efforts.

After the elementary school experience, I began to ponder the good we could do running thousands of programs each year. With future employees, I constantly emphasized that we reflect on the good we have accomplished. Doing something special for others is the best way to express your love, and I wanted our team to be on a mission of service. I learned that people become much more motivated when they reflect on the good they are doing.

***

A company growing into a national effort faces constant change. And changes affect the lives of people. There is nothing more sensitive than a family's paycheck. I visualized a force of 200 well-trained salesmen, rendering service in 48 states, but it all hinged on developing each sales territory to its full potential. We would have to accomplish it in steps as we expanded.

Our territory-development plan required us to hire a band director who sold to other band directors while mastering the business. Since we needed a large territory when we only sold to bands, we developed other product lines for programs with other school groups. After working with bands, our salesmen would target other groups, which often had many more students than bands. These groups could thoroughly canvass neighborhoods and raise a considerable amount of money.

The initial salesmen would receive an override commission on other salesmen hired into their territory, which were usually two other people. When the territory was fully developed, the salesmen could travel a small territory, which reduced travel expenses and increased time at home with family.

If we didn't have these policies in place up front and cut the size of the territory from what we promised, we would have upset the harmony of our sales force. Henco would have lost goodwill among its salesmen. Trust and goodwill are necessary for good communication. With good policies, we had few surprises. We did our best to help people see the future as clearly as possible.

***

After three years, the little building in Bethel Springs was much too small. In 1971, I applied for and received a Small Business Administration guarantee for a $50,000 bank loan. The capital was used to construct the first building Henco would call its own. We selected a small parcel east of Selmer on U.S. 64  *Henco's second location was on Hwy. 64 in Selmer.* and constructed a 3,200-square-foot manufacturing plant.

As our company grew, my main, unmet objective was to find a large bank to be our lending partner. Our local banks did not understand our mission.

I telephoned First Tennessee Bank in Memphis and asked them to send someone to visit Henco, Inc. in Selmer. I hoped the name, Henco Incorporated, would sound like a big outfit and warrant a 100-mile drive to Selmer.

Will Kelley and his associate made the call. I was at my desk in the corner of our new building. Will, who grew up in Brownsville, Tennessee, stood about six and a half feet tall. I am quite sure they were probably thinking they had made a long drive for nothing. I had two chairs near my desk and asked them to sit so I could share my story with them.

Will was truly a good human being, and he listened with respect as I laid out our plan to build a national school fundraising company. I told him we were looking for a large bank to join Henco to finance our fast-growing and profitable company. I gave them our financial statement. I had little equity and included our one-year projections and an extended three-year projection.

"I am not ready for a loan today, but I will be later," I said. "A financial statement, with our sales numbers, will be forwarded to you each month so you can follow our progress. I would like for you to observe us for one year, and then I will come to Memphis for a loan."

I had their interest. They asked several questions. Afterward, they departed with a positive attitude about Tom Hendrix and Henco.

At year's end, I went to Memphis with numbers for the past year and projections for the upcoming year. Henco had exceeded its projections in sales and profitability by 30 percent. The numbers were small but positive.

The bankers were impressed. After our discussion, they asked me how they could help, and my reply was a $50,000 signature loan. They stepped aside for a brief discussion and returned to approve the loan. They drew up the documents, and I signed them.

I left and stepped on the elevator, heading to the garage parking lot, happy that these bankers would finance our fast-growing company. To move from a $3,500 loan to a $50,000 loan was quite a step for this young entrepreneur. A few years later, we were borrowing $12 to $15 million in the late summer to be paid back in December or January below prime rate.

Henco financed its rapid growth of more than 40 percent a year for 10 years with First Tennessee Bank. Doing business with a bank that understands your needs and has the confidence to make the loans is so important to the development of a company. It was essential to have a banking partner that would make loans in increasing amounts. In order for these loans to be made, Henco needed to build financial strength with increasing profits. In the early years, Sherry and I kept my salary low, even though Henco was starting to earn considerable profit.

***

Our first building erected in the Selmer Industrial Park in 1973 was 40,000 square feet. We used tilt-up concrete walls faced with pebbled rock. Every two or three years, we added warehouses and offices until we reached 300,000 square feet during a 10-year period. We increased our land from eight acres to a 43-acre campus. We placed considerable emphasis on the most up-to-date computer department with in-house programmers to write the needed programs. And we outfitted the computer department with new computers every three years or so. Our trucking fleet grew each year as we expanded into most communities in the United States.

We were getting closer to becoming a national company. Financial freedom was within our grasp.

At its largest, the Henco complex in the Selmer Industrial Park, below, covered 43 acres with with 300,000 square feet of industrial build-ings. The first Henco
building in the industrial park, above, was 40,000 square feet.

CHAPTER 11

CLEANERS, CANDLES AND MORE

"Goals are powerful; they activate our mind to search for ideas."

The DRIX All-Purpose Cleaner was a great product, but I always kept my eyes open for new ideas. One day, I made a sales call at a school and saw a candle. It was in a round glass cylinder, flickering on the table. The outside of the cylinder featured a hand-painted design. I saw the light flickering through the glass and thought we could sell these candles in a fundraising program.

I noticed the name "Chicago Candles" on the bottom of the candle. On my way home, I brainstormed how we could produce and sell them. As soon as I arrived, I telephoned Chicago Candles and asked for a price on a truckload of glass cylinders, half full with transparent wax. The candles were nine inches tall and three and a quarter inches in diameter. The company gave me a price that seemed reasonable, and I asked when we could pick up the candles if we paid cash.

Bottles of DRIX

The next week, we had our candles, and we planned to wick and decorate them ourselves. The hand-painted design was beyond our reach at that moment, but I thought we could create a good-looking candle with an acetate wrapper if we could find a company to print them. After several phone calls, I located a small company in Middle Tennessee that agreed to print the wrappers to an exact size so we could glue them to the glass cylinder.

Sherry's talent for creative design prompted me to ask her to design three candles that she thought would sell. She researched monthly magazines, catalogs and greeting cards to stimulate our thinking. Back then, the Vietnam War was in the forefront of American minds. A

Leigh Anne and Susan with our Christmas candles

greeting card we found picturing a white dove with a green twig in its mouth and gold highlights triggered the idea of a promising peace design. For the candle's acetate wrapper, the design of the white dove was on a green background with gold highlights. Because we were entering Christmas season, we contemplated having two of our three candles with Christmas themes; all three would be sold from a colored brochure. We contacted our local school's art teacher for help.

I enlisted Robert Mathis to brainstorm how we could wick the candles, which were half full of transparent wax. I first met Robert in Adamsville when we began Nasco. We had little to work with, but Robert was a smart young man with a creative mind — a practical engineer. In those early days of manufacturing stack stools, he was able to design and construct equipment for pennies on the dollar. He continued to be an asset to Nasco and Henco through the years. Robert was called upon often to solve mechanical problems for Henco in a practical way. His contributions reflected my often-made statement, "You don't build a company, people build companies." I

Robert Mathis

will always be grateful that Robert Mathis was a part of Henco.

We decorated enough candles for our first test program. We saw unbelievable results. The school almost doubled its profit projection, and the candle program almost doubled DRIX cleaner sales. It was almost too good to be true.

My next program had similar results. We quickly realized that this was a moneymaker for everyone — schools, salesmen and Henco. I always believed we created our wealth from good ideas, and this candle was a good idea.

We knew we would experience problems in the manufacturing process. Everything was new to us. Attaching the acetate wrappers to the glass cylinders by hand with glue was tricky. The transparent wax needed to be at a certain temperature so the wax could melt across the candle and the wick could burn with a nice glow. We tested candles for a short time until they revealed a good start-up burn. They needed to perform over time with a nice glowing flame.

Production proceeded well until the weather turned cold. One Sunday morning, before teaching my Sunday school class, I went to check on the candles and heard a ticking sound in the building where we stored several thousand of them. I opened a case of candles to confirm my worst fear. The wrappers were popping loose from the cylinders. This meant the candles we had delivered to schools had the same problem. We even had delivered some to homes, which exacerbated the problem even more.

Immediately, I knew my first priority was to go to the schools in person and address the situation in an upfront, honest way. I assured the school sponsors that we would replace the candles and reimburse them for any problems. It was important to make it right for the schools, knowing we couldn't eliminate all the problems we had caused for them.

Upon contacting the school sponsors, I was pleasantly surprised at how reasonable they were in our attempts to resolve the issue. I think they appreciated our sincerity and the fact we accepted responsibility.

With that fire at bay, our next pressing issue was obtaining an adhesive that would hold tightly in all kinds of weather conditions. We found one and worked through all the issues. Future candle sales expanded.

We had happy school groups and bands.

Within a few years, we were manufacturing millions of candles. Seven or eight tanker rail cars waited outside on our rail spur to be pumped into the huge heated holding tanks inside our building. The wax pumped through a 12-head filling machine so the candles could be wicked on their way to an automatic decorating line. The decorating line, for our special applications, cost several hundred thousand dollars. The whole operation ran smoothly.

The day I first saw the candle in the school with the hand-painted design, I had no idea what it would do for our fundraising business across America. Luck is important to our success. But if one of my objectives had not been to create a product line that would repeat in schools, I would not have noticed the candle flickering on the table.

Goals are powerful; they activate our mind to search for ideas. If you are a goal-orientated person, it is amazing how lucky you will be in life. I believe goals, to some extent, make you a lucky person.

**

In the early years of Henco, our products were candles, DRIX and a degreaser. The degreaser was an excellent product for tough cleaning jobs, such as car motors or projects around the home. The products increased the amount of money raised for the school groups and repeated year after year. People in

An early Henco sales team

179

*Gene Hébert demonstrates
a Millionaire game.*

the community looked forward to band students contacting them each year. The products put Henco on its feet financially, enabling the company to earn millions of dollars in profit and raise millions for schools.

Henco continued to broaden offerings to include a line of household products similar to DRIX, a line of family shampoo and hair-care products, and an assortment of light bulbs for homes and businesses. We also produced a line of greeting cards, personal stationery and assorted paper products.

In later years, the use of more functional products in fundraising gave way to products that were either decorative or edible. The decorative gift items included a wide variety of candles, acrylic ornaments and kitchen accessories. Edible products included candy, cookies, cheeses and snacks.

One highly innovative product line was board games that took advantage of a high interest in table games while providing unique local advertising opportunities. The board games could be adapted to a specific community or special interest.

We perfected our programs until we had the best in the industry. At the beginning of each season, we conducted surveys at shopping malls. The surveys provided us with amazingly accurate percentages of sales and enabled us to produce our products in proper percentages. For example, we asked random people to look at the variety of candles displayed and select their top three favorites. Interestingly, the candles sold in the same percentage in Petal, Mississippi, as Los Angeles, California. Variances were not significant, which gave us an opportunity to manufacture the candles as they were being sold. We had a clean warehouse at the end of our selling season, reducing our inventory.

CHAPTER 12

THE SUN BEGINS TO SHINE

"Henco promoted family life as much as possible."

W hen I started this entrepreneurial journey, Sherry and I always lived within our means. Every dime possible went back into the business to finance its growth.

But in 1976, the sun began to shine. Henco earned enough profit for us to adjust our personal standard of living. The first year Henco made more than $1 million, we thought it was time to raise our salary and enjoy some of the fruits of our labor.

We began entertaining many people at our home. When regional sales managers came to Selmer, our home was open for dinner meetings or offered as a place to relax. We thought about ways to improve it. A recent expansion at Henco added offices around a tropical solarium with skylights, designed by architect Lee Butler. Lee, who was reared in Bolivar, had returned to Medon, Tennessee, from San Francisco. He was a practitioner of sustainable housing designs and had recently built an environmentally friendly home for his family. We asked him to help us create an addition to our home that incorporated a swimming pool with amenities for family living and applied his natural energy principles.

We built a beautiful indoor swimming pool, incorporating a kitchen, sauna and Jacuzzi, which doubled the size of our home. The pool area faced south with glass panels set in redwood beams more than 20 feet high. The space captured the sun's heat, which made it comfortable on 30-degree days. It was environmentally friendly and controlled by a thermostat. It also funneled excess heat during winter months into our main house, reducing our energy cost. It was a unique system for that period of time — a great space to entertain and boost a healthier lifestyle.

Almost every morning, I stepped from our master bedroom to the pool and dove in for a 30-minute swim. It also was a big hit with the kids, and they swam year round. When snow covered the ground, they invited friends for a swimming party. As they grew older, our home became a safe and fun place for teens to gather. Sherry and I wanted our home to be inviting to family and friends of all ages.

Henco also invested in a turbojet to fly district sales managers each week to their different territories throughout the country to work with the salesmen. We named it "Papa Charlie." At the beginning of the week, the plane dropped off sales managers in their territories and picked them up on Friday to spend the weekend with their families. Henco promoted family life as much as possible.

After purchasing the turbojet, we had the flexibility to participate in activities we had never done before. For example, we would invite a couple or two to join us for a weekend in New Orleans. A special treat was Sunday brunch at Brennan's Restaurant before leaving for home. We also picked up fresh seafood and placed it in the nose of the plane — taking a part of New Orleans home with us.

We purchased a houseboat to spend family time at Pickwick Lake. Selmer was only 30 minutes from the lake, and we all loved the water. We partnered with John and Mary Harrison, who were our next-door neighbors when we first moved to Selmer.

Within a year, we sold our interest in the first houseboat and upgraded to a new Burnscraft houseboat, which had more room and nicer features. We enjoyed it for a short period of time and then purchased a new 45-foot Chris Craft Commander yacht.

We took possession of the yacht in early summer in Fort Lauderdale,

Florida, and started a 5,500-mile trip back to Pickwick Lake through New York, the Great Lakes and Chicago.

I shall never forget stepping aboard, climbing up to the bridge, looking over the long bow and questioning myself. What have I done? What will it cost to get this yacht back to Pickwick? How many storms will we encounter? Will our captain keep us safe?

With a positive attitude, our equipment checked and provisions stocked, we headed north as our experienced captain, Warren Elfers, took the wheel. We traveled offshore if the weather was good. But we found the intracoastal waterway to be more interesting. So many sights attracted our attention — marine life, birds, marinas, beautiful homes and other boats.

I operated the yacht part of the time, but it was nice to walk away from the helm and leave everything to Warren. He took his job seriously, and as we cruised, he operated the yacht many hours each day. He was very amiable. When we docked each day at 4 or 5 p.m., Warren refilled our fuel tanks with 300 to 400 gallons of diesel fuel, depending on the day's run. He washed the yacht every day so salt residue would not harm its exterior. He also descended into the engine room to service the engine.

While Warren worked, we had plenty of sunlight left for the girls to get some exercise, ride their bicycles and explore within a safe distance. If the marina was close to a market or restaurant, we picked up supplies or dined out so Sherry could take a break from meal preparation.

We also enjoyed the company of good friends throughout the trip. Generally, one couple would fly into a port city on Papa Charlie and come aboard for a few days. When they disembarked, another couple would board.

One day, as we cruised along the coast of South Carolina, a fisherman brought his boat up to ours and showed us a basket of blue crabs. We traded a six-pack of beer for them. Sherry put the kettle on, and we had a crab feast that evening on the enclosed aft deck as we watched the sunset.

In Norfolk, Virginia, we stopped and scheduled an oil change, which gave us time to visit Williamsburg. We rented a car and made our way to the old

Sherry, Tom, Susan and Leigh on the family yacht in New York Harbor.

city, enjoying the rich history of our great country. Then we continued north, bound for New England.

Our trip had many highlights. One, I well remember, was cruising on the East River in New York City. We looked off to the west, and the Statue of Liberty came into view. I was on the bridge, and I excitedly called for Susan, Leigh Anne and Sherry to join me for a wonderful view of New York. We decided to have lunch on the bow of the boat in the shadow of the Statue of Liberty. It was very inspirational as we moved the bow to the base of the huge statue.

I told my family that I wished there was a Statue of Responsibility standing beside the Statue of Liberty. By being responsible people, we can maintain our freedom in this country. When government takes our responsibility, we become irresponsible. The Statue of Responsibility has not been built, but I wish every small town in America had one to drive home the point: "Be responsible for your life."

Next, we made a course for the Great Lakes.

The Erie Canal will always stand out in our minds. We exited the Hudson River at Albany, where we bought bags of hay to attach along the sides of the yacht as protection from the rough walls of the approximately 30 old locks we would traverse. We traveled through beautiful New York farm country and saw dairy farms on both sides of the narrow canal. We cruised northward slowly, at 10 or 12 miles per hour to prevent wakes that could erode the historic banks. We did not, however, mind the slower speed. We enjoyed the countryside, and we took our time to enjoy Sherry's cooking. One day she made one of my favorite pies — peanut butter cream — like my mother made when we were growing up.

Our Erie Canal cruise ended at Sylvan Beach and the Oneida Lake, where we spent the night at a marina after struggling against a heavy wind that challenged our control of the yacht. The next day, we cruised across the lake and entered the Oswego Canal en route to Lake Ontario. The Oswego Canal is about 24 miles long with a depth of 14 feet. Seven locks span a 118-foot change in elevation.

The water was clear and cool as we crossed Lake Ontario, and the weather was good, despite strong winds. As we docked at Port Weller in Canada, the wind blew the yacht against a docking wall and slightly damaged its side. We rented a car for a day of sightseeing at the awe-inspiring Niagara Falls while the yacht underwent repairs.

We departed the following day for the famous Welland Canal, which is a shipping canal connecting Lake Ontario and Lake Erie. It enables vessels to ascend and descend the Niagara Escarpment and bypass Niagara Falls. The elevation change is 326 feet and the maximum draft is 27 feet.

When we arrived at the Welland, we experienced our first charge for canal passage on our trip. We did not mind the fee because the route saved us miles and time. It was interesting to be up close to the cargo ships — the lakers. At one lock, our captain felt uneasy about the spacing between our vessels, and he strongly requested a delayed entry from the lockmaster. Our yacht was dwarfed beside those huge ships.

As we traversed the inland waterways and the Welland Canal, we encountered a number of drawbridges. If necessary, we called ahead using our marine radio, and requested the bridge master lift the bridge for our passage. In most cases, it was a short wait and we would move along. We continued our voyage and passed into Lake Michigan.

Our first sight of the Chicago skyline was well past sundown. It is one of the most beautiful skylines I have seen in the world, and it was especially beautiful from the bow of our boat. As we grew closer, we hoped to pull into the Chicago Yacht Club, although we did not have docking reservations. It was exclusive and an advance reservation was required. Our captain suggested we press our luck and go in unannounced, hoping the night watchman would relent and allow us to dock overnight. To our surprise, there was no one on watch, so we took a vacant slip. The following morning, we awoke to the sound of someone pounding on the side of our yacht. The attendant questioned us about our unannounced stay and urged us to pay our fee and leave immediately. We did just that, chalking up another interesting memory.

We finished the trip to Pickwick via the Illinois, Mississippi, Ohio and Tennessee rivers.

Three years later, we did it all over again. We purchased our dream yacht — a new 53-foot Hatteras named Susan Leigh IV. It was built in Hatteras, North Carolina, and outfitted in Fort Lauderdale. We flew into Florida on Papa Charlie, and Warren Elfers welcomed us again as our captain.

After provisioning the boat, we headed to the Bahamas for a 10-day excursion. Our new equipment, including a radar system and autopilot, took us to Freeport on one setting. We entered the port, checked through customs and looked forward to beautiful days on the white sandy beaches and exploring the crystal-clear waters.

We toured quaint towns with the streets outlined by brightly painted buildings and tropical greenery. The weather was perfect, and we visited nearby islands with isolated beaches absent of footprints. We anchored offshore, swam in to explore for shells and relaxed as Captain Warren secured the boat.

Upon our return to Fort Lauderdale, we prepared for our 5,500-mile journey home. This was our second cruise, so we were acquainted with where we wanted to dock each day and some of the better restaurants along the way.

One of our favorite ports was at the Chesapeake Bay and Delaware Canal.

Nearing sunset, as we approached, we heard welcoming island music played on steel drums by a group of Bahamians. We ate our dinner that evening beside a large window and watched a huge ship pass slowly through the canal. It felt like we were close enough to touch it.

As we motored northward, dolphins swam alongside our boat and playfully jumped through the waves. We stood on the aft deck, looking over the side rail, while the girls called to the dolphins. They seemed to realize we were watching and put on a show.

Because the trip was longer than two months, we went offshore as much as possible. We could cruise faster in the open ocean than we could in the inland waterways, which often had speed limits or no-wake zones. Warren was experienced, and he would take the boat out to sea when it would be comfortable. The yacht was designed and built to withstand most stormy seas, and with a seasoned captain at the helm, we felt at ease.

The worst storm we encountered was in the Great Lakes. The waves hit the boat, like a picket fence, one after another. Many times the water splashed over the top of the yacht. Susan and Leigh Anne begged us to find a port. We had to choose one where we would not be blown off course and into the rocks of the narrow inlets. We came off Lake Michigan and into the port at Pentwater, Michigan. For two days, we remained docked until the winds settled down enough to continue to Chicago.

Pentwater proved to be a treat. The area was known for its lighthouse, sand dunes, artisan shops and recreational activities. We had a great time! It was an unexpected find.

But we looked forward to Chicago, its beautiful skyline and passing through the heart of the city with skyscrapers soaring overhead. As we neared the city, we wondered again where we would moor for the night because of the lack of marinas.

We tried to slip into the Chicago Yacht Club as we did when we were aboard the Chris Craft, but no slips were available. We made our way toward downtown hoping we could find a small marina. We found one, but the attendant said he did not have a space for a large yacht. We pulled away and went back up the narrow waterway not knowing where we would dock. The marina closed at 5 p.m., so we turned around and arrived at 6 p.m. No one was around. We eased against a wall, which I had seen earlier, because it looked as if it would be a nice place to tie up. It had a great view of the Sears Tower.

We watched the sunset and went to dinner at Eli's — a landmark Chicago restaurant. Our meal, topped off with Eli's famous cheesecake, was one of the best on the trip. In fact, Mr. Eli stopped at our table, which pleased us. He was a legendary personality, a Chicago original. With full stomachs, we hailed a cab and returned to the boat for a peaceful night's sleep. We arose early the next morning and left before the attendant came to work. Mooring overnight in Chicago was challenging on both of our trips.

Our navigational chart showed we could clear all the city's bridges by only two inches. We passed under them slowly, making sure the boat did not bobble and bump the steel girders above. Getting a bridge raised in Chicago could have taken days, so we were fortunate to have clearance.

The Illinois River was fun to traverse because it had great views. The river happened to be at flood stage and had left its banks. We watched for trees, logs and smaller pieces of wood dislodged by floodwaters. We did not want to damage the boat or bend a propeller. I sat on the bow looking for larger logs that the yacht could not push aside. Wood constantly banged against the bow. We were pleased to make it through without incident.

We entered the Mississippi River at Alton, Illinois. We pulled alongside a pier for the night and slept well. But to my surprise, the next morning we found a large log wedged between the pier and the yacht, which had formed a large drift that took us about an hour to free. This gave us a good idea as to what we were in for on the mighty Mississippi. It was a challenging river. There were triple-screw boats pushing 25 or 30 barges and throwing a wake of seven or eight feet. Since we traveled much faster than the barges, we constantly passed them and climbed over their big waves. We spent some nights anchored on the river's edge because there were few marinas. We felt a bit unsafe, but we did what we had to do on the big river.

The Mississippi also was flooded, and we had to contend with all kinds of debris. Once again, we were lucky not to bend a prop. The river was exciting, to say the least, and we were glad to see the Ohio River come into view.

After exiting the Mississippi, we soon reached Paducah, Kentucky, the home of my brother, Carlton, and his family. We noticed a small tributary leading off the river, and our chart indicated a water depth that could accommodate our yacht. So we took a detour, found a place to secure the boat and called Carlton. He and his family met us at the boat for a visit. We were excited to see close family members once again. It also reminded us that we were nearing Pickwick — our homeport.

From the Ohio River, we made our way into the Tennessee River, which was the last leg of our journey. When we cruised into familiar waters at Pickwick Lake, we realized how blessed we were to have the Susan Leigh IV safely at home.

Pickwick Lake, with its beautiful coves where we dropped anchor and spent quality time, was a welcomed sight. It was where we enjoyed swimming, skiing, canoeing, beautiful sunrises and sunsets, moonlit nights and spending time with family and friends. Our voyage had been wonderful — an experience never to be forgotten. Yet, many special times and memories were ahead of us.

On our two boat trips with our family, our cruises were filled with rich experiences. At the time, Susan and Leigh Anne probably did not realize how special the two summer cruises were. We saw so much of our country from the water's edge and experienced parts of history.

***

Our family has an affinity for the water. We enjoyed its bounty, but recognized its dangers, and water safety was emphasized constantly. When our children were young, we swam near the boat. I told them if they accidently fell overboard, they could spend hours in the water as long as they did not let fear control their thoughts. They were fairly strong and agile swimmers. We might stay out an hour without a life jacket, treading water, swimming on our backs, floating and relaxing. Susan and Leigh Anne grew up enjoying water sports and boating, and they fully understood the importance of respecting the water.

Our friend, Henco fleet maintenance director and driver trainer Larry Flowers, taught Susan and Leigh Anne to waterski in our swimming pool at home. Larry was a great teacher, and we appreciated his generosity. He showed them how to manage their skis in the water and taught them how to relax. When they skied for the first time at the lake, their experiences in our pool enabled them to easily pop out of the water on the first attempt. Before long, they could ski on one ski. As they grew older, they often skied with friends, enjoying the ski boat. Our love for the Tennessee River was special because of our access through the years and the relaxing hours we spent at its edges or cutting through the calm waters on our boat.

We also made annual cruises to Knoxville from Pickwick Lake, ascending seven locks along the 400-mile trip. We liked to leave Pickwick on a Monday and leisurely wind our way along, looping through Mississippi and Alabama. We also liked to select a week when the Tennessee Vols were playing a

Cruising to a UT football game

Saturday football game and fall foliage was at its peak.

We invited family and friends to come along on our ballgame cruises. At night, we looked for a quiet place on the river safely outside the channel and away from barge traffic to anchor. We took plenty of food, and we enjoyed our meals with the camaraderie of our guests. After we anchored, it was my job to fire up the grill on the aft deck and chargrill some juicy steaks or burgers. Our last night before reaching Knoxville was at the Fort Loudon Yacht Club about

40 miles from Neyland Stadium. In the morning, we ate breakfast as we cruised along to the stadium, arriving early. As the morning progressed, other boats arrived and rafted off the side of our boat until they were 10 boats deep across the river. And when the Vol Navy was situated, it was party time — time to cheer our team to victory.

On return trips back to Pickwick, we dropped our lines on Sunday morning and cruised at full speed to the Chattanooga Yacht Club. Papa Charlie picked us up at the airport, and we flew back to Selmer for the work week. We flew back to Chattanooga on Thursday and took the yacht back to Pickwick over the weekend.

We took one cruise to Knoxville when the city hosted the World's Fair in 1982. President Ronald Reagan had named my longtime friend and mentor, Dortch Oldham, Commissioner General of the U.S. Government for the World's Fair. We allowed a week to make the trip and attend the festivities with Dortch as our guide. We secured the boat close to the football stadium and the World's Fair Park. Dortch came aboard for dinner, and we laid out our agenda for the next day at the fair. After our excursion, we walked a short distance back to the boat. It certainly was a convenient way to see the World's Fair.

Our cruises to Knoxville were great trips, and we wanted each one to last as long as possible with our family and invited guests. We made the 400-mile river cruise for 10 consecutive years.

CHAPTER 13

EXTENDING HELP OVERSEAS

"We felt it was important to do our part
and help a family settle into a safer, happier environment."

On April 30, 1975, when Saigon fell, we watched dramatic and painful scenes on television of South Vietnamese people trying to flee with the last U.S. personnel. Later that year, President Gerald Ford set up an inter-agency task force that resettled 130,000 refugees from the embattled country.

It was an incredible effort. President Ford was committed to making sure that these innocent victims — allies to the United States — were not abandoned. It was not a popular decision at first, although some people in Congress, including Sen. Ted Kennedy, were helpful. The United States had high unemployment and many were concerned the refugees would take American jobs. The country faced division, and passions ran high. People argued over who lost the war, why it was lost and the treatment of veterans coming home.

When President Ford asked Americans to sponsor a Vietnamese family, we heard his appeal. We felt it was important to do our part and help a family settle into a safer, happier environment. We asked Henco people to join us in our effort. It was not popular with some in the beginning — just like it was throughout the nation. But most people eventually changed their minds.

I phoned the appropriate authorities and volunteered our help in settling a family into our society. It was the beginning of a lifelong relationship.

In March 1975, Trinh Quoc Khuong and his wife, Hoang Tin Du, were in Saigon. Khuong was in the Air Force and worked in a printing shop. Du

PICTURES ALONG THE WAY

Tom and Sherry Hendrix, partners on a journey, ride their bicycle built for two on Main Street inside Henco Furniture.

Jerry Barnes, above, works on the automated candle production line. Henco manufactured and sold several million candles a year. Stacking stools, at left, later to include school emblems and other silk-screen designs, were the first product manufactured and sold by Nasco.

Dan Borlawsky, from left, John Wilkerson, Dick Schroeder and Bob Brooks staff a Henco booth at a band clinic.

Henco's top salespeople are awarded a cruise with their spouses.

From left, Tom and Sherry Hendrix and Jackie and Jeff Capwell are at a Henco Christmas party. Jeff was Henco's President at the time.

Bob Brooks, General Sales Manager, left, and Larry Cromer, Regional Sales Manager, are ready for a national sales meeting with a "Big Top" theme in Las Vegas.

Henco offices were built around an indoor solarium.

Sun floods into the family's indoor swimming pool through floor-to-ceiling windows. The pool was an addition to the Hendrix's Mollie Drive home.

The Hendrix family with Anders Widestrand in 1983

The Hendrix family with Anders Widestrand in Vail, Colorado

Susan and Leigh Anne Hendrix, along with their Swedish brothers, Johan and Anders Widestrand, spent their summers at UT Knoxville selling peaches from the Hendrix peach orchard. Johan, at top, and Anders sit on a Mercedes Benz convertible at the orchard.

Hendrix Orchard peaches were sold at peach stands, like the one at left, in several locations in Knoxville.

Todd Mask, from left, Anders (partially hidden), Susan, Leigh Anne and Tom attend a University of Tennessee bowl game in 1986.

The Hendrix family had two weddings in 1999. Susan and Patrick
O'Connell, above, married in April, while Leigh Anne and Stuart
McWhorter, below, married on August 28 — the same day Sherry
and Tom married 39 years before.

Leigh Anne and Susan in 1998

Sherry's mom, Johnnye Smith, left to right, Susan, Leigh Anne, Sherry and Tom stand in a phone booth in London, England. Tom, above right, returns to the yacht after a UT development meeting.

If you had a problem handling your emus, Tom Hendrix had the answer. Bird gear — similar to a dog's harness — became a popular item in the emu community. The picture, above, was taken from a T-shirt worn to market bird gear.

The ribbon cutting for Henco Furniture in the Selmer Industrial Park

Main Street

Main Street inside the entrance to Henco Furniture featured "shops" of different kinds of furniture and provided a logical and fun way to shop for furniture for your home and office.

Henco's Whistle Stop Café

The oaks on Main Street looked real because of the creativity of artist Victor Moore and his daughters.

Dana Cox, from left, Charles Westbrooks, Grady Barnes and Teresa Parris stand at "Grady's Gas Station" on Main Street during Henco Furniture's Hometown USA grand opening.

Henco Furniture's team

Sherry and Tom Hendrix on Main Street inside Henco Furniture

A Henco Furniture advertisement features "Mr. Henco."

*Johan, standing, from left, Tom and Sherry, and seated,
from left, Camilla (Johan's wife), Susan, Anders,
Leigh Anne and Stuart celebrate Sherry's 65th birthday
in New York City at Tavern on the Green in Central Park.*

The Hendrix family in Summer 2014

Top row, left to right, Stuart and Leigh Anne McWhorter, Sherry and Tom Hendrix, and Susan and Patrick O'Connell; middle row, Clayton and Thomas McWhorter, Sarah Catherine and Sean O'Connell; and front row, Marleigh, Layla and Caroline McWhorter. Stuart and Leigh Anne adopted sisters Marleigh and Layla, who were living in Ethiopia.

worked in the accounting department of the Post Exchange on the base. While they worked, their seven-year-old son, Trinh Chi Thanh, was under the care of a relative in the city. The family feared for their lives as the war ended. Du was told her family could fly out on a U.S. aircraft along with her other countrymen who had befriended Americans.

It was an emotional and difficult decision because her three-year-old son, Hien, was in Da Nang being cared for by his grandmother. As the time for departure grew nearer, she received help from her work superiors to fly into Da Nang and get her son. But when they entered the city, heavy gunfire and shelling prevented them from getting to Hien.

"It's too dangerous," she was told.

As Saigon fell, Du, Khuong and Thanh reluctantly boarded an aircraft for the United States without Hien. They remained hopeful that one day they could return and find him.

After a stop in Guam, they flew to a military base at Fort Chaffee, Arkansas, and their new life began. Military officials introduced them to a new culture and shared the prospects of a host family somewhere in the country.

We received news that the family was arriving at the Jackson, Tennessee, airport after 10 weeks at Fort Chaffee. It was exciting news for us, and we began preparations for their arrival. We found an apartment, put furniture in place, along with a television donated by Henco employees, and stocked the refrigerator and pantry. We pitched in to welcome them to their first home in Selmer.

I met them at the airport. We made the 40-minute drive to their new home — but it would be a much longer journey for them as they assimilated into a new culture.

Sherry and the girls welcomed them as they walked through the door of their new apartment. They were amazed at their new home's spaciousness and the convenience of drinking water directly from the spigot. The refrigerator even had an ice bin, and the milk was cold. A two-bedroom apartment with a living room, kitchen and bath was luxury in Saigon. Water was always boiled before it was safe to drink. Food was purchased on a daily basis because of no refrigeration. Now they had a new life with supermarkets, automobiles and Thanh's first day at school.

On each step of the way, Henco people helped them every way they could. Someone volunteered to pick them up for work, another gave driving lessons and others assisted with shopping. Generous people showed God's love to a family in need.

We introduced Khuong and Du to Henco fundraising, and they began a working career among people who cared about

The Cheng family, from left, Kuhn, Sonja and Thanh with the Hendrix family: Sherry, Tom, Susan and Leigh Anne.

them. Du spoke English reasonably well. Khuong spoke some English, and Thanh spoke practically none.

We introduced Thanh to Patty Taylor, a kindergarten teacher at Selmer Elementary School who had agreed to tutor him. She was interested in his education, and she wanted him as one of her students. With her warm and caring personality, Thanh made great strides learning English and acclimating to his new school. The whole family began an education in different ways.

At the time of their arrival, we were not aware of the son left behind in Da Nang or the circumstances of their departure. As we became more acquainted, Du and Khuong shared their story. We felt their sorrow and were challenged to find a way to get their little boy to the States with his parents and brother.

We related their story to Jack McConnico and asked him to look into the possibilities of retrieving Hien. Jack worked many hours, for several years, and contacted numerous people in government agencies. About seven years passed before Hien, at 10 years old, joined his family. He flew from Saigon to Thailand to Hong Kong to Los Angeles to Chicago and, finally, to Memphis with a tag around his neck and someone helping him from stop to stop. And then the shy little boy stepped off the plane and into the open arms of his mother and father.

Hien's arrival was heartwarming, but everything was so different for him.

He began learning about his newly-found family, his new country, a new language with new customs, a new school and new friends. It was a major adjustment.

We helped the family purchase a nice brick house. The parents adopted the names Kuhn and Sonja Cheng. Their son, Clint, was born. They progressed in their new life and became contributing U.S. citizens.

Time passed and all seemed well. Hien was doing well academically and was well liked. He liked many of the new customs and his new friends. But it seemed his father didn't approve of everything. When Hien was a junior in high school, he left home. Authorities picked him up at a bus station nearby in Corinth, Mississippi. He said he wasn't going back.

Because the juvenile court judge knew about the family's connection to Henco, he called me and told me what had happened. They brought Hien to our house, and we sat down and talked. We had great hopes that his problems with his parents could be resolved, and the family would be back together soon.

We asked them to meet together in our home to find a resolution, but they couldn't. Customs in their home country differed from customs in their new country. Hien's parents gave him an ultimatum to come home and apologize to the family or never again be recognized as their son. Hien refused, and they left him sitting on our living room sofa.

After his parents left, he went to the bedroom and did some serious soul searching. When he had some time to compose himself, I put my arms around him and said that we would be glad for him to join our family. He was a fine youngster making good grades in school.

We noticed that Hien liked to help Sherry in the kitchen and prepare our meals. He especially liked to cook his favorite Vietnamese dishes. Sherry enjoyed having him in the kitchen, and together, they could put a most interesting meal on the table. We tried to decide what Hien might want to study in college. One day, we asked him if he thought he would like to attend a chef's school. He jumped at the opportunity.

Spencer and Tom

We flew to Charleston, South Carolina, to the Johnson & Wales University, College of Culinary Arts, the largest food-service educator in the world.

When he graduated McNairy Central High School, Hien wanted to officially change his name to Spencer. Our friend and attorney, Terry Abernathy, processed the paperwork. Spencer enrolled at Johnson & Wales as Spencer Cheng — a new name and a new beginning.

He completed his associate's degree, worked at hotels and restaurants in Florida and Alabama, and then relocated to Houston, Texas. There he met a beautiful young woman, Suzy Nguyen. When they married, Spencer asked me and Sherry to represent his parents. We were honored to accept. Susan and Leigh Anne were there on their special day, November 27, 1997, and so was his grandmother. Spencer and Suzy are now the parents of four children and are both health care professionals.

Meanwhile, Kuhn and Sonja live in the Houston area. Thanh and Clint are physicians in Houston and College Station, Texas, respectively, with their families.

Sherry and I earnestly tried to help resolve the issues with Spencer and his father. We had and still have difficulty understanding their culture and how someone can disown a child and never know their grandchildren. It saddens us to think of the missed opportunities, but we still hope more time will heal the wounds.

Chapter 14

The Henco Way

"You don't build a business, you build people,
and they build the business."

As Henco fundraising grew, I knew we needed to select capable people to manage the company. I thought about the people around me and their natural gifts. I wanted to find good matches to put round pegs in round holes and square pegs in square holes.

I needed someone who could guide me to make the right decisions. I sought help and found Dr. Paul C. Green, who taught industrial and organization psychology at the University of Memphis. He was excited about the opportunity and said he would give people a two-hour written test to isolate their natural gifts. He told me the test was reliable and could not be faked. After analyzing the results, he would interview each person and give me a written report of the results.

We implemented Dr. Green's program, and I believe it was one of our better investments. As we read his individual reports, I could visualize the person much more clearly. The report made common sense, and it helped us make better decisions in selecting people to lead the company. Putting people in positions that do not fit their natural gifts is a disservice to everyone involved.

Paul included me in the test to determine my natural gifts. Then we met to go over his analysis.

"Paul, tell it like it is," I told him.

He smiled.

"Tom, you are not too smart, but you have as good an understanding of human nature, empathy for people, as I have ever tested," he said. "Your understanding of people will enable you to work with all the departments. Just hire people smarter than yourself."

"Paul, I appreciate your vivid description," I quipped. "I will never forget your interview."

We became good friends, and we still touch base every so often.

In building a business, the first rule is understanding that you don't know it all. With this attitude, you are in a better position to work through people to accomplish your mission. Get good at recognizing people's help, and be grateful. Give them as much credit as you possibly can. It will serve you well over time. Being grateful to people motivates them to do more because they are recognized as a valuable team member. It's the best way to build a business.

***

The top band directors from across the country who came to work with Henco were a competitive group of young men and women who built the best band programs in their states. I appreciated their desire to get ahead.

I remember one of our first sales meetings. We were having a steak dinner at our home, and while I was grilling, Jeff Capwell came to me. He had the idea that, because he was a bit older than some of the other salesmen, he would be a good fit for management. Jeff put his name in the hat to be a leader in the company. I appreciated his thoughts, and I was glad talented people like Jeff wanted to furnish leadership to building Henco.

Jeff was a top salesman, and we gave him an opportunity to manage a few people. After a short time, he began to demonstrate his ability to lead. He was good at seeing problems. When he spotted one, he did his best to solve it. He was proactive, even though he irritated some people from time to time. Jeff went on to be our general sales manager, executive vice president and president. Henco was fortunate to have so much talent within the company as we grew.

We had other very capable people as well. When Joe Utsey became sales manager, one of his strong points was the respect people had for him. He was a man of integrity, and everyone knew that Joe wanted the best for them.

When Bob Brooks joined Henco, he learned the program and became an outstanding teacher. Bob was well respected by everyone, and he became national sales manager, providing exceptional leadership. You cannot carry out your mission unless you surround yourself with good, honest people with a desire to get ahead. Bob was a good listener. He encouraged people to share their input so he could get all the facts before taking action.

Rodney Hendrix — a distant relative — was a young accountant a few years out of college. He opened a CPA firm in Selmer. Rodney began his business with himself and a secretary and grew quite rapidly. He hired another local accountant just out of college named George Donaldson. Rodney constantly added people to keep up with the demand. Rodney and George did Henco's accounting. One day, I paid Rodney a visit.

"Rodney, I want you to sell your business and come to Henco as our CFO," I told him.

Rodney was shocked.

"Tom, I think my business is bigger than your business," he said. "I am proud of my business, and I intend to continue to build it into a successful firm."

I began to paint a picture on how I envisioned Henco's future, becoming a national fundraising company and growing at a rapid rate. I explained how Henco needed a certified public accountant as chief financial officer, and I said I wanted that person to be Rodney Hendrix. I made him an offer and asked him to give me a decision in two weeks.

In my mind, Rodney was a known quantity who was blessed with integrity, which is a must for a CFO. I felt he would be easy to work with and would look out for Henco financially.

"Tom, I will need more than two weeks," he replied.

I wasn't flexible on that point. I told him two weeks was all he had. After that, I would look elsewhere. On the last day, he walked into my office, and I knew he was coming to Henco by the expression on his face.

"This may be the hardest decision I have ever made, but I believe Henco will become a national company, and I want to be the CFO," he told me.

Rodney and I became good friends, and we enjoyed working together for many years.

When Rodney closed his firm, George joined Moore & Gray's CPA firm in Corinth, Mississippi, and continued to do Henco financial work. A little later, George joined Henco as a CPA and has played a key role in Henco's success for more than 40 years. In the early 1990s, George became chief financial officer. He understood the ins and outs of the company as he watched it grow.

Through the years, George became our go-to person when we needed to solve Henco mathematical problems. People with similar characteristics are essential in managing complicated companies. People and situations do not come in perfect packages, but George was about as close as you could get.

Hiring the right people was critical, and my old friend, Jack McConnico, occupied one of the most important leadership positions we ever filled. With a gentle disposition and a bright mind, Jack was the most well-read and unselfish man I knew. He had given more thought to life and could articulate those ideas to keep you on the edge of your seat. Jack agreed to join me in Selmer for the building of Henco. He never asked what his pay would be. This showed what an unusual person he was.

We published a monthly newsletter called "Henco is People." It educated employees and allowed us to share the company's progress. Jack wrote articles regularly. His essays continually encouraged employees to live a better life and grow toward God through service to people. It was a way to highlight our mission of service. Jack also would point to any unfairness he thought we should take note of for improvement. Jack visited with most everyone as they came to work with Henco to discuss how they could join our mission of service. He helped each person get a glimpse of what the Henco service was all about. I promise, they never forgot Jack's visit.

As a company, we strived to base our actions on common-sense values and moral principles, to promote harmony and to give Henco a heart and soul. Jack made sure that Henco had that heart and soul.

He pushed our wheelbarrow. Every school fundraising program we conducted was to be based on our values in order to repeat the program the following year. "Let's grow to our full potential as we upgrade fundraising in America" was Jack's message.

His door was open to anyone with a problem to share. Our employees went to Jack with marital problems, financial problems or to brainstorm an idea. He would patiently listen and ask timely questions.

Marvin Dabbs, one of our plant managers, wanted to start his own business. Jack brainstormed with Marvin about transitioning from Henco to his new business. Marvin decided on a residential and commercial insulation business. Marvin knew Henco wanted the best for him and his family. If his new venture resulted in his leaving Henco, he felt confident we would support him 100 percent — even though we would hate to see him go.

Some of my business friends would ask about Jack.

"What does Jack do?" They wondered.

"I am not sure, other than he is here to be helpful to Henco families," I would reply. "He encourages us to do the right thing. He is the senior vice president of the company because we think his work is that important."

When Dr. Paul Green advised me to surround myself with people smarter than me, I listened. They made me look good as we built the company. Through the years, Sherry and I have been blessed to work with so many talented people. And I always try to remember that the work was accomplished through the talents of others.

You don't build a business, you build people, and they build the business. People don't want to be managed. They want to be led to be a part of the decision making; they want to see the end result of their efforts. This type of leadership inspires more success.

***

We were faced with remaking ourselves with new employees as we grew, and it was a big challenge to find outstanding people to join our team and build the company.

I often tell people that I assembled my Henco team from a little black book, which I carried inside my coat pocket. Wherever I went — civic meetings, school functions or church, for example — I would ask myself if anyone there should be on the Henco team. I also encouraged Henco people to look for talent and make a list of people to help us build our company.

When I spotted an outstanding person, I listed his or her name in my little black book. Then I'd try to learn more about the person through people who knew him or her. Once I was satisfied the person could become a valuable team member, I would call for an interview. I did not look for people who were unemployed. I sought outstanding people who were successful in their work. If we did not have an opening, I would call them when we were ready, giving them time to give their company notice.

This worked well for me. I did not want the hiring process to be a knee-jerk affair. I wanted it to be well planned.

I also found other uses for the concept. Lamar Alexander asked me to be his West Tennessee finance chairman when he ran for governor in 1978. I used my little black book idea to raise money for his campaign. I recruited people to raise a quota for their county in a timely manner, and I gave each county chairman a little black book for his coat pocket.

"The first two weeks, wherever you go, scan the crowd for people who can give to Lamar's campaign," I told them. "First, look for people who have the resources to give $1,000 or $500. List their names in your book. Then scan the crowd for $100 donors, and list their names. Call on the $500 and $1,000 donors first in person. Then, call on the $100 donors. Phone the donors you expect to give $50 or less. After we have raised the money for each county, we will have a big fundraising dinner to include as many people as possible to elect Lamar."

I had never raised money for a campaign before, but this simple plan worked without fail. Lamar became governor of Tennessee in 1979.

***

As the chief executive officer of a national company, I never knew what phone calls would come in each day. On one particular day in 1980, I received a call from Dr. Allen Truex. I didn't know him, but I knew the family name was well respected in Madison County.

"Tom, this is Allen Truex in Jackson," he began. "Youth Town is in serious financial trouble. There are 36 boys and girls who need housing, care and guidance, but there's no money in the bank. Our budget is $350,000 per year to pay the bills, and at present, we have no income. I want you to push back from your desk and meet me at the Old English Inn today for lunch. We need your help with this financial crisis."

Up until the time of Dr. Truex's phone call, the organization was called Tennessee Sheriff's Youth Town. In 1978, all funding from the Sheriff's association stopped. In 1980, Henco fundraising was growing rapidly, and I made an effort to be selective about the requests of my time. I had to protect my calendar because my main responsibility was the Henco people.

"I don't see how I can meet with you at lunch today," I told him.

But Dr. Truex would not take no for an answer. He was passionate about solving Youth Town's financial problems.

"Let me repeat," he replied. "Youth Town is in serious trouble. We need your help, and I want you to meet with me today at noon."

I told him that I would be there. I arrived at the Old English Inn a few minutes early. I sat at a table near the entrance, and I saw this tall fellow walk inside. I was sure it was Dr. Truex. We shook hands, and he got to the point immediately. He told me about the children at Youth Town. Many of them had been picked up on the streets. They had no one to love them, no church life or sports and little discipline in their lives. Youth Town's goal was to help the youngsters live a fruitful life. The organization hoped each youngster would graduate from high school, attend college, rear good families, give back to society and eventually break the cycle of abuse and poverty for the next generation.

"You cannot find a better investment than Youth Town," he continued. "We must find a way to fund this mission with $350,000. Presently, we are selling tickets for a spaghetti supper. I want you to come to a board meeting tomorrow night, and hopefully, we can find a way to pay our bills for the benefit of these kids."

At that time, all I knew about Youth Town was what Allen had just told me.

"I simply do not have the time to get involved in a time-consuming project," I responded.

We ate our lunch, and he asked me to follow him to Youth Town. We drove onto the campus and up to one of the cottages. As we went inside, I saw a boy about 10 years old with blonde hair, a round face and beautiful blue eyes. Allen put his hand under the boy's chin, and I looked into those eyes.

"Now, tell me you are going to help us," Allen said.

"I will be at your board meeting tomorrow night," I replied.

At the board meeting, they told me about the ways they were raising money in the community.

"Tom, you have been very quiet," Allen said. "How do you see this situation?"

"I don't have a solution this minute, but $350,000 is no small amount of money," I replied. "We must come up with a $350,000 idea. We cannot piecemeal a budget of this size. Let me give it some thought."

The meeting adjourned, and Youth Town's future seemed bleak. As I drove back to Selmer, I racked my brain to find a way to fund the budget. By the next morning, an idea hit me — put a capable person on the road to tell the Youth Town story. Don't ask anyone for less than a $500 donation. Select a person who will make this his or her mission.

I knew that I could put together a convincing Youth Town story. However, the question in my mind was who was the person who could tell the story convincingly enough to raise $350,000?

A young man representing Boy Scouts of America had lived in Selmer, but recently moved with his family to Arkansas to assume a position as an executive in the organization. As I thought about Darryl Melton, I became convinced that he could carry out this mission.

My assistant, Anita Graham, located his phone number, and I called him.

"Darryl, I want you to come here for an important interview with me tomorrow morning."

I am sure Darryl thought the interview related to a Henco position. When he arrived, I explained Youth Town's problem and passionately told its story. Darryl listened without blinking an eye.

"We can help these kids grow up and hopefully rear a good family, breaking the cycle of abuse and poverty," I said. "I think you are the person to carry out this important mission."

"I will pray about it and give you an answer in the morning," he replied.

He returned the following morning.

"I cannot turn this down," he said. "I am ready to get to work if I can support my family."

We worked out his salary to match his Boy Scout pay. Now the question was: How would Youth Town pay Darryl? Youth Town was still in debt without any income. I telephoned Dr. Truex. We set up a meeting, and he called some of the key board members to attend. I presented my idea, and they liked it.

My next step was to call my friend, Benard Blasingame, founder and president of Aqua Glass Corporation in Adamsville. I shared the Youth Town story with him, and he asked pointed questions. I told him our plan would raise the money needed to keep the organization from closing its doors. I asked Benard if he would help me pay Darryl's salary.

"That's a lot of money," he said.

"That is the reason I am talking with you today," I replied.

Benard agreed, and he generously mailed a check for many months.

Darryl Melton, on behalf of Youth Town, worked long hours. He called on service clubs and caring, generous people to fund the budget of $350,000.

I was asked to serve as president of Youth Town's board. Dr. Truex and I became good friends. A number of dedicated people put in many hours on behalf of Youth Town, but if it had not been for the driving force of Dr. Allen

Truex in 1980, Youth Town would have closed its doors. Allen had a soft heart and strived to do what was morally right for people.

Darryl Melton also is due a lot of credit. When I resigned the position of board president, the bills were current, and Youth Town had money in the bank. Darryl was the person who made it happen.

***

Making a positive difference in people's lives is one of the best things we can do. I like business because it provides opportunities to do that for hundreds, even thousands, of lives. Henco's goal was to help employees grow to their full potential. Our message was "let's grow together" as we upgrade fundraising in America. I was a businessman under construction, just as they were. I learned just as much or maybe more.

When the sun begins to shine on your hard work, you see the fruit of it. You see it, for example, when an employee who is truly on a mission of service to others earns enough money to move into a new home. This is one of the gratifying parts of building a business.

I am reminded of a young man who was not coming to work regularly because he was having problems at home. He was on the verge of losing his job at Henco. His managers would say, "he's a great guy, but he must come to work."

I asked them to send him to my office. As we talked, he shared with me that his wife had left him, and he was caring for his two small daughters and living with his family. His brother was in prison — it was complete chaos. He said he had to find a place of his own for his children, but didn't have the money to make the move. I asked him to put together a plan. We helped him make his transition, and he later became foreman of our manufacturing plant with about 200 people. All he needed was a little help to turn a difficult situation into a positive where he could rear a good family and make an outstanding contribution to his company.

***

We wanted our employees to feel free to speak their minds. The person who was closest to the work saw the work more clearly than anyone else.

"Tell us how we can improve" was the Henco attitude.

We constantly shared the spotted cow story: "A cow may be beautiful on one side, but on the other side, she may have been gored by a bull. It's not a pretty sight."

We encouraged people to tell us how the cow looked from their side. We wanted them to walk around a problem and find the best solution.

Henco could grow faster and render more service by promoting freedom and openness to better harness the brainpower of its employees. We wanted employees to know that their thoughts and ideas mattered. Doing what was right by people was a big thing for us. The freedom to speak up was important. I told them, "It's not who's the boss. It's what's right that counts." We did not want a manager muzzling people and preventing them from telling their side of the story — how they saw the cow.

I always reminded people that my office door was open. If they had something to share or thought they were being mistreated, I wanted them to talk to me.

People are more motivated when they can see they are an important part of the company's progress, and they can plainly see how their work fits into the service being rendered. They are not just working. They are a part of a service mission — something much greater than "just making a living." Our employees could see the good of their work. At Henco, it was understood that success must be built on generosity and fair play.

***

Just as we practiced in our own lives, we taught servant leadership. We sought to hire the best person for the job, then the manager would teach the how of the job description. We taught managers to do anything they could to help the new hires be successful. We also taught them to make it a team effort.

Henco was in the service business. If people failed in their job description, they would let the Henco team down, but more than that, they would let our customers down. And without good customers, our employees would not have paychecks to support their families.

At Henco, we were determined to motivate all team members to join the service mission. Our service began by elevating our employees, helping them grow to their full potential. If we asked our employees to join us in our mission of service to our customers, then Henco leadership needed to be on a mission to serve our employees. It all went hand and hand.

One of our teaching points was to help everyone see work as a blessing. Few things affect our success and happiness more than our attitude toward work. The happiest people I know are those who are working — not because they have to work but because they want their life to be a mission of service. They are people who constantly strive to increase their knowledge and skills so they can increase the quantity and quality of their services. This principle also can be applied to family life and to the community.

It's the attitude! If we are to be happy, we must contribute to other people's happiness. To have friends, we must be friendly. To get what we want, we must produce goods and services that others want or need. I was extremely proud of the Henco attitude and the harmony among our people.

I have always liked the quote: "Know that there is so much good in the worst of us and so much bad in the best of us … that it behooves any of us to not talk about the rest of us."

We made sure employees understood how they fit into the service. Mules were created to work, but we were created to render service to our fellow man.

This attitude of service added dignity to our work and helped provide our employees with self-worth. They felt better about their lives, and they were happier. Henco created a corporate culture that people appreciated.

***

We must make a decision on our mission in life, and there are so many areas of service that accomplish great benefits for people.

Business and entrepreneurship appealed to me as I visualized free enterprise. I saw free people exchanging their services with one another in competition to see who can render the best service. I saw Americans deciding who will serve them with their hard-earned dollars. If a business doesn't get the support to ring the cash register, it fails. This is freedom and people power at its best.

In this competitive system, businesses cannot be greedy. They must render a quality service to survive. The spotlight shines on the best service. It appealed to me to think I could survive with quality service. As I made the decision to pursue entrepreneurship, creating payrolls and services to people, I thought about how I would manage money, because I fully expected to earn a considerable amount.

One day, I brought up the subject with Jack McConnico.

"How can a person manage money, in a positive way, for it not to dominate his life?" I asked.

"Money should be a tool in your tool chest along with other tools, but money should never be the goal," he said. "If money becomes the goal, a person is apt to sacrifice his values for it. Remember, service is the goal. The more you render, the better you will do. But money is one of the most important tools in the chest."

His words were so true. It takes money to solve problems for the good of people.

When I taught the Sunday school class, we had discussions about being more Christ-like. One of the young men in class asked:

"Can a rich man be Christ-like?"

"Yes," I replied. "I want every person in this Sunday school class to become a multimillionaire in service to your fellowman. Use the money you earn to render more service."

About anything we do requires money. Human needs cannot be fulfilled with empty pockets. So, I say, don't apologize for earning money in service to people.

As I view it, we get money one of three ways. We could steal it, but we are apt to go to jail. We could inherit it. For example, our parents could leave us some money because they love us. If that happens, we should celebrate all the way to the bank and use our inheritance for good. Or, we can earn our money, in service to people, which is how most of us acquire money. In essence, money represents services rendered.

An educator, teaching in the classroom and helping students live a more productive life, earns a check at the end of the month. A doctor, setting a broken arm, receives a check for his services. We are paid to do good things in life. Therefore, we should celebrate the money we receive for services rendered.

Many times civic and school groups made a path to Henco's door, asking for donations to different projects. They asked other businesses in the community as well. Sherry and I responded to community needs and causes often. One of our more unusual requests was from the cafeteria manager at McNairy County High School who wanted a chandelier for the school's commons area. She showed us a picture, and we helped her get the beautiful chandelier that added a bit of elegance to the commons area.

On another project, Henco helped to put artwork by graphic artist Knox Everson of Germantown on the walls of the lobby of the new Selmer Middle School in 1981. In visiting schools, Sherry and I were familiar with Everson's work. As construction progressed on the new middle school, we visualized graphics depicting personalized images related to Selmer Middle School's students. Sherry and Estel Mills, Superintendent of McNairy County Schools, paid a visit to a school where Everson's work was displayed. Estel was impressed and agreed with the concept of enhancing the interior of the lobby.

It was satisfying to view the completed art work and to realize that students for years to come would view a piece of school history as they passed through or lingered in the lobby. Participating in projects like this for the betterment of our community was a way of saying thank you.

***

Too many times people refer to businessmen as profit-making money-grabbers. My experience has been far different. I have observed that when communities need money to solve problems, they contact the business community, which is often filled with generous people. Successful business people are problem solvers and have the money and tools to be helpful.

Today, we see business people donating billions of dollars to find cures for diseases, dig wells in Africa so children can drink safe water, feed the world's hungry and help other humanitarian causes.

An untold number of problems need to be solved abroad and here at home. Thanks to the generosity of people, many of whom are business people, critical problems are being addressed for a favorable outcome. We need more people to give their time and money to help alleviate human misery around the world.

***

In 1981, we had our best year ever. We added another 120,000 square feet of warehouse space. Our sales were $30 million for a profit of $5.4 million. We paid $2.6 million to the federal government.

In 1968, our first financial statement for two months ending July 31 was: sales, $12,183; operating expense, $2,579; income before taxes, $6,978; federal taxes, $1,535; and net income after taxes, $5,443.

Henco had assembled a fine team of people as we pursued our goal of upgrading fundraising in America. Starting from scratch, with only $3,500 in borrowed money, Henco was competitive with companies that had been in the market long before us. We created a service that was in demand, and we grew at a phenomenal rate of more than 40 percent each year for more than 10 years. It was a testament to our approach to service, putting our employees first. We were profitable every year for more than 15 years, and plowed our profit back into the company to fuel our rapid growth.

People must have harmony to work together productively. As I observed Henco's progress, I came to believe that the company was 95 percent people and 5 percent economics. Much of our success is measured in how we deal with each other.

For instance, are we fair? Are we considerate? As supervisors, we are simply not right all the time. If we are wrong, we should admit it at once. By admitting our mistakes quickly, we increase our effectiveness and improve the way people feel about us.

Henco Financial Highlights

(in millions of dollars after 1968)

	1981	1980	1979	1978	1968*
Sales	$ 29.6	$ 21.2	$ 15.4	$ 9.7	12,183*
Profit Before Taxes	5.6	4.2	3.1	1.7	6,978*
Income Taxes	2.7	2.0	1.5	0.7	1,535*
Profit After Tax	2.9	2.2	1.7	0.9	5,443*
Calculated in 2014 $					
Inflation Multiplier	2.62	2.89	3.28	3.66	6.85*
Sales (in millions)	77.5	61.3	50.6	35.0	83,441*
Profit Before Taxes	14.7	12.2	10.3	6.0	47,792*
Income Taxes	7.0	5.8	4.9	2.5	10,513*
Profit After Tax	7.7	6.4	5.5	3.5	37,279*

* 1968 figures are in thousands of dollars and for two months only

The chart shows sales, profit and tax figures in Henco's early years. All figures for 1968 are for two months only. The chart then figures in inflation and reports the same figures in 2014 dollars.

Many times we talk when we should be listening. Using newsletters and speeches, we promoted fair play to create as much harmony as possible to be more effective working through people. We wanted Henco to be a happy place to work as we pressed to meet our deadlines. We strived to never walk over people to get there. I wanted the Henco philosophy to be full of common sense — the right thing to do. (Please see "Henco Faith, next page.")

It was important that the employees see the good Henco was doing. For example, we paid more than $6 million in a three-year period in federal taxes, which was a 49-percent rate and much too high. In today's dollars that $6 million would be $14.7 million. Though taxes were extremely high, they helped pay for the government to operate and provide services.

***

Henco Faith

We believe that we live in a universe guided by moral purpose and governed by laws designed to effect that purpose.

We believe there is a plan for mankind, that the plan grows and evolves through the centuries as does any flower, tree, or other thing, according to the immutable laws of God that govern the universe.

We believe that man determines his own fate by the degree to which he cooperates with or opposes the will of the Creator operating the plan.

We believe that man is free only when he controls himself.

We believe that to cooperate with the will of the Creator voluntarily is to live. This entails struggle and growth. To cease growing is to die.

We believe that man is mature when he can look at the universe, including himself, objectively, recognize the inevitable necessity of complying with the laws that govern the universe and voluntarily seek to understand and comply with them.

We believe that the moral purpose of the Creator, implemented by the laws built into the universe to effect that purpose, is causing a larger percentage of each generation to mature.

We believe that every mature person has an obligation to help others grow to maturity.

We believe that the family is the basic unit of society and that growth toward maturing must begin in the home.

We believe that an alliance of mature people operating through a vehicle that communicates directly with the home can be of value in cooperating with the will of the Creator.

We believe that the profit motive is a basic drive of human nature and essentially moral, and that private competitive enterprise as practiced in America is the strongest force that can be devised to constantly improve the ethical standards of the human race.

I wanted Henco people to see the free enterprise system as a service system instead of a system of greed. In our sales force, some would raise three times more money for school groups. Sure, they earned a considerable amount of money, but they did three times more good for others. I wanted everyone to see money as a measurement of the good they were doing. Yes, it is good to earn money in service to your fellowman.

Freedom was the centerpiece of the Henco philosophy. We prosper to the extent that we are free. When I initiated a review of our free enterprise system, reading many biographies, it was evident that freedom was at the core of success. They were free to set out on their mission and realize their dream. The more freedom within their company, the better they did, which enabled people to become neck-up employees to participate in the company's problem solving. They knew they were free to make mistakes as they pursued their mission.

I have always been impressed with the parable of talents in the Bible. When you are given talent, you must do something with it. Don't bury the talent out of fear, afraid you will make a mistake. Accept freedom, mistakes included. It's a fact: The more mature a person, the more freedom he or she can handle.

I have said "you can measure the wealth of a nation by the freedom it possesses." With freedom, you have incentives. With incentives, you get work done. I promoted freedom every way I could to help our people be more productive. At the outset of Henco, when we created $5 mystery houses in communities as an incentive for students, we gave every salesman a Henco checkbook. The salesmen had the freedom to write a Henco check based on projected sales. Many times it would be for $100 or more. When the sales force grew to about 150 people, hundreds of Henco checks would be written each day. When I first mentioned this idea to our chief financial officer, he warned against it.

"Tom, you can't do that!" He said. "They will abuse the privilege to buy tires and other things. And, how will we know what we are spending each day?"

But we marched ahead with the policy of allowing salesmen to write Henco checks while promoting their programs in the way they thought best.

"This policy may be a first in our country," I emphasized to the sales force. "Giving each salesman a company checkbook is unheard of today." I told them I was proud of their high level of integrity.

The salesmen were impressed with our confidence in them. I reminded them that this policy was based on an honor system, and we expected them to live up to it. Abuse would not be tolerated. Checks could be written only to promote their fundraising programs.

After several months, however, we learned that our top salesman was abusing the policy. After I fired him on the spot, several people came to my office to object.

"A stern warning would have been more appropriate because he is the top salesman," they said.

"I'm against stealing," I replied. "He is fired. I don't want to water down the integrity of the sales force, because they have the integrity to continue writing checks without abuse."

This reverberated through the sales force, reminding them the privilege was not to be abused.

***

More and more families moved in to Selmer's corporate offices to help expand our services to schools across the nation. As part of an expansion to our facility, we built an office complex overlooking a beautiful solarium with numerous green plants and fountains. Trickling water could be heard from inside opened office doors. We wanted employee offices to be an inviting place — a place as nice, or nicer, than their living room. Sherry spent a great deal of time working with them to make sure their offices had personal touches while conforming to our corporate standards.

Henco people took active roles in the community. We wanted Selmer to be a good place for them to rear children. I encouraged them to take an interest in schools and churches and to consider joining a service club, such as Rotary. I wanted them to be catalysts to make their community a better place.

I had been an active member of Rotary for years, and it was natural for me to ask others to consider membership. Henco people constituted more than one-third of the Rotary membership. We met periodically in our boardroom to discuss how to make the club better. Because Henco was in the business of raising funds, we had the skills to organize for success.

Henco people also took active roles in their churches. They led choirs, taught Sunday school and looked for ways to actively participate in their church's progress. I would estimate that about one-third of the membership of the First United Methodist Church choir in Selmer was made up of Henco people. And the choir was directed by a Henco employee who had been a school band director. People from our company made the choir bigger than life, and they were appreciated very much by the membership.

CHAPTER 15

OTHER ROADS

*"Entrepreneurship is truly an interesting way to live. I don't think
I have ever been in a project where I didn't enjoy the challenge."*

In 1982, we finally achieved our goal of becoming a national company. Our sales-force had grown to 209 people. Our annual payroll exceeded $10 million. Henco's tractor-trailers delivered products to schools throughout the nation with "Professional Fundraisers" imprinted on the sides.

We did our best to live up to that graphic. And I was proud of the money flowing into the pockets of our employees, sending kids to school, paying doctor bills — all the things we do in America to live the good life.

Henco was a vertical company with a great profit margin. We manufactured or packaged the product, sold it and delivered the merchandise to schools across the country with our trucking fleet. Our salesmen supervised everything that went into customers' homes with a computerized printout of all the items little Johnny sold and the exact amount he was to collect from Mrs. Jones.

We had grown financially to the point we felt we should diversify. We looked for companies that would complement our operation — companies we knew how to operate, but not outside our field of expertise. We appointed five people to a development board and asked Ken Marston to be chairman.

The first company considered was the Goo Goo Candy Company in Nashville. It was made famous through radio advertisements for many years on the Grand Ole Opry. The company had an outstanding reputation with a fine, quality product. We asked ourselves if the candy could be sold through

Rodney Hendrix, back row, from left, Terry Abernathy and an attorney (whose name I do not know); and seated, David Landreth, Curtis McMahan and Tom Hendrix gather for Henco's purchase of the C-MAC Oil Company. The company's name later was changed to Spectrum.

our schools' fundraising programs and not conflict with regular sales channels. After a thorough study, we felt that selling the candy through the schools would be a conflict, so we declined the offer.

The next company we considered was the Marinette Boat Company in Louisville, Kentucky. It manufactured small aluminum yachts. The aluminum hull gave many advantages over fiberglass because it was lightweight and long-lasting. We declined this offer. We realized that if we decided to move the company's operations to a location on the Tennessee River, the union's attitude could complicate the move. The boating business also is cyclical and more sensitive to the ups and downs of the economy.

Then we studied an oil packaging company in Hornsby, Tennessee, named C-MAC Oil, which made blended-oil products used in lawnmowers, for example. We thought it had room to grow, so we purchased it. The company was not that profitable, but we knew it would be with the right management.

We named it Spectrum Corporation and appointed a proven, professional team of people at Henco to run it. David Landreth became Spectrum's president. Randy Rawlings, one of Henco's top fundraising salesmen, became general sales manager and was asked to develop national accounts, such as Wal-Mart, Husqvarna and others. The previous owners had only sold small accounts. We felt certain we could expand the business rapidly with national accounts. Another Henco salesman, Lewis Waynick, was given the manufacturing responsibility. Billy Brown, with his background in accounting at Henco, was tapped to fulfill the position of accounting and office management.

These men were new to the blended oil business and had to master it quickly. Their Henco experience gave them an enormous advantage, bringing a positive can-do spirit to the staff. The company grew rapidly. By the third year, Spectrum earned in excess of $1 million. In today's dollars, that would be about $2.5 million.

In late 1986, when Henco bought Princeton Industries from Herff Jones, it expanded its sales force by 200 salesmen. Above, left to right, are Jim Hackl of Herff Jones, Henco Attorney Don Malmo, Tom Hendrix and Henco CFO George Donaldson.

We then purchased the C.E. Roser Handle Company in Savannah, Tennessee, which manufactured hickory replacement handles for striking tools. It had been in operation for many years, and we thought we could sell its products with the Spectrum line of merchandise. Our salesmen were not as excited about the idea as we were. We struggled with the company for several months until we sold it for a small loss. We decided that just because it's a good idea, it doesn't mean it will work in the marketplace, and we wanted to concentrate on developing Spectrum.

Another purchase was Pro-Sports Inc. in nearby Adamsville. It held licensing agreements with the NFL for production of team posters and other products, providing good product line potential for Henco's fundraising business.

***

While Henco looked to diversify, I kept my eyes open for side projects to invest in personally. I always enjoyed a challenge. Because I grew up on a farm and studied agriculture at UT, I had farming in my blood.

My good friend, Julius Hurst, was my favorite teacher from Bethel Springs High School. He was a true professional in the classroom with high expectations of his students. He took an interest in each one of us, measuring our progress with one-on-one conversations each month. He even came to our farm and visited with my father about a Future Farmers of America project, which was a first for our family.

Julius was superintendent of McNairy County schools for several years. He furnished the leadership to build a new school on the cutting edge of design and curriculum.

At the end of that experience, I persuaded him to go into the real estate and auction business instead of accepting other job offers on his desk. One of his listings was a thousand-acre farm near Rose Creek with promise for growing corn. I bought the farm to Julius' surprise, and his commission was as much as his last year's pay as superintendent of schools.

When Julius passed away, his family asked me to eulogize my good friend at his funeral service before an overflowing crowd.

I continued to buy land until I owned 2,000 acres, which prompted me to think about a hog operation to consume the corn we grew.

I went to UT Martin and looked for an outstanding farm manager. I hired Fred Grossner, a young man who had been working at a large hog operation similar to the one I had in mind. We flew to different parts of the country to investigate the most modern and successful hog operations we could find.

We bought 350 sows from a Minnesota herd. They were long and lean for quality meat with much less fat. The sows stood in crates. Their feed was dispensed automatically with the appropriate amount to match their weight and condition.

They were beautiful animals that produced large litters because the boars were given proper care and management. It was a pig factory — a farrow to finish operation. We went to market with 6,000 to 8,000 hogs each year.

I left my desk at Henco sometimes in the middle of the day for a quick trip to the hog farm. On my return, everyone turned their head. The smell of the hogs permeated my clothing. When I went home for the evening, my family could still smell it.

"You have been to the farm!" They would exclaim.

Sherry, Susan and Leigh Anne did not like to go to the farm with me because they did not want to smell like hogs.

Ultimately, the operation was more fun than profitable. Hog prices dropped below the break-even point, and I began to lose several thousand dollars per week. After a while, it ceased to be fun. Hog farming was like riding a roller coaster at the amusement park.

Farmland prices also sank considerably for the first time in my lifetime. People always told me that land was the only sure thing to appreciate in price, but I learned that even with land, nothing ever remains the same. It took many years for it to return to its original price.

Entrepreneurship is truly an interesting way to live. I don't think I have ever been in a project where I didn't enjoy the challenge.

**

In 1991, I purchased Bolivar Aviation — the largest, privately owned flight training school in the country. Lured by the glamour of flight and the thrill of educating young, energetic pilots, I thought it would remain a profit center.

If you were to have asked someone to name the third-busiest airport in Tennessee, they probably would have answered Memphis, Knoxville or Chattanooga. It would have been a long shot for someone to say Bolivar, a city with a population of about 6,500. But it was. Bolivar had more takeoffs and landings than all the airports in Tennessee except for two.

Extremely expensive flight-training costs, an abnormal amount of bad weather and lengthy waits for flight testing caused a shortage of pilots overseas. Typically, it would take European pilots one to two years and $60,000 to $80,000 to earn their pilot's license. At Bolivar Aviation, they could obtain their license in about six months for $22,000. Tuition included books, instruction, flight time and dormitory housing. International students made up about 60 percent of our entire student body.

The Federal Aviation Administration strictly regulated the flight training school. We followed extremely rigid guidelines in every aspect of the business. Bolivar Aviation even had seven FAA administrators on staff to grade tests.

The training facility had two campuses: one in Bolivar and another at McKellar-Sipes Regional Airport in nearby Jackson, Tennessee. Enrollment averaged about 300 students year-round.

The purchase of Bolivar Aviation turned out to be one of my entrepreneurial mistakes. I relied too much on the owner, whom I had known for many years, and his description of the business. I should have completed a more detailed due diligence. Bolivar Aviation had 80 or 90 planes and several flight simulators. We should have taken the time to have an outside inspection of each plane and each simulator's mechanical condition in detail. It would have taken some time to accomplish, but we would not have moved forward once we understood the problems involved. I should have been more hands-on to make sure we knew what we were buying. Deadlines that were set too close should have been ignored.

The flight school was in a state of change in several areas that would have been difficult to know at the time of purchase. Students were coming from around the world, paying for the flight training at the time of enrollment. But the federal government changed the rules, requiring students to pay as they received training, which turned our cash flow upside down.

Terrorist threats at that time made parents more cautious about their sons and daughters going abroad for training, and the regulatory oversight of bringing in foreign nationals began to tighten.

I am sure the owner knew the winds of change were on the way, and he was not under any obligation to tell us what was likely to happen.

With dozens and dozens of planes in the air each day, flown by young pilots in training who sometimes landed in nearby cotton fields, Bolivar Aviation never seemed to have a dull moment. I regularly called in to ask: "What has happened today?"

Shortly after our purchase, four Italian young men, who came to Bolivar Aviation for advanced training, checked out two planes, which they were qualified to fly.

Then tragedy struck. All four were killed instantly in a mid-air collision. I don't think I will ever forget their mangled bodies; the scene was atrocious.

The National Transportation and Safety Board determined that the students were practicing illegal and dangerous maneuvers — actually taking photographs of each other as they played dogfights over the Tennessee River. Though it was proven to be no fault of the flight school in any fashion, the crash cast a pall over the school for some time that further complicated recruitment.

Before long, I knew I had made a mistake, and it was totally my mistake. I sold the business shortly afterward. In hindsight, I took a risk without doing my homework. The seller pushed for a quick closing date, and I should not have agreed. Bolivar Aviation could have been the only business I did not enjoy.

***

We ultimately sold Spectrum to John Sorey for a considerable profit. John kept the management team in place, with the exception of David Landreth. A few years later, Randy Rawlings, Billy Brown and Lewis Waynick bought the company from John. About a year after that, they sold the company again at a good profit. They became financially free to live the life of their choosing.

These highly capable young men were the type of people banks wanted to back financially. The day we asked them to join Spectrum, they had no idea what would unfold before them, which points to the value of freedom and entrepreneurship. Looking back at what the company was like when we bought it and watching the good the company brought to people's lives is gratifying.

Tom, left, gives his brother, Ray, a 10-year service gift from Henco.

My brother, Ray, joined Henco in 1971 as warehouse and delivery manager when we had only one truck. Like me, Ray developed his management skills, and as the years passed, he directed his focus to warehousing and distribution with Spectrum. When Spectrum was sold, his expertise paved the way for an opportunity with the company. He became president of Spectrum Distribution for 15 years, and now he is the manager of their warehouse and shipping across the country.

I have enjoyed watching him mature into an outstanding businessman as he managed increasing responsibilities through the years. When Ray and I were growing up on the Hendrix farm, we never dreamed we would furnish leadership to a national business operation. That is the beauty of life — traveling roads you never dreamed you would travel.

CHAPTER 16

JACK'S LIBRARY

On December 21, 1982, I met with Jack McConnico and Ken Marston. We were developing a script for a film — Henco's Philosophy — and Jack was to be the star of the show as narrator.

Jack telephoned me that afternoon, but I was out of the office. He then called Joe Utsey, Henco's sales manager, to say that he thought he was having a heart attack.

Joe bolted to his office and hurried Jack to the hospital. When I found out, I rushed to the hospital to meet them. I saw Jack on a gurney being rolled into the emergency room. He was very pale, but he began to talk.

"Jack, just relax," I said.

As they rolled him through the doors, he gave me a thumbs up with a smile, as if everything was fine. He was dead within three or four minutes.

My longtime friend and mentor had passed away. His heart attack occurred while he was at his office, involved in projects and associating with people he loved. It was a shock at first. He was active, and we were not expecting his death at age 75. It seemed too young for Jack. We celebrated his life with a beautiful memorial service in Selmer. In his unselfish manner, he donated his body to science with the request that his family spread his ashes around his beloved family church — Tabernacle in Brownsville, Tennessee.

We wanted to do something special in Jack's memory to emulate his unselfish life. As the news spread, Henco team members and his many friends asked how could he be memorialized. We decided a memorial related to books was appropriate, because Jack was a student his entire life as he searched for truth and enrichment. Contributions began to come in.

Selmer's Public Library — a small library within the Shiloh Regional Library System — was housed in a portion of the former Shackelford Funeral Home. We contacted one of the service clubs that had discussed the need for library improvements. Three women from the

Jack McConnico

service club came to my office, and we explained our vision. They were excited. Next, we brought together a cross section of the county's leadership, including the Selmer mayor, school superintendent and city aldermen. We described a modern, up-to-date facility to benefit thousands of McNairy County residents, young and old, for years to come. The library would be named the Jack McConnico Memorial Library. We further emphasized that everyone needed to be on board with their support if we were to raise the $400,000 to $500,000 needed to build the library.

It was interesting to read body languages as the bold plan unfolded. Most comments about the library were positive except for a few questions.

"Do you really think we can raise that kind of money in this small town and county?"

"Yes," I replied. "If we adjust our thinking to believe we can. To start the ball rolling, Henco will donate $75,000. And, we will call the governor to see if we qualify for a state grant."

I went around the room asking each person if he or she would support the project. Each said "yes." It was one of the most interesting meetings I have ever conducted. A small community was coming together to do something special for the benefit of people for years to come.

***

Gov. Lamar Alexander had asked me to interview candidates for his commissioners. I knew him quite well.

We contacted his office immediately.

"Is this a community effort to build a community library or a Henco project?" He asked.

"We will have another community meeting with a cross section of leadership, and your people can observe the community's commitment," I said.

We scheduled another meeting and drew a sizable crowd at Selmer's middle school. The governor's representatives came to observe and report back to his office. At the end of the meeting, Robert Bedwell, Henco's superintendent of manufacturing and project engineer, was introduced as chairman of the project, and everyone was asked to give him a round of applause.

Robert was intelligent, soft-spoken and very capable to lead the effort. He was surprised to be the chairman of the library project, but we knew it needed strong leadership, and no one would be opposed to Robert. The project became a part of his Henco job description.

With the community's positive response, Gov. Alexander agreed that he and his wife, Honey, would lead a 5K walk-a-thon to kick off the fundraising effort to build the library. He had initiated a statewide effort to celebrate Homecoming Tennessee, commemorating our heritage while inspiring improvement and development in small communities across the state. McNairy County's library project was exactly what the governor had in mind — something special for the community.

Lamar and Honey led the walk-a-thon and played baseball while Alexander's Washboard Band entertained. A luncheon at our home for the governor and county leaders was followed by a planning session. Later in the afternoon, Nashville recording artists gave a free concert. Afterwards, we had an auction to raise money with numerous donated articles. The Governor's plaid shirt was a popular item.

It was a great day. We raised $17,000, and with Henco's contribution, we were off to a good start.

Gov. Lamar and Honey Alexander, above center, lead the walk-a-thon to raise money for the library on festival day. Julius Hurst, far right, auctions off one of the Governor's red plaid shirts. Gary Garner, a Henco employee, is in the foreground.

The governor and his wife improved our chances of getting the Community Development Block Grant, and within a short period of time, the state approved one for $350,000. The only caveat was that we needed to guarantee that we could raise the remainder of the money necessary to complete the library; another $100,000.

Robert Bedwell came to my office after he heard the news about the grant and told me that neither the county nor city would sign the guarantee. So I signed it to keep the project on track.

***

The $350,000 state grant was wonderful, but government grants do have a downside. The grant stipulated a fair-share wage rate. In essence, this was a union's pay scale and caused the cost of construction to increase considerably. From my prospective, big government did not think the McNairy County citizens had enough sense to build a library without dictating what we were to pay the people involved.

It was our tax dollars that were being granted to us, but when money passes through government's hands, it becomes its money, with all the strings attached, driving up costs. With the union scale rate, I am not sure how beneficial the grant was in building the library.

We raised a great deal of the money by making a list of people in the county, including those who had been reared in the county but were residing elsewhere. We sought people who could donate at least $5,000 or more. After the list was made, we made a presentation to them. Every single one of them wrote a $5,000 check to build the library.

I never cease to be amazed at the generosity of the American people. We are, by far, the most generous nation on this earth.

We raised the money and built the library. We presented the keys to the county, debt free, to serve our community. Not one dime came from local government. At the final settlement, Terry Abernathy, H. J. Maxedon and I took care of the remaining $30,000 that needed to be paid.

Because the building was much larger than the old library, we asked for a small increase in the library's budget, but some members of the county commission fought against it. They thought the grant should have been used to build a ballpark. They did not understand that the grant was for cultural projects as part of the Tennessee Homecoming initiative. The library budget eventually was approved by a few votes.

As I left the courthouse, one of the men leading the fight against the budget increase came to me.

"I sent my daughter down to interview with Henco, and you wouldn't hire her," he said.

I did not know that his daughter had ever interviewed with our company, but I did know that Henco hired people based on their qualifications.

You can't build a company hiring your friends or the children of a politician. I have often said that it takes an extra measure of patience to build a large business in a small town. I think the McNairy County people, whom I have had the opportunity to get to know, are the salt of the earth. They are hardworking, honest people, and Henco hired a number of sons and daughters to build our company and provide our services.

***

The request to get more money for the new library reminded me of when I was on the county court in the 1970s. Not much had changed about its conservative approach to the budget.

As a member of the county court, I followed the dictates of my conscience, with the idea of doing what I thought was right and what was best for all the people in McNairy County. I let the chips fall where they may, and I did my best not to play politics.

I would ask myself, if everyone in the county had the facts, how would they vote? I didn't get it right every time, but studied the issues to get my facts. If I felt strongly about something, I armed myself with as many facts as possible and used my communicative abilities to persuade members of the court to my point of view. I was successful most of the time.

I was appointed chairman of the budget committee, and that was a tough position. People had strong feelings about their tax dollars, as they should. When we had our first oil shortage during President Carter's administration, the price of fuel skyrocketed.

McNairy County Schools consumed large quantities of energy for heating and cooling and running school buses. We were working on the budget for the coming year during the time many county court members were running for re-election. I went before them to explain our dilemma with energy costs, giving numbers that entailed a sizeable amount of money. We had been cutting back every year to pass a lean school budget, but we couldn't pay for the extra energy costs without raising property taxes.

"If anyone has an idea about how we can make up this short fall, I am certainly open to suggestions," I told them.

No one put forth any suggestions, and two or three people took the floor to say they had promised their constituents they would not raise property taxes.

"Have you explained our problem to them?" I asked.

"I can't get elected talking about raising taxes," one of them said.

"If we pass an inadequate budget that we know will not pay the bills, you will be back here some time next year in an emergency meeting to figure out how to pay those bills," I said. "And, with the tax rate set, where are you going to get the money? The McNairy County people elected us to be problem solvers, not problem creators. I say it is time to level with our constituents as a responsible court."

The members voted against the property tax increase. The following year they called an emergency meeting to solve their problem, without any money to solve the problem they created. To me, elected officials should do what is right — even if they never get elected again. In my experience, if you are honest and up front with people, it is amazing how reasonable they can be.

After the budget fight, my term on the county court ended. In many ways, I was glad to be able to focus on my busy life building Henco and my family.

***

The year 1982 turned out to be bittersweet. It's the year Henco finally became a national company and the year we lost Jack McConnico.

But I was happy on that day in December 1984 when we dedicated the Jack McConnico Memorial Library.

CHAPTER 17

EXCHANGE PARENTS

*"So much good can happen when you get to know
a young person who has been reared in a different country
with different values and a different worldview."*

Months before we dedicated Jack's library — on a cold January day in 1983 — I sat at my desk and received a phone call I had not been expecting. It was from a woman representing foreign-exchange students.

"Mr. Hendrix, you have been approved to sponsor an exchange student for the school year," she said.

I had never considered sponsoring an exchange student, but for some reason, it struck me as a great opportunity for our family. I replied immediately.

"Yes, I would like a boy!"

"Sir?" She questioned.

"Yes, I would like a boy," I repeated. "When can you visit with us to see who the young man might be?"

She said she had the biographies of two teenagers — one was from Sweden, the other's home was Finland. I asked her to describe the Swedish boy, whose name was Anders Widestrand. She read highlights of his story, and we set a date for her to visit.

When I arrived home that night and sat down at the dinner table, I announced that I had scheduled a meeting about sponsoring an exchange student. Exchange programs were familiar to us. The Rotary Club sponsored students from around the world. But with our active lives, we had not considered inviting a young person into our home for a school year. As we talked, though, our discussion was favorable.

Sherry, of course, thought it would be a great experience for Susan and Leigh Anne if they became friends with a young lady. When I said I wanted a boy and discussed a Swedish teenager with the representative, Sherry was concerned. She questioned the idea of a teenage boy from a liberal country being so closely associated with our teenage daughters for an entire school year. But, the more we talked, the more positive we all became. Susan and Leigh Anne thought it would be fun to have a brother.

The representative came to our home, and we reviewed the biographies. I read Anders' story, and I was absolutely sold on him. By the age of 16, he had completed two marathons. He was a straight-A student from a solid family. His mother was employed with a bank in their hometown, and his father was an educator. He had a younger brother, Johan.

We reviewed biographies of young ladies, but Sherry realized how important it was to me to have a boy. We let the representative know that we wanted to invite Anders to our home and be part of our family.

Many decisions are made in our lifetime. This decision was one of our better ones, though we did not fully realize it at the time. So much good can happen when you get to know a young person who has been reared in a different country with different values and a different worldview.

We exchanged letters and pictures for several months, becoming better acquainted and more excited about our new adventure.

Other families in Selmer and surrounding communities, including some of our friends, also hosted students. Our McNairy Central High School teachers were to have new experiences as well.

August arrived, and Anders landed at the Memphis International Airport. We gathered at the gate with anticipation. Down the gangway and through the gate he came with a big, enthusiastic smile. He was light on his feet, as I expected a young marathon runner to be.

We greeted each other and he introduced himself.

"Hello! I'm Anders, from Sweden," he exclaimed.

Little did we know then how often we would hear that greeting through the coming months and years. It was a great day.

Anders was well-versed in the English language. He was fluent in German and also studied Spanish. During his time in the United States, he wanted to improve his English and communicate more comfortably. We, of course, could not communicate in Swedish or German. However, we overcame any language problems quickly. Anders had his English handbook for assistance, and he made unbelievable progress.

He seemed to be relaxed with us from the very beginning. Jim Tucker, piloting Papa Charlie, flew us home from the Memphis Airport. Anders sat in the co-pilot's seat and sipped his first soft drink from a pop-top can.

We arrived home on tree-lined Mollie Drive during a warm August day. We walked into the house, and Anders spotted our indoor swimming pool and heard the sound of its recirculating water. He quickly changed into his swim trunks and dove in.

The next morning, we headed to Pickwick Lake, boarded our yacht for the weekend and introduced him to the Tennessee River. We anchored in a cove, and he dove into the water. He was shocked. The water temperature was above 80 degrees — far warmer than he expected and unlike the colder water temperatures from his home country.

He was physically fit, and he learned how to waterski quickly. By the following weekend, he could ski on one ski just like Susan and Leigh Anne. He liked our new ski-boat, and he liked exploring the river with the girls. I soon taught him how to operate it.

Later, in his first full week with us, we flew to The Greenbrier in White Sulphur Springs, West Virginia. It's one of the most beautiful resorts you will find anywhere. We were conducting a Henco fundraising regional sales meeting there.

Anders was a good tennis player, and he became friends with a few of our regional managers, including Tom O'Neal and his wife, Lucy; Gene Hébert; and John Waite.

We had a good sales meeting and a great time. Then we returned home to Selmer for a busy week at work. Before I went to the office, I asked Anders to go with me downtown to watch the guys at the pool hall. We sat and watched them play for about 15 minutes. As we stepped outside, I told him that Middle America was somewhere between The Greenbrier and the pool hall.

We traveled often at that time to sales meetings around the country. Anders' wardrobe was limited, so we purchased suitable clothing for business meetings and our busy lifestyle.

We were determined to expose Anders to as much of the United States as possible during his school year. Because I traveled quite a bit with our business, I wanted Anders to take the vacant seat on the Henco plane whenever possible to further his education. We discussed the plan with his high school principal, David Hurst, and he agreed that it was all right with him if Anders missed some classes for travel. I promised the principal that Anders would still make straight As, and he did.

We broke one rule set forth by the exchange program's officials. Because of safety issues, students were not permitted to drive a vehicle during their stay. Anders was much more mature than most 16-year-old boys, and I wanted him to experience the freedom most teenagers in our country had. We contacted his parents about his getting his license, and they agreed. He studied on our way to the driver testing station and aced the test. I did not worry about him showing off or putting anyone in danger. He was grateful, and he did not take advantage of his special privilege. The first time he drove our red 450SL Benz convertible, heading out to pick up his date, his smile was contagious. With the wind in his hair, he experienced freedom like many American teenagers. I knew how he felt.

His school year in Tennessee came to a close, and Anders prepared to return home. Just before he left, his parents and younger brother came for a two-week visit. We arranged for them to stay on our yacht to enjoy time together

Anders, second from left, joins the Hendrix family on a trip to White Sulphur Springs, West Virginia.

and the lake's atmosphere. We entertained them and tried to make them feel at home. Johan was delighted to be on the Tennessee River. We grew fond of Johan and invited him to spend a school year with us outside of the exchange program — just family to family. He thought it was a great idea.

Their visit was over, and we bade them farewell. It proved to be the beginning of a wonderful relationship.

We gave Anders an opportunity to attend the University of Tennessee in Knoxville with Susan and Leigh Anne. He graduated from his Swedish gymnasium and finished his year in the military. He then called us to say that he was ready for big UT.

Two years later, Johan arrived, and we were delighted. Susan and Anders were at UT Knoxville. Leigh Anne and Johan were high school seniors. We did our best to expose Johan to as much of our American culture as possible — as we did for his brother. He was popular on campus. He participated in school activities, excelled in school projects, played tennis and dated. He also took the Tennessee driver's test and drove the red Benz convertible.

We often visited Susan and Anders on the UT campus. When the leaves began to fall, we planned a boating trip to Knoxville. We made the cruise in our 24-foot Cobalt with a cuddy cabin. I asked Johan if he would like to ski as we made our way. It was about a 400-mile trip, and Johan skied a good part of it. He was athletic, physically fit and loved to ski.

The two of us spent some quality time together, and after a year, Johan returned to Sweden. But we remained close to him and his brother.

On spring breaks, our family vacationed in Vail, Colorado, to enjoy some fantastic days on the slopes. Before one ski trip at Christmastime, we invited Anders and Johan to join us. They flew into Denver and came aboard Papa Charlie for the short flight over the mountains to Vail.

Johan, Tom and Anders in Vail, Colorado

Anders and Johan, as experienced skiers, could not get enough of the powdery slopes. They grabbed the lift to the top early each morning and stayed late. After a full day of skiing, we were tired and ready to enjoy some good food. During one meal, we looked up and were surprised to see former President Gerald Ford. He wore a full-length fur coat, and his party walked by us to get to their table. It was a nice treat, especially for the Swedish boys.

After three days of intense skiing, we flew home. The boys renewed friendships in Selmer and then returned home.

During another Christmas holiday, our family of six soaked up the sun's rays in Hawaii. We jogged on the beaches, did some sightseeing around the island and took a dinner cruise. Anders, Johan and the girls were the center of attention as four young hula dancers.

The boys appreciated their American experience, and we were so fortunate that they became part of our family. Both young men were smart, respectful, energetic and full of fun.

As expected, Johan and Anders became successful businessmen. We are proud of them and their outstanding accomplishments, and we remain their "Tennessee Mom and Dad."

***

In late autumn 1986, an exchange program coordinator contacted me and asked if we would consider being host parents again of a young man from France for the remainder of the school year.

Nicholas Trehet had been placed with a family in Memphis. When the arrangement did not work out, he was placed with a second family.

After a few weeks, it became obvious that he needed another home.

Sherry and I discussed the situation at some length, questioning whether we could make it a successful stay and good experience for all of us. In the end, we agreed to meet Nicholas and his coordinator at a Germantown restaurant to determine if we could be compatible.

Nicholas was cordial and mannerly. He was a tall, nice-looking young man, but he was reserved. Knowing something about his previous two situations, I was firm about what was expected if he shared our home. I emphasized that I was chairman of the board in our home, and if he could accept it, we would have a good start at getting along. We shared our family's lifestyle and our thoughts about his having a good experience. He placed his luggage in our car, and we said goodbye to the coordinator.

As time passed, we learned more about Nicholas. His parents were divorced, and he lived primarily with his mother on the French Riviera. His father was a movie producer and had remarried. Nicholas was an exuberant teenager, riding his motorcycle and enjoying life in France. It seemed his parents felt he needed more structure, so they gave him a choice of enlisting in the military or becoming an exchange student.

He chose the exchange program.

The first two American homes in which he was placed were quite different from his lifestyle. He found it hard to adjust. He was unhappy, and his host families were unhappy. The exchange program director was faced with sending him home if we had not agreed to take him in.

When he moved in with us, he called home often, but he adjusted.

At the end of the school year, his father and stepmother came to California on business. They planned to accompany Nick on his return home. While visiting us, we suggested they stay at our Pickwick Lake home to relax and enjoy the scenery.

While they were at the lake, we had a young man maintaining the lawn. He went to the house to mow and trim. When he looked up toward the sundeck, he saw a woman sunbathing in the nude. He was shocked and distracted. He could not concentrate any longer on his work, so he came home earlier than expected. His scenery that day was quite different from his normal Pickwick day, and we had a good laugh.

Nicholas' experience in Tennessee ended well, I believe. We exchanged Christmas cards that year, but we have not since communicated. His desire to be an exchange student was not anything similar to Anders' or Johan's. He did not view it as beneficial or rewarding. He did it because his only other choice was the military.

Nevertheless, we appreciated our time with him.

***

Our exchange students and Spencer were a blessing to our family. We learned so much from each other, discussing different viewpoints and life experiences. They all loved our dinnertime discussions, which encouraged everyone to speak up. Sherry wanted everyone to look forward to our meals together — good food and good conversation with the exchange of ideas. We talked about values and current events throughout the world, and I enjoyed directing the conversation. I could hardly wait for dinner each night because I could see our family learning from each other as we expanded our worlds.

I wanted the boys to understand our free enterprise system of service — how we, as a free people, exchange our services with one another. I wanted them to see the good that comes from free people exchanging their services with as little government interference as possible. They read books on free enterprise, and we had many discussions. I tried to make sure they understood to value a service system instead of a system of greed.

Ultimately, I believe all of them became sold on the magic of freedom.

CHAPTER 18

PARENTING AND PEACHES

"The decisions you make will determine your future.
Crummy decisions, crummy life! Good decisions, good life!
Successful people are good decision makers."

When a child is born, instructions for parenting are not included. We derived most of our ideas from our parents based on traditional family values and stability. Sherry and I always believed we could deal with situations and problems with good old-fashioned common sense and sensible practices directed by the teachings of Christ.

The year Susan was born, Dr. Benjamin Spock's *Baby and Child Care* was a top seller. The pediatrician had gently coaxed post World War II parents to trust their own common sense. His handbook encouraged parents to think things out for themselves. It empowered parenting.

Our world news was sobering the month before Susan's birth. The Tet Offensive had erupted during the Vietnam War. Families were uneasy, questioning our country's involvement. There were protests and the Kent State University debacle. It was a turbulent time for the American people. We yearned for common-sense answers.

With determination to teach good values reflecting much of what Christ taught, we approached our jobs as parents much like our parents, who were our role models.

We hoped we could prepare our children for the struggles or crises they might encounter. To do that, we needed to spend time with them. We found plenty of opportunities around our dining table, driving to church or family events, on our boat, or beside their beds at night. As they grew older, we adjusted our manner of teaching to best fit their situation.

At the dinner table, I would listen to their conversation to connect to any problems they might have in school. I wanted to know their attitude and how they dealt with those problems.

"Regardless of your age, you must take ownership of your decisions," I told them. "The decisions you make will determine your future. Crummy decisions, crummy life! Good decisions, good life! Successful people are good decision makers."

A neighbor's teenage daughter ran away from home for several days with a man in his 20s. I pointed out that decisions had consequences — good or bad. For example, if the girl became pregnant, her life would be changed forever. We discussed the problems she might create in her life.

I wanted them to talk through the problems created by dumb decisions and to internalize the reality that decisions have definite consequences. I knew it wasn't what I said, but what they accepted and believed that determined my success as a teacher.

Sherry and I did everything we could to make meals a happy time together. It was rare for us not to have dinner together each evening. It was a time for family discussions, and it encouraged conversations, which gave us an opportunity to teach. I did not want to come off as preaching to them, but rather, sharing ideas with them that made sense at their age.

I guarded against boring them. I watched their body language and eyes to see whether they were receptive. If their body language was negative, I took a different approach.

***

When Susan was in her two-year-old phase and became a little more difficult to deal with, I spanked her a couple of times. It bothered me a great deal. I decided to change my approach. When I came home from the office, I picked her up in my arms and walked outside, through the trees in our back yard. I told her how much I loved her. I told her how smart and pretty she was and that her mother and I wanted her to be a good girl. We wanted her to be happy. She laid her head on my shoulder, put her arms around my neck and said, "I love you, Daddy."

Susan looked forward to our walks through the woods. It was a happy time for us to be together. Other times, I placed her in the rumble seat of our bicycle built for two, and we went for a ride. She

Tom and the girls at Disneyworld

threw her arms into the air and screamed with joy. After our walks, rides and talks together, times were more harmonious, and we had no more spankings.

Sherry's recipe, when they were small and happened to get into mischief, was to find something else more interesting. She attempted to be proactive instead of reactive. Her idea was to keep them happy, and it worked like a charm. You can do business with a happy child.

I learned it required a lot of patience to teach values. As children grow up, it takes different techniques for different ages.

One Friday evening, I returned home from a week of traveling. Sherry said Susan had a cold, and the doctor prescribed cough medicine, but she would not take it. I picked Susan up and sat her on the kitchen counter.

"Susan, if you take your medicine, we'll ride the bicycle to Mr. Estes' store for your favorite sucker."

She took the syrup into her mouth, I put her in the bicycle's rumble seat, and we pedaled to the store for the sucker. She chose her favorite sucker, and we rode home. I unwrapped the sucker and handed it to her, and then she spit the cough syrup out of her mouth. I made her take the medicine again, and this time she swallowed.

"I wondered why Susan wouldn't tell Mr. Estes goodbye," I said to Sherry later at the dinner table.

"Me had me mouth full," Susan replied.

Little minds see things differently than grownups. We tried not to treat Susan and Leigh Anne like kids, but like little people who were growing up to be outstanding people.

The girls knew they had a privileged life, but they also knew the honor of hard work, and they were taught that all jobs were honorable. When they were old enough, they worked at Henco during the summers. Their first jobs — in the mailroom and on the production line — were at minimum wage. They became part of the Henco family.

Sherry and I had some of our best years with Susan and Leigh Anne when they were teenagers. They were well-rounded, participated in school and church activities and dated. Their lives unfolded before our eyes.

***

We read about a custom within the Joseph Kennedy household that we put to use. Mr. Kennedy would post a topic on the family's bulletin board before he left for his office. The children checked the board each morning for the topic to be discussed at the dinner table that evening and prepared to offer their viewpoints. We found it to be a good exercise.

At the dinner table one night, I announced that the topic of conversation would be about dating successfully to find the right person with whom to spend your life. I asked Leigh Ann to start. She gave us her thoughts as to what she thought was important. I then asked whether you should date someone you would not consider marrying. The question stimulated considerable discussion. I looked across the table and saw Johan sitting quietly.

"You haven't said much," I told him. "How do you see it?"

"I think finding the right person to spend your life with and raise a family is, by far, one of the most important decisions we'll ever make," he responded. "In fact, I don't think we should leave anything to chance if we can avoid it. It makes sense to me to live together for a period of time before making the final decision."

Remember, this was 1987. Sherry almost stood up from the table.

"Johan, living with a person is not necessary to make a good decision," she said.

Leigh Anne laughed silently. Standing his ground, Johan said it could prevent a divorce one day. He stuck to his guns, and we continued our lively conversation.

I believe these dinner discussions paid off in the lives of our children. We looked forward to coming together each evening at the dinner table. It was the family's time to connect and Sherry's and my time to teach. We talked through real-life situations with a common-sense way of sharing our experiences.

We had few discipline problems, and through respect, we parented with love, high standards and high expectations. Susan and Leigh Anne knew it didn't matter to us if they said, "everybody else was doing it."

When Susan was about 16 years old, she had a car accident. She was driving too fast on her way to cheerleading practice, and she lost control on a slick street. She called me on the car phone. I asked if she was okay, and she said she was but didn't think she could drive the car. I asked her if she could get out of the car, and she said "yes." I told her I would be there in a few minutes.

When I arrived, she was crying. I told her that we did not want the wrecked car to ruin her evening. I took her to practice and told her we would talk about the accident later. I did my best to have a happy conversation with her. She wrecked the car because she made the decision to drive too fast on a slick street. She certainly did not plan to have an accident.

The next day, I asked Susan to meet me at 3 p.m. in our formal living room, where we had serious discussions from time to time. Susan was waiting when I walked in, and she embraced me.

"I love you, Dad," she said.

"I love you, Susan," I responded. "You are a responsible young lady, and because of that you are permitted to drive Anders, Leigh and yourself to school. But Susan, last night you made an irresponsible decision when you drove entirely too fast on a slick street. You lost control of the car. Decisions have consequences. I have asked the owner of the body shop to give us an estimate to

The family gets dressed up for the 50th anniversary celebration of Tom's Aunt Ruby and Uncle Russell McDaniel in January 1983.

repair the car. It will cost about $2,000, and I expect you to pay the bill. Once you have saved $300 from your weekly allowance, and the money is placed in my hand, the car will be moved to the body shop. Until then, the car will sit here in the driveway. I want you to see the car every day until it is repaired. You are not to touch a steering wheel until it's fixed, and you are to pay the bill from your allowance and bank account."

I asked Susan if she had any questions, and she didn't. We embraced one another with no ill feelings. This did not change our relationship whatsoever. She never mentioned driving while she was saving her money, but I knew it saddened her to see the car sitting in the driveway.

When she had saved $300, she called me at the office and said that she wanted a meeting with me at 5 p.m. in our formal living room. I told her I would be there. Susan began our meeting by counting out $300.

"This wasn't easy," she said. "Let's get the car fixed. I can't wait to get behind the wheel again. I have learned my lesson."

When we went to pick up the car, she wrote a check for the balance.

"Why don't we have collision insurance?" She asked.

I explained that we could if she paid for it.

Sherry thought I was too hard on her. I may have been, but Susan is a lot like me — always in a hurry with Type A behavior. I wanted the experience to stick in her mind so she would be a safer driver. I didn't see this situation as punishment. I saw it as a teaching point that had good results.

A year or so later, Leigh Anne was driving our red convertible Benz at Pickwick. As she waited for the car in front of her to make its way onto the highway, the driver moved forward and then stopped abruptly. Leigh didn't expect his quick stop and hit him in the rear. She was afraid that she would get the same lesson as Susan. But I explained that accidents such as that one could happen to anyone, and in fact, the same situation had happened to me. Leigh was more like her mother — a careful, thoughtful driver. I cannot remember her having a fender bender after that.

When Susan and Leigh Anne attended UT, they drove a BMW with the freedom to vacation in the Florida Keys and other places of their choice with their friends. We gave them freedom, but they assumed responsibility for their actions to live up to the Hendrix values.

On some weekends, they would come home to Selmer. One drove as the other pored through newspaper articles to get ready for that night's discussion at the dinner table. They knew they would be quizzed on current events.

We also visited Knoxville often when they were students. Occasionally, we docked our yacht by the stadium for tailgate parties before football games. Their friends joined us, and we celebrated the prospect of a win. If we flew into Knoxville aboard Papa Charlie, the girls met us at the airport with happy faces. Sherry and I were pleased we could spend quality time with them, and they felt comfortable sharing their problems with us, knowing we would not overreact. Our close bond made for good communication. I think they knew we wanted the best for them as their parents. They knew, in any given situation, we were there for them with an open ear and reasonable conversation.

Every parent knows making tough decisions with tough love is difficult. The parent loves his or her child, but we must make those tough decisions for their well-being. I think every parent wishes they could do some parts over, making tweaks here and there, but we only have one chance. It is so important that we not miss that opportunity.

Values were important to us, and I wanted to make sure our daughters understood that. I often wrote them letters that shared our love, but also to reinforce a value or discuss a concern I thought important at the moment. My handwriting is atrocious, so the letters often were typed on Henco letterhead.

We visited one weekend, and I noticed Leigh Anne was tired after staying up too late at a party the night before. It was her freshman year, and she was only 18. When I got back, I addressed the situation in a letter. I reminded her of the Henco family values and the importance of getting enough sleep.

Leigh Anne always wanted to please her Mom and Dad. College was exciting but more demanding than high school. It was hard for her to make her grades and maintain the social scene. I required my daughters to give me a plan for the semester — courses, their goals for grades and allotted study time to achieve the grades.

"Without goals, we are like a ship without a rudder," I wrote them. "Successful people have goals. Unsuccessful people do not. The more successful people have goals in writing. You are growing, and I am proud of you. Life is made of ups and downs, but winners use the downs as a stepping stone to get up and go again."

I sent Leigh Anne a tape about setting goals and asked her to listen to each side before passing it on to Susan. It provided a common-sense approach to good planning. I was worried her grades would suffer if she didn't pay attention to them. I didn't want her to fall into a hole with poor grades and have to spend the rest of her college days climbing out of it. I put my thoughts in a letter.

"You are going through a period of life that requires a lot of discipline. Becoming a disciplined person requires some growing up, but you are fully capable. You have so much going for you. You have a bright mind, a good attitude and a loving family that will do anything that we can to help you. You are so fortunate — be thankful, take advantage of opportunities, and live the good life. I love you very much!"

As it turned out, Leigh Anne's grades fell a bit short of what we expected.

So Sherry and I went to Knoxville and took our daughters to dinner at a favorite restaurant. After we finished a delightful meal together, I told Leigh Anne her grades were unacceptable if we were to continue paying for college expenses and the good life they were living.

"At the end of the semester, you can go to work for one semester and earn your living," I told her. "Ask yourself if you need a degree."

Leigh Anne was shocked with the idea.

"What will I do?" She asked with a tear.

"There are opportunities in many places," I said. "For one thing, go interview at one of the nicer restaurants in town, and as you wait tables, make it a beautiful evening for families. You'll also learn how to communicate with all types of people — some nice and some not so nice."

Leigh Anne worked at Copper Cellar near campus and became an outstanding server. She certainly grew a notch or two. At the end of the semester, she was back in school full time and focusing on her education.

Leigh Anne wrote me a three-page letter telling me how unfair she thought I was at the time, and then saying it was the best thing that had ever happened to her. I cried as I read it. It was a masterpiece — daughter to father.

Another time, I wrote Susan out of concern of how she was managing her time. "You know when I write, I generally have something on my mind that I think needs to be said, and I think you know my constructive criticism is out of love for you. I am concerned you don't manage your time or your life better. You can control your life within or you can control by external forces, and the latter is a sure way to fail. To succeed we must have strength of mind to plan our lives and implement those plans according to what we think is good for us."

A few months later, I wrote a letter to Susan to encourage her to live a healthy life. She had started a diet and had begun exercising regularly, so I wanted her to know she was making good decisions.

"Wherever I go, regardless of the weather, I do what is necessary to maintain my good health," I wrote. "It's the way I live. It's the good habits I've developed. Life is a matter of good and bad habits, and hopefully, we have more good habits than not."

In that same letter, I gave her some fatherly advice about boys.

"Susan, I admire you for not hanging onto a boy all the time and having the confidence to feel good about yourself as you do it," I wrote. "There will be that special person for you one day. In the meantime, have fun being busy becoming that person for that special person. You are on track."

Later that year, Susan asked me about working for Southwestern. I was all for Susan selling books with Southwestern, but Sherry had concerns about her safety if she took a job as a door-to-door saleswoman. So I wrote her a letter in an attempt to guide her to selling peaches from the new peach orchard we were developing, which we felt would be much safer.

"Your summer experience needs to be a learning experience that will round out your educational life," I wrote. "These summer experiences should bring the best out of you, and I think selling does just that. In fact, Susan, if you dedicated yourself to the peach project, it can be invaluable — very rewarding. Selling peaches can be almost as rewarding as selling books, except for the sales training. Southwestern has the very best sales training, in my opinion. Maybe we can get some formal sales training if we set our minds to it."

***

With our children in Knoxville, I searched my mind for a positive family work experience — a worthwhile summer project for students. I wanted them to have a valuable selling experience like I had in college. And I wanted them to be productive.

So I hatched the idea about peaches — and we developed what turned out to be the largest peach orchard in Tennessee.

I knew Mike Searcy, a young man working with our University of Tennessee Extension Service in McNairy County. He was a UT Knoxville graduate with a degree in horticulture, specializing in orchard management. He had family ties in East Tennessee. Mike told me that East Tennessee orchards had been successful in years past. But most tree-ripened peaches sold in the

Knoxville area were trucked from eastern South Carolina. We thought an orchard near Knoxville would provide the perfect work experience for our family.

We found land to lease in Dandridge, located in the rolling foothills of the Great Smoky Mountains and about 30 minutes east of Knoxville. The site had been productive in years past, so we decided to establish a 100-acre peach orchard with more than 10,000 trees and 12 different varieties that would ripen about every two weeks. We planned to have a plentiful supply of tree-ripened peaches to sell from June through September.

Mike agreed to manage the Hendrix Orchard. Before we began, he researched forest trends from the previous 50 years. The data he found indicated we might lose a crop or partial crop every six or seven years. We could accept those odds and still have a successful orchard.

Mike hired a crew of people to plant, prune, thin, mow, spray and pick the fruit. He ran a professional orchard operation that was year-round work. They thinned the peaches to a size that would have the most market appeal. They created a spraying schedule to prevent insects, especially worms, from attacking the fruit. They fought off pesky rabbits chewing bark off young trees.

It proved to be a tricky operation.

At critical times during the season, freezing temperatures were a huge threat. As we waited for our first bumper crop, an unexpected April freeze killed the young fruit. It was the first such freeze in 20 years. Weather continued to be a problem, despite our best efforts to protect the peaches during freezing temperatures. We lost a crop or a partial crop every two years or so. The weather was an aberration for that time period. Farming certainly can be unpredictable.

With the unusual frost problems, the orchard was not as profitable as desired, but it was a good family experience with great educational opportunities and many advantages.

On a hilltop at the edge of the orchard, we built an open-air market with a large refrigerated section and an office. White fencing lined the drive up to the market site. A billboard near the highway advertised our tree-ripened peaches with the Hendrix Orchard logo. We put a couple of swings at the market. It was a relaxing and peaceful spot for our customers to sit with a view of the Smoky Mountains. Families enjoyed their trips to the market and orchard.

During our first peach season, Sherry lived with Susan and Leigh Anne in our condo near campus. Anders lived on campus. After completing my workweek at Henco, I made the six-hour drive to Knoxville.

At the beginning of the season as we set up our market facilities at the orchard, Sherry, Susan, Leigh Anne and Anders arrived early each morning. One morning, Sherry woke up a very sleepy Leigh Anne.

"It's time to rise and shine!" Sherry said. "We need to get to the orchard. We have lots of work to do."

"Just fire us!" Leigh Anne replied, which drew a laugh.

Despite the weather's impact on supply, we had a top-notch marketing plan that attracted attention from residents in Knoxville and surrounding areas. We put peach stands throughout the city and outlying communities. Sherry and Robert Bedwell, Henco's project engineer, designed and built them to look like peach baskets. They used sheets of lattice-style wood on the sides of a 10-foot-square structure with a white bale made of PVC pipe across the top, which they accented with brightly colored graphics of ripe-looking peaches. They put Hendrix Orchard flags on the corners and an American flag in front of the basket. The stands were picture-perfect replicas of peach baskets full of ripe peaches.

We also designed a tasting barrel — an oak barrel cut in half, lined with fiberglass and with a Plexiglass top that was hinged in the middle. We placed crushed ice at the bottom of the barrel beneath a plate of sliced peaches segregated by variety and pierced with toothpicks. Customers could taste our fresh, tree-ripened peaches and select their favorite variety to purchase.

The mayor of Knoxville was a personal friend, and he was helpful in finding high-traffic locations for our peach baskets throughout the city.

Our star summer salespeople included Susan, Leigh Anne, Anders,

Spencer Cheng, Kim Vermillion, Jennifer Graves, Jimmy McLeod and other UT students who were friends of the girls. Sherry designed their outfits — white T-shirts with our Hendrix Orchard logo on the left crest and khaki shorts. It was a good-looking, comfortable outfit for the students.

We conducted sales training at the Holiday Inn near campus. We kept it simple. They were taught to give Mrs. Jones a big smile and a warm welcome when she came to the peach stand and opened the tasting barrel.

"The proof is in the taste," the student would say.

As Mrs. Jones began to taste the different varieties and make her selections, the student would close the sale.

"Hendrix Orchard peaches ripen on the tree, which makes them extra sweet. Would you like the large basket or the smaller one?"

Then they thanked Mrs. Jones for her business and asked her to help spread the word.

The students loved their summer job selling Hendrix Orchard peaches. We had a professionally run operation, and they liked every part of it. They got to know their customers and looked forward to seeing them on their next purchase. They also liked the generous tips they received.

Anders' daily duty was peach delivery. Each morning, he woke up between 3 and 4 a.m. and drove to Knoxville before the traffic rush to deliver fresh peaches to sales stands in our refrigerated truck. Anders and Susan were our sales coordinators, making sure we had peaches available at each location. If one location needed more stock, they redistributed the peaches. They also drew up the order for the next day's sales.

I taught Anders how to sell peaches on the street after making his deliveries. He sold them from the back of our red pickup, creating a scene and a lot of excitement. People loved the good-looking, full-of-fun, young peach salesman from Sweden. After Anders got the hang of it, he could earn $100 a day to offset some of his college expenses. Moms would bring their daughters to see Anders many times. Other ladies brought him freshly baked peach cobbler as their way of saying thank you. Anders relished every minute of his sales experience.

He developed empathy for the American people and learned how to communicate, which complemented his UT education.

Each day, Mike's team picked and transported the peaches to our hilltop market, where they were sorted, packed and shuttled to a refrigerator, the market floor or the delivery truck. If we had more peaches than we needed, we shipped the extras to a farmer's market in nearby Jefferson City. If we had over-ripe peaches, we called on knowledgeable locals to fire up their black kettles and create tasty peach butter. During the latter part of the season, we also sold fresh apples along with our last crops of peaches.

Hendrix Orchard made quite a name for itself in Knoxville. It was a fun project that even brought Governor Winfield Dunn to the orchard on one occasion for a news conference. He spoke about the benefits of locally grown tree-ripened peaches to the Dandridge and Knoxville areas.

I was proud of our children. They worked long hours on hot summer days doing whatever needed to be done. They had great attitudes. It was a perfect work experience that taught them some great life lessons.

However, Mother Nature's frosty years ultimately iced our operation, which shows that even with well-laid plans, entrepreneurship is risky.

I have said many times that there is never a dull moment when living a risk-taking life. I believe it is an exciting way to live. The people who try the most and fail the most are our most successful entrepreneurs. Risk-taking is a must for a vibrant economy and a good life.

***

Our daughters grew into fantastic young women. They made wonderful decisions about who they chose to marry, and they are successful parents.

Even after Susan and Leigh Anne graduated college, I continued sending them letters. Susan, who was a traveling salesperson, said to me, "I pulled to a roadside park and read your letter. It was almost like visiting with you."

My emotions welled up. I found out later they kept most of my letters.

A few years ago at Christmastime, I sent a letter that encapsulated my thoughts on parenting …

"Rearing your children is, by far, your most important assignment in life. I do not doubt your ability to get the job done for outstanding results. My grandchildren are in good hands, and I am truly grateful.

"The greatest gifts you can give your children are the roots of responsibility and the wings of independence. If our children get everything they want, they will soon want nothing they get. Teaching the child the giving habit is paramount. A giving, generous attitude toward life is essential to a happy successful life, and we have to be careful as we teach this important concept. So be a close observer, analyzing everything you do to make sure your kids understand that a good life is not what they get but what they give. Merry Christmas! Love, Dad."

CHAPTER 19

HENCO IS PEOPLE

"I am prouder of Henco's investment in people
than anything we have ever done."

As Henco continued to grow, we had ongoing training programs to make sure we had the highest quality fundraising service in the country. We were never satisfied because we knew we could improve our service for the benefit of millions of people. It was serious business, and it wasn't just the mission of corporate executives. Our sales force had strong feelings about being the best in the business — running well organized programs that raised more money in less time and with less interruption to the schools. They also wanted it to be a positive experience for students. The mission of upgrading fundraising was good for everyone, enabling salesmen to repeat their programs more often.

Our people were our best business investment. Whether it was in Henco work or another career, they were much more productive. I am prouder of Henco's investment in people than anything we have ever done.

***

In the first sales meeting with rookie salesmen — a room full of band directors with master's degrees — I would hold up the Henco Sales Manual.

"You can no more fail than water can run uphill if you master what is between these covers," I'd tell them.

"This is your sheet music. Learn your sheet music. Just as your band students did to win band contests. Climb your financial mountain in service to people as we upgrade fundraising in America. Let's make it happen!"

Our professional sales training was focused on teaching the business through weekly phone calls that could last 30 minutes or more. We also routinely rode with salesmen to verify their presentations were carried out according to the written script, which had been tested for several years. Observing the salespeople in action was a way for managers to confirm and compliment what they were doing well and suggest improvements in their less effective areas. The salesmen looked forward to our managers' visits.

Gene Hébert was one of our best teachers. When I was in the field riding with his salesmen, they kept close to the script as they made their presentations. Their results were excellent with more money raised for the school groups.

Rookie salesmen were asked to memorize the sponsor and student presentations, as written. They had to give them before a video camera on the last day of our sales school. We asked them to wear their best suit because we emphasized being well dressed; if you dress well, you feel a little better and you walk a little taller throughout the day. The exercise became competitive, and they knew that mastering a well-organized presentation would raise a lot more money for schools. We had a contest to see who could do the best and win "the boiled egg award." The crazier the prize, the better!

Why did Henco require the presentation to be given as written? Because I had given it hundreds of times, and it worked well. The presentation had been written from experience, which gave me an opportunity to share what I had learned with new people coming into the business. We constantly improved the manual as salesmen made notations to be considered for improvements the following year.

The Henco presentation told our fundraising story much like viewing a movie. You lived the story being told, and you didn't think about the actor's lines being memorized. We covered all the details in simple language. It was eight or 10 minutes long — short enough to reach busy educators between classes. The sponsor never thought about it being a memorized script because it was professionally presented. The Henco presentation enabled inexperienced salesmen, who knew we had the best fundraising program on the market, to sell professionally and earn professional pay. Their sincerity made them more convincing.

When we arrived at a school to make a call, Henco salesmen were well dressed and carried a service attitude. Most drove a Mercedes-Benz because of the car's proven safety record and efficiency. The salesmen also liked the professional touch the cars gave them. When we had a sales meeting, I saw Benz autos coming from every direction.

***

We invited some of the most outstanding speakers of the time to address our Henco sales force and staff members. It helped us see more clearly how we could have the good life in service to others — a way to stimulate our growth together.

Joe Sills came into my office one spring day, and I asked him why his spring sales had almost doubled. He said Denis Waitley's training program changed his life. Waitley was a respected author, keynote lecturer and productivity consultant on high-performance human achievement. A graduate of the U.S. Naval Academy at Annapolis and a former Navy pilot, he counseled sales and management executives and leaders in every field from premier athletes to Apollo astronauts.

We invited him to speak to our employees and were excited because his philosophy of winning was so closely associated with Henco's. The win-lose playbook suggested there must be a loser for every winner, and that winning by intimidation is obsolete. The win-win playbook was at the core of the Henco philosophy. It meant if I help you win, then I win, too. The real winners in life get what they want by helping others get what they want.

Waitley emphasized that independence has been replaced by interdependence. There will be no peace on earth until there is a piece of pie in every mouth. We must face the inescapable fact that we, as individuals, are vital but single organs of a larger body of human beings in the world. One cannot succeed or even survive for long anymore without the other.

Waitley brought new insights to how we could work together as a team with more harmony to improve our service to our employees and our customers. He got us thinking about how we could live a more productive life.

Henco invested millions in teaching the how of the Henco business. Besides Waitley, we invited other renowned

Working in Henco's office systems department were, clockwise from top, Manager Loretta Hendrix, Brenda Kilburn, Debra Qualls and Peggy Griffin.

speakers of the time, including Jim Rohn and Glen Bland. They were intelligent, master communicators and left a lasting impression. We would have 200 Henco people in the room. Some were affected more than others, but everyone benefited.

I felt it was vital to have a constant educational program for Henco to grow as a group and help each person feel good about his or her Henco life. Our speakers brought new ideas to consider and new insights to stimulate our thinking. They were a breath of fresh air for our former educators because this was a new venture for them.

***

By the fall of 1983, Henco dominated school fundraising in the United States. We had a mature sales force, of which most had a master's degree and 15 years of experience in the school fundraising business. Henco fundraising operated in 40 states with approximately 160 sales representatives.

Each year during late summer, Henco typically organized regional sales meetings with an emphasis on conducting successful fundraising programs and identifying new opportunities. In late January and early February, we conducted a national sales meeting. The events featured various seminars by selected Henco salespeople, a nationally recognized motivational speaker and the introduction of the new fall brochures and products.

The 1985 national sales meeting was held in Las Vegas. The meeting's theme was "Henco High School Reunion." It featured reunion T-shirts and Henco High School cheerleaders who conducted cheer sessions throughout the event. At the end of the meeting, the region with the most spirit was awarded the Spirit Stick.

One evening around the pool, we orchestrated a Henco High pep rally. As with any pep rally, ours included a speech by the principal and football coach, cheers led by the cheerleading squad and music by the Henco High band. Music played a big part in Henco meetings because we had a large supply of professional-level musicians in the sales force.

The introduction of the new fall-fundraising brochures and products highlighted the meeting. Marching band music played to create an upbeat mood as the sales force gathered. We introduced and explained the new brochures with a slide presentation and factual information about each product.

After the session, the room lights turned off, and the opening fanfare for the 1984 Olympic games began to play. The wall at the back of the room slowly opened to reveal all the new fall products on a brilliant display. We invited the sales force to see, taste and handle the new products.

The second highlight of the meeting was the awards banquet where individuals were recognized and awarded plaques for achieving various sales levels.

Our national sales meetings were expensive, so we needed to achieve maximum results. We wanted to make sure we kept the enthusiasm and excitement of the sales force alive so when they returned home, they hit the road running.

The overall purpose of these meetings was to educate and motivate. In an earlier year, one of our motivational speakers told us: "You are either climbing or slipping." Our sales management team had a single focus: to keep the sales force climbing.

Dick Echols at a sales meeting

One of our pilots, Buddy Jones, was a special member of our Henco team. He believed in the good that could come from a company of people growing to their full potential together. Buddy said he wanted to work with the manufacturing team and keep the option to fly the company plane when needed. He was a retired Air Force major — a test pilot who flew supersonic jets in all types of conditions. He was a smart and courageous guy with a soft heart. He loved Henco's philosophy to elevate people.

We worked out a plan to accommodate Buddy's request. His goal was to meet with each person to create a plan to help him or her grow. He could visualize them attending night classes and getting their degrees over time. But after two or three months, he came to me and said that he was disappointed with the negative responses he had received from many of his team members. He looked at me and asked how we could motivate these people. I expressed how I appreciated his sincere efforts on behalf of the manufacturing team, but it was wishful thinking to believe they all would buy into the idea of growing to their full potential.

"But look at the people who did join you in growth and the good that will come from your efforts," I told him. "These people can be a good example to everyone."

Encouraging people to do the right thing takes patience and persistence. Over time, you can make a big difference in the way people view themselves. Through the company's honest efforts to be helpful to employees, we sent a positive signal that we cared about them and wanted the best for them. This attitude, in itself, created a good environment. Employees saw how they were working with a company that had a heart and soul and believed in what was right. It created employee *esprit de corps* for less employee turnover and a better place to work.

***

In the early 1980s, we hired our first female salesperson. We learned immediately that we had been overlooking great talent ideally suited to fundraising. The women were as communicative as the men when they gave presentations to parent-teacher associations, band moms, sponsors and student groups. In many cases, they became our best salespeople.

It was a great feeling to walk into a large meeting room with men and women dedicated to upgrading fundraising in America. Giving equal opportunities to women was one of Henco's better decisions in building a national sales force.

In one of our summer sales meetings in Las Vegas, I made a promise to the sales force: The person who sells the most that fall will drive a new 300SDL Mercedes-Benz for one year. The contest created furious competition, and Elisabeth Jonas was the winner. She almost fainted when her name was announced. Elisabeth later wrote me a letter.

"I will never forget driving that amazing car from Memphis home to Orlando with the sun roof open and my arms in the air screaming, 'I won it! I won it!' I will never forget that day!"

Elisabeth was one of our most outstanding sales people. She soaked up every word during training and did the most possible for every group for which she worked. She espe-

Elisabeth Jonas in the new Mercedes-Benz

cially liked the Jim Rohn training.

"I still have my notes," she told me years later. "I absorbed every single word he spoke. It was a life changer for me. 'Design your life' is one of his best lines, and it stuck with me for all these years."

***

I first met Joe Utsey, one of our best salesman and a good friend, in 1968. It was his first year as Director of Bands at Meridian High School in Mississippi, and I was just starting Henco. I told him about Henco and DRIX, our all-purpose cleaner, and how our organized program would raise money for his band in only two days of taking orders. Sold on the idea, he invited me back to a band booster meeting. I told our story again, and they signed up.

Later, Joe told me that after I left the band booster meeting, one of his parents said, "I have never seen anybody dramatize a bottle of soap like that man."

A year of so later, Lewis Muhondro walked into Joe's office and invited him to visit Selmer for an interview and become part of Henco's mission to change school fundraising across the country. Joe was one of the best hires we made.

As I was writing my autobiography, I asked Joe to write down his feelings about being a part of the Henco experience. In part, he wrote ...

"That trip to Selmer changed my life forever. The thing that I remember the most was a statement made by Tom. 'Joe, we have a philosophy at Henco. We believe that philosophy is important because what we believe determines what we do. And, what we do, determines what happens to us.' That philosophy, combined with the emphasis of positive and forward thinking, was constant throughout my career at Henco and still is a guiding force in my life today. Tom also talked about Henco's training. He made the point that with the training Henco provided, combined with the right attitude, we can 'drop you out of a plane anywhere in the United States, and you could earn more than you need to live.'

That played out in my life after leaving Henco. I was able to start a new chapter in my life, eventually creating programs for inner-city youth to teach

Regional sales managers, from left, are Gene Hébert, Larry Cromer, Bob Brooks, Joe Utsey, Tom O'Neal and Jim Stackhouse.

the life skills of planning, time management and positive thinking that I learned at Henco. As an independent contractor for AMRO music stores, I also was able to create piano lab programs for Memphis City Schools and group piano programs for adults at AMRO. Henco's training and philosophy was critical in getting those programs off the ground.

"A day never goes by that I don't use the tools that I learned while at Henco. The company's mission statement of helping each employee reach his or her full potential was true."

***

Sherry and I attended the Wilson Learning Center in Minneapolis. The program pushed a consultative approach to selling, suggesting that successful sales did not require manipulation. Founder Larry Wilson, at the age of 29, became the youngest lifetime member of the Million Dollar Round Table in the life insurance field. He was a speaker and an author of several books.

We wanted to investigate the possibilities of incorporating his ideas into our sales school. The course was too expensive to send several Henco people to Minneapolis, so I contacted Larry, and we worked out an arrangement. He trained some of our key people as instructors and allowed us to use his training materials. It was one of our better educational programs for our employees.

Henco awarded the top salesmen each year. Pictured, from left, are Tom Hendrix, Lee Knowles, Jim McGonigal, Von Beebe, Rob Koen, Dave Buhman, Jerry Brown, Brad Bartlett, Henco president Jeff Capwell and Sales Manager Otto Feddern.

The Wilson training course was designed to help people better understand human nature. We are all different — amiables, expressives, analyticals, drivers — and we all see our world differently. The course helped us better communicate and create more harmony as we worked together. Communication is complicated when we view things differently because of our differing personalities.

I telephoned our school superintendent in McNairy County to say Henco would like to conduct a Wilson seminar for the county's school teachers to help them better communicate with students.

Tom O'Neal, whom we recruited to join Henco from the University of South Carolina, led the seminar. He was a skilled band director, having taught for many years, and he became an outstanding sales manager with Henco. He later served as our human resources director. Tom was witty, and his approach was interesting for the teachers. They loved him for his teaching ability.

***

We decided to complete three-year planning sessions with all of our sales families. I gave an overview to the sales managers as to how the interviews with the couples would be conducted. We scheduled our visit in advance so they could arrange for a babysitter while their sales manager treated them to a quiet dinner at a nice restaurant.

Afterward, we gathered around their dining room table as the couple shared what was important to their family that we could help them accomplish. The sales manager directed the conversation with questions. The interview covered their financial needs, vacations, their faith and anything they thought was important for a successful year.

These annual planning sessions were one of the most appreciated initiatives Henco ever did with our sales families. We left their home with a written outline of what was important to them — sales projections, social goals, investment strategies, home furnishings and whatever else they listed. After the meeting, the manager typed the plan and sent it to the family for any additional input before a final draft. We sincerely wanted it to be an important event in their life. We had taught the importance of planning, and this was a way to put those teaching sessions in action for great results.

Through the year, sales managers worked with families to reach their goals. We emphasized realistic goals for the good of the family, and we managed from the plan.

The following year, the families would show us the goals they had reached, such as a new car, new furniture or a vacation to the beach. This was when they became convinced that to be successful, you must have a plan. Spouses were involved in reaching their goals as much as the salesperson. Many times, a spouse would do the paperwork, and in some cases, a spouse would make phone calls to the fundraising sponsors to free up more time for his or her spouse to make more sales.

***

Pat Kroken, the wife of Henco salesman Bruce Kroken, was one of the spouses who learned about the Henco way of doing things and later used those principles to become highly successful in her own consulting business. Bruce died in 2003. Pat struggled at first, she said, but then the principles she learned from her husband's Henco training kicked in. She wrote me.

"While Bruce received the formal Henco training, I pirated every tape, book, article and lecture note he had and applied what I could glean from 'the Henco way' … Henco initially introduced us to a better life in terms of income, education and opportunity for growth. Ultimately it has taught (and reinforced) some timeless values, philosophies and techniques to provide resilience. Yes, members of the Kroken family have numerous accomplishments on our resumes. More important, however, has been the ability to pass along those values to others with whom we interact and to reinvent ourselves and our lives when facing events and circumstances beyond our control. In those instances some people just fold up and live in the past for the rest of their lives. We cherish the lessons of the past, but Henco (and Bruce Kroken) have taught us the value of thoroughly enjoying the wonder of today and the promise of tomorrow."

***

We knew we must do more than talk about the Henco philosophy — we must implement concrete programs that could make a positive difference in an employee's life. One of our initiatives was a wellness program. I had been running four miles per day for years and believed strongly that diet and exercise was the way to live an energy-filled life. God endowed us with an incredible body that should be respected and maintained for a successful trip from the cradle to the grave.

They tell us our heart beats about 36 million times per year, fueling 60 miles of veins and arteries and pumping more than 600,000 gallons of blood. Our body has five quarts of blood and 32 billion red blood cells. Each second, two million of our red blood cells die and are replaced with new ones to give us vitality. God has done his part. It makes common sense that we should focus on wellness if our bodies are to serve us as they should.

Henco established an annual wellness day for a team of doctors to check our state of health. If you were overweight, for example, you went to a class that discussed the merits of diet and exercise. If you were a smoker, you went to the smoking class to be convinced to change your lifestyle and quit. A good percentage of employees made common-sense decisions to change their lifestyle for good health. We think everyone attempted to make some improvement in their health. Our objective was to create a culture of wellness.

We placed further emphasis on wellness by providing an in-house health facility for daily use. Our health spa included a weight room, racquetball court, sauna, Jacuzzi, lounges and meeting rooms. The health spa was an active place before and after working hours and during lunch periods. We also designed a fitness trail through our adjoining Henco park and organized aerobics classes.

Company policy required us to show a film highlighting the benefits of diet and exercise and healthy living at each sales meeting.

It was wishful thinking to believe everyone accepted the challenge to live a healthy life, but Henco could see the difference we were making with our employees. It was much appreciated, regardless of whether they participated. Some people do not have the will power to replace bad habits with good ones. Our goal was to do our utmost to encourage employees to grow to their full potential, and good health was a vital part of that.

We organized group runs, and it was gratifying to see how many people brought their running shoes to sales meetings. We had a lot of fun running for good health, and we inspired each other to do more.

When Henco bought Princeton Industries in late 1986, Mark Kissel came to us as a general sales manager. When I met him on our company plane trip back to Tennessee, I thought he needed to lose about 100 pounds. The next week, I went into Mark's office to tell him about the Henco wellness program and that is was beginning again soon.

"A team of doctors will be at Henco to evaluate our employees' health," I explained. "After the evaluation, you will have an opportunity to enter into a wellness program designed for you to live a healthier lifestyle."

Mark did participate and later told me that the wellness meeting changed his life forever. He began a diet and exercise regimen and lost 91 pounds. He also achieved his goal of running the New York Marathon in 1988.

***

As a company filled with service-minded people, we also looked for ways to serve our community.

Jim T. Hamilton, who by this time was a district judge in Middle Tennessee, addressed our Selmer Rotary Club one day. He outlined problems of child sexual abuse, which came before his court. It was a gut-wrenching presentation.

After he closed, he walked over to me.

"Tom, you are in a perfect position to implement a prevention program within schools across America, which could make a positive difference in the lives of thousands of children."

I returned to my office and could not get out of my mind the horrible conditions he had dramatized.

After about two weeks, I called Jack Hawkins to visit with me. Jack was one of Henco's top salesmen and an outstanding manager. Before joining Henco, he taught at a small North Carolina University. I thought Jack could develop a comprehensive prevention program to help young children get out of an abusive situation, and more importantly, help prevent it.

I gave Jack an overview of the judge's presentation, describing the horrendous circumstances around child sexual abuse. I challenged him to develop the most up-to-date child sexual abuse prevention program in the country. I asked him to contact people who were presently involved in prevention measures and go wherever he needed as he compiled useful information. Jack concentrated on contacting the most influential people he could find, and we met weekly to discuss his progress.

The extensive research he compiled revealed that one in four females and one in seven males were sexually abused before the age of 14. Much of the abuse occurred at the hands of family and friends.

Henco set into motion a study with several child psychologists to see what could be done to impact child sexual abuse at the elementary school level. We determined that age-appropriate material could be presented in a non-threatening manner that would provide information about child sexual abuse and how it could be prevented.

Jack met with the Child Welfare League of Chicago, which had done extensive studies into this matter. They suggested using some type of coloring or activity book and videotapes. He also met with the Walt Disney Company, which had an award-winning video, *Now I Can Tell You My Secret.* After much discussion, Disney agreed to allow Henco to use its video at cost because Henco was not using it for profit. This was a major plus for the program.

Henco also discovered that Marvel Comics had produced an issue of a *Spider-Man* comic book that dealt with child sexual abuse prevention, and they agreed to allow us to use it at cost, too.

We developed two coloring books with help from many organizations. One was for grades one through three, and the other was for grades four through six. The Western Publishing Company printed the coloring books at cost. We also prepared materials for teachers and parents.

We contacted several civic organizations to see if they would help fund the effort and promote the program in their local communities. Every group we asked wholeheartedly agreed to do so.

We felt we needed a national spokesperson for the program and approached Barbara Mandrell, a popular country music entertainer. Sherry and I had met Barbara, her husband, their children and her father during a time we were boating on Old Hickory Lake near Nashville. Our children were about the same ages. We asked Barbara if she would write an introduction for the program, and she agreed. She did not ask for any monetary consideration.

A major video production company made an introductory video at cost. It included testimony from a well-known child psychologist and presidents of civic organizations stating they would support the program and help fund it for their local elementary schools. The chairman of the Tennessee State Department of Education also endorsed the program on this video.

We introduced the campaign to the Henco sales force during the 1987 winter meeting, and they enthusiastically endorsed it. Several members of the sales force even opened up about abuse they had experienced as a child and said the program could have been helpful for them. I stood in the back of the room and witnessed salesmen wiping tears away from their eyes.

We continued research and development into the spring of 1988 to see how best to place this program. In the summer of 1988, we launched "Think Safe, Stay Safe" and provided the materials for use by the Henco sales force.

Our salespeople placed the program in schools throughout the nation, and thousands of students took advantage of the training. In every school, students raised their hands during training sessions, indicating abuse. School officials notified authorities about the possible abuse.

We knew we had a good program, but we did not anticipate the negative attitudes we faced as we implemented it. In 1987, our society was struggling to come to grips with the facts and the enormity of the problem. Schools were still in denial that a significant percentage of children were being sexually abused. Many wanted to avoid the sensitive issue because it might produce a negative response from parents or lead to false accusations. They felt they had enough problems already. And even though Henco did not profit from the program, teachers and parents had to pay a nominal charge for the materials or get financial support from the community.

But our sales force had no doubt about the facts, and our employees were driven to implement the program for the good of students wherever possible. Their determination was bolstered by the results the program achieved in schools when children admitted they were in an abusive situation. The Henco sales force was a special group with a generous spirit, giving their time with deeply felt empathy to help kids in abusive situations. The salesmen made a small commission to pay their expenses. The driving force was their generosity and knowing the good that "Think Safe, Stay Safe" could do in preventing child sexual abuse.

"Think Safe, Stay Safe" was recognized as the most comprehensive child sexual abuse program ever developed. We saw the campaign as an opportunity to give back to the schools — our way of saying thank you.

Henco also was invited to Washington, D.C., to present the program to a Congressional committee to determine if it could be used for elementary schools on U.S. Army bases across the world.

Of all the services we rendered, the "Think Safe, Stay Safe" program was Henco's finest hour — thanks to Jack Hawkins and our courageous sales force. Thank goodness we met many educators who felt as strongly as we did. It was time to take action and expose the perpetrators, for the safety of children.

***

The fall season was the busiest time in our fundraising business. Our warehouse was filled to the brim, but space opened up as we neared Christmas.

Since our warehouse would be near empty, we would have a big Christmas party inside. Henco had a sizeable art department, and the artists' talents were called upon to decorate the warehouse with a stage and backdrop. With a crystal ball rotating above the large dance floor and our cylinder candles on the tables, we created a festive atmosphere. The evening was open to employees, salesmen from across the country and invited guests. It was a celebration — a fun evening for more than 500 people.

Townspeople would ask me in August for an invitation so their kids, who were college age, could come along with them. Local ministers came most years, endorsing the Christmas event to the community.

Two bands provided music. The musicians alternated on the stage to give us a continuous variety. Because many Henco salespeople were former band directors, they also played their instruments and took over the stage for a short time. They loved to show off their talent. The audience joined in with applause, encouraging them to play their best.

Henco made the Christmas season a special time for many people — the Henco family as well as the community.

We asked Project Engineer Robert Bedwell to build a 35-foot-tall metal tree with synchronized colored lights where 75 people could stand and sing Christmas carols. Each year, one of our in-house band directors would take charge of our singing Christmas tree program. Several practice sessions were required because the community expected the best from Henco. Our employees joined with vocalists in town to perform the carols.

Henco invested a considerable amount of time and money to help our employees and the community celebrate Christmas. It was another way to do something special for people, another avenue of service.

We loved our community, and we loved our people — the best investment we ever made.

Henco's singing Christmas tree, directed by Ernest Cadden, Henco Personnel Manager

***

McConnico, Donaldson, Brooks, Hébert, Rodney Hendrix, Utsey, Capwell, Graham, Cadden, Barnes, Ray and Loretta Hendrix, and hundreds more, are names synonymous with Henco. Each one made significant contributions to the building of its success. The names used here are representative of countless others whose individual stories could be told. Each talent, packaged in a unique personality, pushed the company forward.

CHAPTER 20

FREE ENTERPRISE

"The free enterprise system is the most dynamic economic system in the world."

The story of my life is the story of the success of free enterprise. I am a dreamer and a risk taker, and free enterprise was the vehicle that helped me to achieve my dreams.

I was an entrepreneur for 55 years, and it all began in a college dorm room when I met Dortch Oldham. My life changed the day I signed up to sell Bibles. I took a big risk, and it paid off.

In those early days of college, I made the decision to do something that most other students wouldn't do. I chose not to take the steady job with the guaranteed paycheck. The freedom that came with entrepreneurship lured me in, and I was never the same after that.

My first few days of being an entrepreneur, I felt like a failure. I couldn't sell even one Bible, but it was only a year later that I assembled and trained my own team. I learned more that summer selling Bibles than I did in all my college studies.

Free enterprise taught me to have assurance in my own potential. It taught me to serve others above serving myself. I also learned about human nature and how to communicate with people. The work was incredibly satisfying.

Every time I knocked on a door I had a lesson in human nature. It gave me confidence. I had so much more courage after that first summer that I believed I could earn money doing anything. I flipped cars and paid for my tuition. I made money selling Japanese shower shoes (flip-flops) because no one else was selling them. And then finally, I decided to be a leader and assemble and train my own selling team.

Many of the Bible boys went on to be successful. Those summers taught us to take risks, to take advantage of our own potential, and most of all, to serve people.

Russell Caldwell started an office supply business from scratch after college and became a prominent businessman in Tennessee. Ted Welch became the COO for the state of Tennessee in 1971. I was there when Ronald Reagan put his arm around Ted and said that Ted was the greatest political fundraiser that the country had ever produced. Jim Ayers went on to build a chain of nursing homes. He later became a banker and has made it possible for qualified students in his county to go to college. All had gained much of their experience and financial freedom during those summers selling Bibles.

It wasn't about making a living but more about living life. It made me set even higher goals because I knew that I could reach them. Being an entrepreneur had taught me to work with my mind, not just my back. Taking risks and working hard is an excellent way to maximize your God-given potential.

I began to read autobiographies about successful people. Over and over again I would read about their passionate missions and their desire to serve. I decided that my mission was to serve through entrepreneurship.

After years of succeeding in business because of free enterprise, I was determined to leave a legacy by creating a Chair of Excellence in Free Enterprise at the University of Tennessee Martin. My goal was to help people better understand our free enterprise system — a free people exchanging services with one another in competition for the best service. The customer calls the shots as he or she decides who will provide the service needed. We call that "people power" — freedom at its best.

My legacy was announced on a Saturday afternoon in January 1985 in a crowded room at the University of Tennessee Martin, where I had attended college. The room was full of educators, businessmen and government officials. Governor Lamar Alexander was holding a press release in his hands.

Gov. Lamar Alexander, above left, and Tom Hendrix listen to speeches at the announcement of the Chair of Excellence in Free Enterprise. At right, Tom talks to Dortch Oldham.

I was on the stage waiting for him to speak. My wife, Sherry, and our two daughters were sitting on the front row. Dortch Oldham, my longtime friend and mentor and the one who started me on this path, was there, too.

As I waited, I thought about that first summer selling Bibles and how naive I had been. The disaster of that first day and the success that had followed led me to where I was today. Free enterprise had taught me to be my own man, and I was so thankful for it.

Finally, the governor stood up to speak, "The reason we are here today is to announce the University's first million dollar endowed Chair of Excellence… the Tom E. Hendrix Chair of Excellence in Free Enterprise … It is especially fitting that it be named for Tom Hendrix who has had a brilliant career in private enterprise."

I was thrilled and felt so honored to be sitting in that room that day.

I'm glad that I didn't stop after those first two terrible days of failing to sell a Bible. Entrepreneurship had become my passion, and now I was leaving a legacy that would help others to understand and use free enterprise as well.

I stood up and thanked the Governor and others who had helped to establish the chair.

I said, "There is at least one thing I have learned in life and that is to get things done you must take action … It is my hope that this Free Enterprise Chair will promote a better understanding of our economic system, to help insure our productivity and freedom."

It was our hope that the chair would accomplish several things. First of all, we wanted to expand the research into the free enterprise system. We wanted the university to be able to offer more courses in economics. We wanted to teach elementary and secondary teachers about free enterprise so they could, in turn, teach their students. Finally, we wanted the general public to understand and appreciate the free enterprise system and its benefits.

That day I reminded the crowd that between 70 and 80 percent of public school students will earn a living from the free enterprise system. It makes sense for those students to understand that system.

That was a proud day for me. The gift that I gave made me UTM's largest living donor. At first, I funded the chair annually. Then one day the UT people came for a visit to explain that if I would give $250,000, the chair could be endowed for one million dollars. I wrote the check. I gave more than $400,000 in 10 years to the school, and I was proving that free enterprise was not a system of greed, but a system of service.

I reminded a crowd of businessmen about this in Jackson, Tennessee, years later. I told them that our objective as entrepreneurs is to grow towards God through service to our fellow man.

Not everyone succeeds as an entrepreneur. I told them that the free enterprise system has a built-in pruning device that eliminates those who fail to serve. You can be a nice guy, take your savings and open a family restaurant in a great location, but if your food and service aren't great, "you will be pruned from the vine." That is as it should be. That's why the free enterprise system is the most dynamic economic system in the world.

In fact, I have always been such a believer in the free enterprise system that I made it part of the Henco statement of faith.

"We believe that the profit motive is a basic drive of human nature and essentially moral, and that private competitive enterprise as practiced in America is the strongest force that can be devised to constantly improve the ethical standards of the human race."

In 1985, I also was awarded the Herman W. Lay Memorial Award. Herman Lay started with a single snack food truck and went on to become the Chairman of the Board at PepsiCo, Inc. Herman was just as generous as he was successful. The Association of Private Enterprise Education select the recipients of the award based on the individual's pattern of success and philanthropy.

They select the person who made the most annual contribution to free enterprise education.

Free enterprise is about taking opportunities and risks. Dortch Oldham made me understand the opportunity that was in front of me that day in the dorm. I took the risk. Now I hoped to help others see the

Tom Hendrix receives the Herman W. Lay Memorial Award.

opportunities created by free enterprise and encourage them to take the risk because the reward is so great.

CHAPTER 21

A SHARP CURVE

"Nothing ever remains the same in business."

In the mid 1980s, Henco began to face an unexpected problem that would plague us for years. An import company entered the market, selling items through school fundraising. These products were of poor quality and overpriced, but they looked good on the colored brochures used by student groups to sell to their communities.

The products were primarily made in China with cheap labor, and they had special appeal because of their price. They could be purchased for pennies on the dollar compared to items manufactured in U.S. markets. Importers could sell these items with an unusually high markup, which increased profits for salesmen and school groups. It was a win-win for everyone except Mrs. Jones, who purchased cheap, overpriced products.

Henco, at the time, had the most prestigious and successful sales force in the fundraising industry. So the import companies went after our top producers, telling them they could double their commission while increasing profits for school groups. It was difficult to resist because it all looked good on the surface.

Importers wanted our salesmen because they wouldn't have to train them. Henco had already paid that cost. They also wanted our most valuable asset — our customers, with whom we spent years developing relationships by providing an outstanding service.

Our salespeople had signed a no-competition contract. If they went in business on their own, they could not sell to Henco customers for a year. Ideally, that would give us enough time to hire and train a replacement to protect our relationship with the customer. But importers told our salesmen that our non-compete contract could not be defended successfully in court. Our corporate lawyer also had a negative attitude toward the contract and made a half-hearted effort defending it. We lost in court.

Each year, importers converted some of our best salespeople to sell their cheap products. Their plan was working — reducing our sales and gross profit while increasing our sales cost. Henco would hire a new salesman, put him through a training program to cover the territory. Then he would have to compete with a successful former Henco salesman who had close ties to the customer and had offered good service through the years. Our former salesmen had an inside track with our customers, and our new salesmen would fail within a few months.

When these top salesmen left Henco, they took what we called incremental business, which is where most of your profit is realized. Meanwhile, Henco added considerable sales cost, hiring and training, for a failed effort. We also incurred large legal expenses in an effort to defend our non-compete contract. We went from a company with a 40 percent growth each year to a company barely making a profit.

Many of the salespeople who had agreed to sell the imports came to our fall sales meeting, and Henco paid their expenses. Then they returned to their territory and began selling imported products. We did not have enough time to hire and train new salesmen to compete for the business. All the talk of the top salespeople leaving and making exorbitant sales commissions hurt morale and created turmoil in our remaining sales force.

Many of our people wondered what was happening to our company. They once believed Henco could do no wrong.

This situation went on for several years until I received a phone call from John Hubbard, an attorney in Omaha, Nebraska, who specialized in defending non-compete contracts. He confidently said he could give us a victory in court.

He also advised us to make small changes in the contract our salesmen signed. John's legal fees were much higher than I had ever paid an attorney. He defended his fee by saying he was more efficient and spent less time to achieve success.

We gave John three signed contracts, and he won all three cases in court. The court awarded damages, and the wins allowed us to protect our territory for a year while forcing our salesmen to think twice about breaking their contract.

It seemed so easy for John in the courtroom. He had the strategy to win. If we had known about him in the beginning, Henco would have remained a profitable company and retained the most outstanding sales force in the fundraising industry. By this time, however, the company had been weakened. The horse was already out of the barn.

With Henco's profit in a tailspin, we asked our auditors and tax attorneys to devise a plan for Henco to make a maximum contribution to the employee stock ownership pension plan. The contributions came from shares of Henco stock and existing shares held in the Henco treasury. The large contribution created a net operating loss for tax purposes, enabling Henco to recover some of the high income taxes we had been paying.

We were careful to get a reputable, independent and qualified third party to make sure the stock evaluation was done according to IRS rules. We knew that when they were asked to give back, even by their own rules, the IRS would question it.

***

You may have heard people make the statement, "timing is everything." My experience has taught me timing can be your friend, and it can be your worst enemy. In Henco's case, timing was our worst nightmare.

We lost our best salesmen to imports, and our bank's real estate portfolios were in trouble. The banks began calling in loans from companies, like Henco, that had an unprofitable year. The IRS decided to do everything it could to undo our pension plan contribution and recover its tax dollars. I had considerable business experience, but I did not have the experience to cope with the oncoming freight train. Everything seemed to go against Henco — all at the same time.

Banks were facing new pressures from the federal government in the late 1980s. The value of many properties dropped substantially after changes in tax laws relating to write-offs of depreciation. Investors had been taking write-offs that were far beyond the amount of cash they had invested. The government's change in tax laws set off a chain of events. When tax deductions went down, property values went down. Banks now had loan amounts that were greater than the value of the underlying properties. The loans became "classified" loans, and banks could not count interest on them as income because they might default. Banks moved to get out of those loans, causing values of large properties to drop substantially. The whole banking world went into disarray as it related to financing large properties. Many tax shelters became insolvent because the government changed the rules in mid-stream, creating financial havoc and devastating many people financially.

Loans to operating companies like ours that showed losses also became classified loans. Banks called these loans or refused to renew them. Henco had short-term loans and lines of credit to finance inventories and receivables to get through the fall season each year. Three months in the fall produced about two-thirds of the annual volume of business. It was necessary for us to build inventory and receivables, with collections coming later to pay the loans. And Henco had an excellent record of paying its loans, a good relationship with banks and an outstanding rating from Dunn & Bradstreet.

I was on the board at First American Bank in Jackson and Memphis when the board's chairman, Ken Roberts, announced the bank would pull every loan made to companies that were losing money. He said the strength of the company's balance sheet did not matter. That statement sent shock waves through board members.

"You mean you would pull Sam Walton's loan if Wal-Mart had a bad year?" One board member questioned.

"We might have to reconsider that one," Ken said. "But gentlemen, this is a new day at First American Bank."

Within weeks, Ken and the president of First American were fired, and some of the board members were replaced. The federal government had taken over the bank and began calling loans. Henco was caught in the middle.

Our loans were called, causing great duress. And because the banks were in disarray, it was impossible to move the loans to another bank.

I recognized that my primary responsibility at this point was for Henco to continue as a viable company in order to save as many jobs as possible. Our families needed to continue receiving checks in their mailboxes. We decided to contact a respected competitor, Cherrydale Corporation in Pennsylvania, about Henco's sales force joining their company. Our salesmen would retain their customers, only the product lines would differ. We reached an agreement with Cherrydale for a considerable amount of money, and most of their payment was spread out over a five-year period.

Many of our salesmen had high incomes, and their families enjoyed a high standard of living. I thought it was important to give them the opportunity to maintain that. Most salesmen retained the customers they had worked years to develop, and with the Cherrydale product line, they continued to serve them successfully. We knew that as they made their way to Cherrydale, their business life would never be the same. The Henco way of life was special, and Cherrydale could not fill that void.

Relinquishing Henco's sales force was a bitter pill to swallow. The evening I made my final speech to the sales force and looked into their somber faces, I thought back to the first time I interviewed each of them in my office. They were just beginning their journey in the fundraising business to develop into professional business people and become financially free. It was an extremely emotional time. I knew many of them blamed me for their uncertain future, and I could understand why they felt that way. My only consolation was that they would practice the Henco philosophy and live a successful life in whatever they chose to do. Most of them shook my hand and thanked me for their

Henco training and experience. I had an empty feeling as I said goodbye.

Meanwhile, the IRS decided to audit Henco because we retained more than $1 million in tax refunds from the pension plan contributions and resulting net operating losses. The audit dragged on for a long time. The IRS proposed large tax amounts to be due from Henco and its officers who sold shares to the pension plan. The agency took the position that the shares of Henco stock had been valued too high, which would reduce the amount of the pension plan deduction. This would have meant that officers sold shares at values beyond the fair market value, creating a prohibited transaction — a transaction the IRS wanted reversed. This also would penalize the officers and require them to give back the dollars they had received. In my case, it was $500,000. Some of our officers used the money to pay down debt that had been incurred to buy the shares several years earlier.

***

In February 1992, under constant pressure from the over-reaching aggressiveness of the Internal Revenue Service, Henco filed for Chapter 11 bankruptcy. The agency began garnishing bank accounts and "seizing" Henco real estate by putting up signs on the property to that effect.

While the bankruptcy was in process, our law firm fighting the IRS resigned, saying a conflict of interest could exist between Henco and its officers, and the firm had represented both. We hired a second law firm, which also resigned after some time. By this time, the IRS had assigned someone new to manage our case.

Faced with having to hire a third firm, Henco's bankruptcy attorney and CFO put together an offer to IRS, and the IRS accepted it. When the IRS audit was finalized, the agency processed a refund of $185,000 to Henco. I received a $95,000 refund. Henco officers were not required to repurchase any shares and did not owe any taxes. But the agency's actions forced us to file for bankruptcy protection, and the company lost more than $10 million.

The fact is that the IRS owed Henco money that it refused to pay, but it still had the power to attach our property and bank accounts. Many people who understood what happened would ask, "Does this make you bitter toward our government?" My response was, "No, I still believe this is the greatest country in the world. I certainly wouldn't move."

Our settlement with the IRS cleared the way for Henco to file a plan with the court to exit Chapter 11. I went to my local banker for a Henco loan, which I personally guaranteed, to pay the remaining debts and go forward with operations. We paid the bank back within the next couple of years with continuing receipts from the earlier sale of the sales force and the Spectrum Oil subsidiary.

We outlined for the court the collection of money from Cherrydale Farms and how we would pay off our creditors, who were given a choice to receive 50 percent upfront or the full amount if they waited until all the money was collected. Some opted to settle; others waited until we collected the balance of the money.

Henco was not allowed to launch another business until we had fully implemented the plan filed with the court. We had some disgruntled minority stockholders who filed a suit against Henco for not maximizing profits — even though we were under a court order to wait. At the end of long litigation, a judge declared the suit frivolous and ordered the participants to render their stock to pay court costs.

Today, the IRS would not be allowed to proceed in the manner it did, placing large signs on the doors of our building and garnishing our bank accounts. Congress had extensive hearings, and people in similar circumstances testified that the IRS had overstepped its authority, forcing them into bankruptcy. In fact, I wanted to testify, but when I telephoned, I was told that too many people were slated to testify, and they had scheduled all of their allotted time.

The IRS claimed it had evaluated our stock, but we thought it was most interesting that we had never talked to anyone at the agency about it. Our valuation had been properly done by a qualified, independent, third-party firm in accordance with the IRS guidelines, and it was closely observed by an accounting firm and Henco's tax attorneys.

Also, instead of owing millions, we recovered refunds, but by the time it was over, it was too late. Henco was forced to take Chapter 11 to fight for what we knew was right. We won, but it devastated the company financially.

When Henco concluded Chapter 11, the judge fervently spoke about the company's case as the most successful case he had conducted. He said it was a company that would continue to serve people. I appreciated the judge's comments, but I had personally witnessed a fine company be destroyed financially. I had profound mixed feelings about the Chapter 11 experience. But it was a new day for Henco, and we were anxious to begin the next chapter.

When business people and entrepreneurs are on the top of the world and leading the pack, they tend to get the idea that no one can challenge their position. In business, capital flows toward profit centers. When a company is highly profitable, it attracts considerable attention from other business people to get in on the profit. That is exactly what happened to Henco, and the import company took advantage.

We became complacent with our competition, not recognizing we could have changed the dynamics. In Henco's case, I had strong feelings about business being conducted for a win-win for everyone. I felt that no one should be short changed. I still believe that's the right thing to do, even though things can get complicated when you actually try to do the right thing.

***

If you observe geese flying south in early winter, you will notice they all fly in formation, and they know exactly where they are going. The lead goose flies point, and the others follow in a V-shape formation. Their job is to honk encouragement. The lead goose soon will drop back in the formation and another goose will take its place. By flying in formation, each goose gets a minimum of 70 percent more lift, enabling them all to fly much faster and farther. If a goose gets wounded or sick and goes to the ground, two geese drop out of formation and stay alongside the goose until it flies or dies.

God programmed this flight plan into their DNA. Man, on the other hand, has not been programmed. Man has been given free will to make good or bad decisions.

Henco had been in front of the line with a determined effort to make it fair to everyone — a win-win for our company, our employees, the schools and their customers. But if I had the sense of a goose, I would have been the first person to China, checking out opportunities for fundraising products. In an ideal world, it still would not have been a win-win situation, especially for Mrs. Jones, who buys the fundraising items and should get a quality product at a reasonable price. But then you must consider whether maintaining that win-win for all is worth destroying a profitable company with almost 1,000 employees who receive paychecks to support their families. You could say that imports are sure to come to the fundraising industry. So I will be the first one to import the cheaper merchandise and do my best to improve its quality to give Mrs. Jones a good product. It may take a year or two, but with determination, we can achieve the goal in favor of Mrs. Jones and find a true win-win.

Entrepreneurs should realize nothing ever remains the same in business. Competition forces change. We should never become complacent, regardless of how well we are doing. We must think outside the squares, looking for new ways to succeed.

Henco was financially strong with the resources to pioneer the import business to schools. I was too prejudiced against imports because the products were of poor quality, but we could have improved that quality.

A businessman fills needs as he gives people what they want, and you cannot dictate to the American people with your personal, idealistic view. You may say it's not right to sell imports and ship American jobs overseas. If you were to say that to American shoppers, they would be apt to reply: "We want as much mileage as possible from our hard-earned dollars, even if that means buying lesser-quality imports."

With school fundraising, Mrs. Jones was buying the cheaper, overpriced imports because she wanted to support little Johnny next door. But I still think she should have gotten her money's worth.

When our top salespeople left Henco to sell imports, they put their extra commission in their pockets, and so did the school groups. The school groups saw a 50-percent profit, and Mrs. Jones was left holding the bag. We might call that greed.

The fundraising imports grew in quality over time. So I ask: Why can't the Americans compete with China? My simplistic answer is that the corporate tax rate is much too high, and businesses operate in an over-regulated environment.

The son of a friend, who is 10 years old, is industrious. He has a few chickens, and he wants to sell his extra eggs. But he can't sell his eggs at the local farmer's market without a government permit and fee. When I grew up, we sold our eggs, and I thought nothing of it. It is much more complicated to start a new business today than it was in 1960. Today, we have to jump through a lot more hoops to comply with government regulations.

I keep saying that you can measure the wealth of a nation by the freedom it possesses. With more freedom, we have more incentives to get the work done. In my opinion, we are replacing freedom with government nonsense. We must have a lawyer at our side to do business today, and that must change if we are to compete with the countries around the world and keep our jobs at home.

Chapter 22

A New Path With Travels and a Few Emus Along the Way

"Entrepreneurs experience many experiences,
and we educate ourselves with each one."

A fter having been so active in business, being in limbo was different for me. We had successfully emerged from Chapter 11, and we followed the plan filed with the court to pay our creditors. I was ready to try something new, but it would take awhile to settle all debts, and Henco could not start another business until all was settled.

So, we used the time to travel and to try a quite unusual business.

First, we took an extended western trip in our motor home. We visited Las Vegas, the Hoover Dam, Yellowstone National Park and other historic sites. I had traveled in every state on business trips, but had never taken the time to see the sites in a leisurely manner. It was a time for us to relax, rejuvenate ourselves and appreciate our beautiful country.

Back at home, we attended a revival at our Methodist Church. The Reverend Wayne McClain, whom I knew well, came from his home in Slidell, Louisiana, to conduct the services. Wayne was a star basketball player at Selmer High School in the 1950s when the team won state championships. Wayne and I talked after one of the services, and he told me about a project he was working on that was profitable and exciting — the emu business.

I hardly knew what an emu was, much less that the flightless birds could be raised domestically for market. But with my past farming ventures and my agricultural degree, the idea of raising emu chicks for the breeder market interested me.

My friend, Estel Mills, with whom I was drafted into the army and worked with after Korea, had recently retired to his farm in Michie, Tennessee. Estel and his wife, Mary Ruth, were progressive farmers with livestock and pecan and walnut trees. I contacted him, and we investigated Wayne's claims about emus being a profitable venture.

We found out that emus are soft-feathered, brown, flightless birds that reach up to six-and-a-half feet in height. Their long legs allow them to take strides of up to nine feet. Emus use their strongly clawed feet as a defense mechanism. Their legs are among the strongest of any animal, allowing them to rip metal wire fences. Commercial farming began in Western Australia in 1987, and the first slaughtering occurred in 1990.

Ostriches and emus were being raised in a number of states for their meat, leather and oil. We learned that emu meat is lean and similar to venison. It is lower in cholesterol and fat, and it was promoted by the American Heart Association. We also learned that emu oil has anti-inflammatory potential and anti-oxidant properties. People apply the oil to the skin for relief from sore muscles and pain from aching joints. Jewelry and decorative arts and crafts were made from the feathers and eggshells, which are a beautiful jade color. The leather, with its distinctive patterns, is used in small items such as wallets and shoes, often in combination with other leathers.

Emus, apparently, are versatile birds.

We built long open pens for emu pairs in a section of a shady pecan orchard on Estel's farm. Each pen had a feed and water trough, and eventually, we automated the supply of water. In the wild, they drink infrequently, but they take in copious fluids when the opportunity arises. Emus breed well in captivity. So we installed incubators for the eggs in the Mills' garage and planned to sell the chicks when they were about two months old.

After making inquiries of emu breeders and constructing pens, Estel and I traveled to a farm in Texas to launch our project. Emus were expensive in this breeder market. We bought seven pairs at $15,000 each. We handed over our $105,000 check, and prepared to load the birds into our trailer.

Our host emu farmer called his professional bird handlers to the pen. They stepped inside with cautiousness and determination. Emus, when in protective mode, jump high and forward with their legs and their sharp talons, which can rip your skin to the bone. The birds were curious and watched us with large dark eyes and long eyelashes.

The handler grabbed a bird around the neck from the side and straddled it as he held on to its short wings. With a firm grip, he walked the bird out of the pen and towards our trailer. It was a force of wills, but with mighty arms, the emu went into the trailer. The handler had 13 more to load.

It was a workout.

We were astounded with the bird handler's methods and realized the dangers. As farm boys, we led our horses and cows to a pen or trailer with a bridle. When we returned to Estel's farm, I began to brainstorm emu gear to move the bird more easily. After a few inadequate starts, I used nylon webbing similar to a dog's leash and clasps from life vests. I designed the webbing and clasps to adjust to the size of the bird and to form-fit the bird similar to a large dog harness. The harness enabled two people to walk along the side of the bird and guide it in any direction. Most importantly, we could guide the emu from a safe position, and it was not harmful or stressful to the bird. We tested the harness on our emu ranch with great success. We filed for a patent for the design and called it Bird Gear.

Emu and ostrich conventions were held in various states to provide resources and demonstrations, offer retail opportunities, and share farm practices. With bundles of Bird Gear, we McNairy County emu ranchers attended a convention in Texas. We leased a booth and advertised our invention for sale. We produced a video demonstrating the ease of moving and loading emus and received the attention of our fellow ranchers.

During the convention, bird handlers held a live demonstration of controlling emus. They showed off their skills to the amazement of the crowd.

When they finished their demonstration, Estel and I led a large emu around the ring with our Bird Gear. It walked along very calmly, which was an eye-opener for other ranchers. We showed them the best way to safely move an emu.

At the conclusion, we announced that harnesses were available at our booth for only $29. Bird Gear sales boomed. We sold out and took orders.

We advertised Bird Gear in the exotic bird magazines and attended conventions in Tennessee, Missouri and Washington, D.C. We demonstrated the gear and showed how it solved a big problem for ranchers while being safe for emus.

After one convention, a female rancher near Washington, D.C., telephoned me. She asked if we would help her load her emu pair, transport them to a convention at the Hilton Hotel nearby and then take them to the pen inside the hotel's atrium. We said yes. It proved to be an interesting experience.

Sherry and I enjoyed the drive to her farm, and we easily guided her pair into her trailer for the trip to the convention site. At the hotel, the convention's leadership and a local television crew were waiting for the arrival of the star attractions. We pulled up in front of the hotel lobby and attached the Bird Gear on the emu. Out we came toward the front entrance.

With Sherry on one side and me on the other, the tall, long-lashed and wide-eyed brown bird pranced toward the cameras. With a royal demeanor, she walked through the lobby, her clawed feet slipping along on the slick marble floor, to her home away from home — the atrium of the Washington Hilton. The crowd loved every minute. The evening news carried the convention's information and pictured Sherry and me with the emu prancing through the hotel. Our experience was an experience!

We rapidly grew our herd to sell breeder stock. In 1994, we sold our emu chicks for $750,000. The profit was excellent, but the longer we were in the emu business, the more convinced I became that the commercial market would not develop successfully. Breeders sold to each other, which was profitable at the time, but I could not visualize a successful, long-term future.

On a Saturday morning, a young man came to the farm from Georgia. He bought one emu chick for $4,000. As he drove away in his little Pinto, with the back seat out and the bird cooped in the space for the ride home, my thought was that the young man would not get back the money he had invested. I decided that morning that I would find a way out of the emu business. Estel, Mary Ruth and her brother and sister-in-law, Ray and Martha Holt, bought our stake.

Entrepreneurs experience many experiences, and we educate ourselves with each one. As I have said before, risk takers, like me, live exciting and interesting lives. It's a fun life — I would not have made the trip by another route.

***

In 1995, we began to discuss retirement. We thought about traveling in our motor home, spending time at Pickwick Lake and downsizing. Susan and Leigh Anne were well situated in their first careers after earning their degrees from UT. Bob and Terry Parry told us if we ever decided to sell our home on Mollie Drive, they would be interested. I called Bob, and within two weeks, we sold the house to them and made preparations to move after 25 years on the street. We revamped a suite at Henco and quickly made it our Selmer residence until we could find a home at Pickwick.

Our Swedish friends had invited us to visit numerous times. After our move, we began planning a two-week family vacation to Europe with a starting point in England. Sherry's mother loved English history, and she especially enjoyed reading about the monarchy. Sherry's father passed away in March, and we thought it would be meaningful for her mother to come with us. We coordinated with Susan and Leigh Anne and booked a flight in July.

Johan met us in London, and we were thrilled. It had been several months since we had seen him because he was attending Lund University in southern Sweden — his father's alma mater.

Sherry and I had been in London a few years earlier on a Henco awards trip. We were somewhat acquainted with the buses, trains and getting around the city to see the sights. We celebrated Independence Day in downtown London and patriotically waved our American flags in redcoat country.

We rented a traditional black car and drove to the birthplace of Winston Churchill, Blenheim Palace near Oxford and the nearby church in Bladon where Churchill is buried. On the way, we stopped at an inn with a thatched roof and window boxes filled with colorful flowers, and we ate an English breakfast. We visited Oxford with its one-way streets and saw the university and Christ Church. We traveled south to the shore of the English Channel and returned to London in busy traffic. It was quite an experience driving on the opposite side of the highway and maneuvering through the roundabouts. We had a lot of fun in our English car.

From London, we traveled to France on a high-speed passenger train via the Chunnel, the 31-mile tunnel beneath the English Channel at the Straits of Dover connecting England and France. It had just opened the year before. We continued by train to Paris where we explored the picturesque city, visited the Louvre and Versailles and made the most of our brief stay.

We rented a nine-passenger van in Paris and traveled through the countryside dotted with vineyards, sunflowers and sheep to our next adventure — the Alps. We randomly chose a quaint stone inn along our route and stayed overnight. The innkeepers spoke little English, and we did not speak French. Johan knew some words, and with Susan's handbook, we arranged for rooms and ordered our evening meal.

The following day, we stopped at a sizeable market and stocked a cooler with good cheeses, meats, bread and fruit for picnics as we drove through the Alps. The road carried us by picturesque lakes at the edge of the mountains on our way to Lucerne, Switzerland. We walked across the ancient covered bridge and marveled at our surroundings. Johan's knowledge of the German language helped us with our accommodations for the evening. We ate dinner outside, underneath an awning by candlelight. Our surroundings and weather were better than we could have imagined.

We wanted to spend more time in Lucerne, but our next stop was Frankfort, Germany — the largest financial center on the continent and Anders' home at the time. After UT, he completed graduate studies at Essex in England before accepting a position with a multinational corporation based in Frank-fort. We met him at his apartment. He showed us his office and guided us on a tour of the city. We visited a biergarten for apple wine and currywurst, cruised the Rhine River and viewed castles that were several hundred years old over-looking the river.

Anders placed his bag in our passenger van and joined us for the next leg of our journey. We crossed sections of Germany on the autobahn, with Mer-cedes-Benz autos speeding by us at more than 100 miles per hour. We dropped off the van, our Hendrix bus, at the German coastal city of Hamburg. Then we boarded a ferry and crossed the Baltic Sea to the Swedish coast. We took an overnight train to Stockholm, Sweden, and Bo and Anita Widestrand met us at the station.

It was wonderful to see the Widestrands once again. It had been several years since they visited us in Tennessee. They escorted us in their two cars to a photogenic lakeside resort for the evening. The following morning, they made arrangements for us to travel into Stockholm by boat from the resort's pier. The skies were clear, the air was crisp, and it was a grand entrance to the colorful, historic city. After several hours of viewing notable buildings and mar-kets, we returned to prepare for our next day's journey to Tranås, Sweden, and the home of the Widestrands.

The drive from Stockholm to Tranås was picture-postcard perfect. Old barns, homes and cottages painted copper red were interspersed with more modern buildings with yellows and whites. We drove past fields of vibrant yel-low rapeseed, dense forests, dairy cattle farms and age-old steepled churches.

For three days, we scheduled an array of Swedish traditions. Anders and Johan shared their lifestyle with us, and it was terrific for us to experience a small part of it. We shopped in their open-air market and visited the 800-year-old Saby Church, their father's boyhood home and the bank where Anita worked. We saw their school, indulged in their favorite foods and created many memories.

As our vacation was ending, we were escorted by ferry to Copenhagen by our wonderful Swedish friends to experience the picturesque city. We saw the famous statue of the Little Mermaid, inspired by Hans Christian Andersen's fairy tale. We also toured the beautifully landscaped Tivoli Gardens — a famous amusement park and pleasure garden.

After an overnight stay in Copenhagen, we reluctantly said our farewells and boarded a plane for home. Our fast-paced vacation was packed with attractions for all our senses. It was great that our immediate family could be together. Sherry's mother fulfilled a dream. The Widestrands shared their heritage. The trip was educational and immensely gratifying.

***

When we landed stateside, we hit the road again. In those days, we traveled often in our motor home, driving through several states across the country. We were especially fond of our western trips where we spent time in Nevada, New Mexico and Colorado. Some of our sightseeing stops included Taos, the Grand Canyon, Salt Lake City and the Mormon Tabernacle, and the Painted Desert.

During one memorable trip, we joined a caravan through Copper Canyon in Mexico. It was an adventure we will long remember. We traveled through the canyon with the motor home loaded on a flatbed rail car as the track carved its way through the mountains. At night, we disembarked and explored interesting and historical venues as a group. We began our tour with the caravan in El Paso on the Texas border and ended in Nogales, New Mexico.

After a few trips out West, we returned home and planned a trip up the Eastern seaboard, which is especially beautiful in the fall.

Our destination was Old Lyme, Connecticut, the ancestral home of Sherry's maternal family, the Tinkers. It was October 1995. We were accompanied by Sherry's mother, Johnnye Marie Tinker Smith; aunts, Allie Mae Stevens, Mary Sue Carrington and Nellie Jo England; uncle, James Lawson England; sister, Jonetta Smith Vise; and cousin, Nancy Burton Ivy. Family members boarded our motor home in Parsons, Tennessee, and we began our journey to the Northeast.

Tom stands at the door of the motor home.

We traveled along the Shenandoah Valley, through Washington, D.C., and New York City, and we reached Old Lyme's historic district and cemetery where several Tinker ancestors are buried. Sherry's cousin, Allen Tinker, who lives in Vermont, met us at the cemetery to share family history. At the picturesque cemetery, which also contains the gravesites of original settlers, we shared an emotional and special time together. Jonetta kept a journal.

"Had a refreshing picnic lunch under the trees with the leaves falling, decorating our table and blanketing the ground," she wrote. "We felt we were standing on Holy Ground."

Their ancestor, Nathan Tinker, fought in the Revolutionary War.

The following day, we traveled to New London, Connecticut, and toured one of New England's oldest and best-documented dwellings. It's made of two buildings: the 1678 Joshua Hempsted House and the 1759 Nathaniel Hempsted House.

Joshua Hempsted lived there his whole life. He filled many roles and recorded events and the weather in his diary daily for a lifetime. His diary has served as a wonderful resource for later generations. The Tinker family is thankful because he recorded events pertaining to their ancestors.

From New London, we returned to Old Lyme and Old Saybrook. We then took a scenic route north along the Connecticut River to admire the fall colors. At East Haddam, Connecticut, we ate lunch and toured the home of the historic Goodspeed Opera House, which opened in 1877 next to the Connecticut River. With history buffs and educators in our family group, we also toured the Nathan Hale School House, one of two in Connecticut.

After two full days in the Tinker homeland, traveling back in time, we said goodbye to Allen and began our trip home. The returning leg of our journey carried us through six states: Connecticut, New Jersey, New York, Pennsylvania, West Virginia and Kentucky. I was the chauffer for the entire ride, and Sherry was our navigator, reservation clerk and hostess. Her relatives rested in the evenings at hotels, and we sought camping facilities to service the motor home. We had picnics at roadside parks. We ate dinner at nice restaurants. Sherry's aunts enjoyed singing hymns and their favorite popular songs as we drove along, sharing childhood memories and having discussions about their family tree.

We said goodbye to Sherry's family and returned to Selmer. The trip became a treasured memory.

Then, as temperatures in Tennessee dropped, the prospect of warm, sunny days in southern Florida beckoned us. We packed our summer clothes and headed to Naples for a few weeks.

After Florida, we decided to explore the southern part of Texas and Padre Island for the remaining winter months.

I have always been appreciative of being mobile and active. Our country has a wealth of beautiful and historic areas to explore, and we generally don't take the time for them. Our 42-foot motor home was spacious. With its amenities, it was our home away from home. And, with our car in tow, we explored it all.

CHAPTER 23

A RETIREMENT PROJECT
WORTH THE DRIVE

*"Experiencing experiences is the best way to live
and grow a notch or two."*

After traveling to different parts of the country, I began to ponder my next project. Sherry and I discussed retirement, but I did not want to retire at age 65 — the most productive time of my life. I did not want to spend my time going to the next town, which could look a lot like the town I just left. We met many families along the way who had sold their homes, purchased a motor home and traveled throughout the country, creating a somewhat unusual lifestyle in their retirement years. Their winters might be in Florida and their summers in Colorado. There is certainly nothing wrong with this lifestyle, but I felt I could do better.

I felt it was time to get back to work and do something that was worth my life. In my opinion, if you are not making a contribution, you are not living. All we have in this life is time, and the best way to spend your time is doing something special for others. When we give time to something, we are giving a part of our life. Your work must be special.

We searched for a new business idea that we could feel happy pursuing. I laid awake at night thinking about possibilities. Finally, we decided on retail furniture — partly because I wanted to try my hand at a new experience.

The Henco property consisted of 300,000 square feet of office and warehouse space that was debt-free. The primary question was whether we could motivate families to drive to Selmer's industrial park, traveling past furniture stores on the way. Could we create a happening, become a destination store and entice families to drive long distances to furnish their home?

It's impossible to see the future clearly. That's why we call it risk taking.

As we brainstormed the idea, we wondered if we could create the most up-to-date furniture store in the Mid-South. We wanted a store that would be so much fun that the kids would cry when it was time to leave for home. We did not have any retail furniture experience and would begin with a clean slate. At least we did not have any bad retail habits.

With strong desires and goals, we proceeded to buy some furniture pieces from a business in north Mississippi. We arranged the pieces in a section of our warehouse space and began our learning experience.

We felt that although we knew nothing about selling furniture, Sherry and I knew how we would like to be treated if we were furnishing our home. If we could create that experience, families would like our service.

The venture required opening an operation with the bare essentials. We could only offer goods for cash or checks with local delivery. We did not offer financing. We placed a relatively small advertisement in the *Independent Appeal,* our county's weekly newspaper, and prepared for a small number of customers. We did not want to be overwhelmed at our initial opening.

Henco Furniture's opening day came, and went, with no customers.

At about 3 p.m., our friend, Gary Kerby, who owned a neighboring business, stopped by.

"How is everything going?" He asked.

"You are the first person to come in today," we said.

After Gary left, we sat in a couple of glider rockers and discussed what might be ahead of us. The day was a stark reminder of the difficulties of opening a retail furniture business in the Selmer Industrial Park. It rekindled my determination to create a happening in the park — one that would make us proud. Sherry, as always, stood by my side, and we found inspiration to build our dream store.

During the first few months, problems arose that I had not anticipated. For example, major furniture manufacturers, such as La-Z-Boy and Lexington, would not return my phone calls. When manufacturers asked where our store was located, and I replied the Selmer Industrial Park, they were pessimistic. Furniture representatives who came to check us out thought we would never succeed with our lack of experience and poor location. They were not excited about selling us furniture to say the least.

I realized I had to put on my selling britches and show them a determined person who would build a successful business in spite of the address and lack of furniture retail experience. If a vendor was negative, I faced him head on to change his outlook. With my new determination, their attitudes turned positive.

I went to Action Lane's home office and manufacturing plant in Tupelo, Mississippi, and met with one of their top people in management. After they checked my credit, I asked for a solid commitment to stock their line of furniture, and they agreed for Henco to be a dealer.

In October 1996, we went to the International Home Furnishings Market in High Point, North Carolina, and sought commitments from other major vendors. We convinced Lexington, a prestigious line with name recognition and affordable prices, to set us up as a dealer. We also contacted Drexel Heritage, which was one of the higher quality lines in the furniture industry. These top lines gave other vendors confidence to do business with us.

The furniture reps began talking about the guy in Selmer, Tennessee, with big plans in the furniture business. I painted a picture and laid out our plan to visit the top stores in the nation and ask them to be our teachers as we designed our furniture business. Our vendors changed their minds and wanted us to stock their lines. Soon, they were knocking on our door from far and wide.

Sherry and I were definitely not skilled furniture buyers, and we were not astute at reading the pulse of our customer. We made some bad buys, but we learned quickly from our mistakes. We asked our most trusted vendors to help us, and they did. I warned them if they sold us furniture that wouldn't sell, this would be our last buy from their company. They began to look out for us.

And this time around, we were smarter about imports. Many companies fought them instead of asking how they could retail the imported furniture with a better price and do their best to improve the quality over time. We watched furniture companies in the United States resisting change as they went broke.

Shoppers sometimes asked me where the furniture was manufactured.

"Is your furniture imported? I want American-made furniture."

I explained that they could be out of luck. We stocked furniture that sold, and many of our products happened to be made in other countries. We would show them an American-made bedroom suite and compare it to an imported suite across the aisle. The imported suite sold for 30 or 40 percent less, and the quality was about the same. Customers purchased the less-expensive suite 90 percent of the time.

***

After we were able to buy top brands of furniture, we thought it was time to expand our knowledge and learn from the pros of the industry. We devised a plan to locate and visit the most admired and up-to-date furniture stores in the country. So we hooked the Jeep behind the motor home and began our journey.

Upon arrival at a store, with our yellow pad in hand, we explained who we were — that we had just entered the retail furniture business and that I had come out of retirement at 65 to develop the store. We also shared our goal to create the most up-to-date furniture store in the Mid-South. We needed all the help we could get, and we asked them to fill our yellow pad with good ideas that had made their stores so successful.

In almost every case, they responded in disbelief.

"Do you know what you're getting into?"

"Probably not, but I need your best ideas," I replied. "We're students, and we're here to learn as much as possible. I have always believed that if you want a cool drink of water, go to the head of the stream. That's the reason we're here."

Without fail, the store manager or owner would stay with us and share information he or she thought would be helpful, along with policies and procedures. After a day of exploration, talking with employees and gathering brochures, we left with their telephone number to call them if we needed.

Sherry and I visited megastores that generated $50 million to $100 million per year in sales. Some were owned by Warren Buffett. Sherry seemed to understand the furniture business better than me. I saw right away that she had an eye for furniture and store design. She was a much better buyer than I was, and I relied on her judgment.

After our extensive travels to larger-than-life stores in Virginia, Nebraska, Texas, New York, Massachusetts, Colorado, Florida and Mississippi, we recognized their differences, but saw a common thread of uniqueness. All had a special calling card and a deep-seated philosophy about their brand of service.

One unique store was Green Front Furniture in Farmville, Virginia. Richard Cralle, fresh from college, was given the task of overseeing operations of this relatively new venture in the mid 1960s by his father. He learned to buy and ship goods directly to save customers money. He paid cash wherever he could to avoid debt, and he chose a location that was more rustic than ornate. It featured 12 massive tobacco warehouses acquired with the help of the city. Slowly and steadily, the store grew into its success story of today. Now, customers up and down the East Coast and across the nation cram into warehouses full of stunning Oriental rugs and furniture pieces from all corners of the globe. He did it all with little advertising — just word of mouth, an excellent reputation and a love for an honest deal.

Most of the warehouses were not heated or cooled. All they had was furniture at the best price.

When Sherry and I visited, we saw large yellow arrows on the street directing people to Green Front Furniture. The store's shoppers brought new businesses to the small, once-dying town. It reminded me that entrepreneurs have done so much for this country — creating untold numbers of jobs and waking up little towns that have died on the vine. We need more entrepreneurs to create jobs and spread the wealth.

***

In Selmer, we were determined to keep our expenses to the bare minimum. To save money during the winter months, for example, we kept the thermostat at about 50 degrees. If someone appeared to be cold, I had a supply of coats on hand.

"We keep our thermostat low because all costs are passed on to the customer through the price of the furniture," I would say. "If you wear this jacket, you can save a lot of money."

Customers would laugh and wear the jacket. We no doubt had the best prices around.

To promote the store, we bought small spreader knives and gave one to each person who made a purchase. The inscription on the handle read: "Henco Furniture — Spread the Word."

"I want to thank you for your business and make a special presentation to you today," I said as I gave a customer a knife. "With this little spreader knife, I want you to become our official word spreader in your family and your community, which will help Sherry and me build our business. Will you be one of our official word spreaders?"

With my fun presentation, we would have a big laugh. Customers left with their spreader knife and a special kinship to our store. The next time they came to see us, so many of them would say they've been spreading the word and sending us business. I would hug their neck and warmly thank them. Sherry and I celebrated their presence and their actions on behalf of our business.

Our official word spreaders were doing an unbelievable job helping build our business. Our sales grew each month as more and more people talked about Henco Furniture in the middle of the Selmer Industrial Park.

"It's like finding a pot of gold!" They said.

***

In the beginning, Sherry and I did sales. Sherry kept track of them and handled the paperwork involved. Our long-time, loyal Henco fundraising employee and friend, Grady Barnes, helped me load furniture and make deliveries.

I came up with the idea of renting billboards on Highway 45 north and south of Selmer, as well as Highways 57 and 64, which run east and west. I telephoned a billboard company for monthly rental prices and learned they were $400 to $800 per billboard.

"We're going to build our own billboards," I told Grady. "I need to find landowners who will agree to having one on their property in areas where they qualify for a state permit."

I talked with landowners where a billboard would qualify. I explained that I would pay $200 per year, and if they needed the land back for any reason, I would remove the sign in two weeks without question. One landowner said, "It's free — build your sign."

We drew a plan for the billboard to be 10 feet by 36 feet. I went to Pickwick Electric Cooperative to ask about their discarded utility poles. Grady and I built the billboard in two days. Grady did the measuring and cutting, and I climbed a ladder to nail everything in place. With a little practice, I drove those nails like I once did on the farm. Paying $200 per year for a billboard was much better than $800 per month. There are many ways to cut costs in building a business.

We then secured a 48-foot billboard on the busy Highway 45 Bypass in Jackson, across from Walmart. We thought it could effectively communicate our message to a large number of West Tennessee families. Sherry wanted the colors to be American-flag red, white and blue with yellow wording for emphasis. We wanted our message to be simple, with as few words as possible so drivers could read it while zooming by.

The Jackson billboard company called and said the layout was ready for our approval. Upon arrival, it was exactly as we had envisioned it.

"We need directions to the store on the bottom of the board, and I have some suggestions," the designer told me.

I looked over three of them and had an idea.

"Put Selmer — It's Worth the Drive!"

I don't know how that idea came to my mind. I had been looking for a connective statement as a slogan that would encourage families to make the drive to Selmer.

"Do you think they can find your store?" The designer asked.

"We'll see," I replied.

We began driving south on Highway 45, returning to the store and talking about how things were falling into place. We felt more positive than ever that we were on track to build one of the most-up-to-date furniture stores in the Mid-South.

After we got our furniture legs under us, and our customer base grew, we decided with confidence that we were ready to expand our efforts. Our next step was television advertisements to reach a broader market in West Tennessee and parts of Mississippi, Arkansas and Missouri. We began advertising with WBBJ, an ABC-affiliate in Jackson, about 40 minutes north of Selmer.

I had taught salesmanship and built two national sales forces. I knew I could communicate after I became more relaxed in front of the camera and lights. It was important that we write our own TV ads because we knew more about our store than anyone. It was our story, and we felt we should tell it with strong feelings.

I did not know anything about writing television commercials. However, I thought it best to follow my instincts — just tell our story before the camera. I knew our commercials would not be the slickest ads on TV, but they would be truthful and explain our service in simple language. A simple message would be best in the long run. I ended each television ad with a big smile and our slogan: "It's worth the drive!"

I had been interviewed on television through the years and was comfortable in front of a camera. Television ads, however, were different. They were time-sensitive and allowed only 15 or 30 seconds to communicate your service.

Too many times, we had too much to say, which made it a contest to complete the script without being rushed.

It was difficult.

With the bright spotlights turned on, I stood ready to perform my lines. Then someone noticed my nose needed makeup. We began to proceed only to stop to straighten my tie.

"You need to straighten your shoulders a bit, too," I was told.

By this time, I almost forgot my lines. As I began to deliver them, the videographer stopped me again.

"I'm sorry, but you need to go a little faster," he ordered.

Then I overdid it, and he told me to slow down to pick up two seconds.

"Yes, I am relaxed and smiling," I thought, with the bright lights shining in my face.

After a while, I adapted to all those nonsensical things. Many times, I delivered my lines correctly, with strong feelings, on the first take.

Our TV ads brought families from six states to see what we were all about. At the outset, it was a problem to communicate the size and scope of our store. We produced a television spot with me walking across the top of our 200,000-square-foot building to help everyone visualize what was under the roof. Next, we produced an ad picturing me walking along the 50-yard line of the football field at the Liberty Bowl stadium. In the spot, I said our store had four football fields of furniture. We received many comments about the two ads. They certainly communicated the overall size of Henco Furniture and the scope of our large showroom.

My daughter, Susan, joined me in developing the ads. She was much better than me in the beginning. She was a natural before the camera. Families loved her, and they especially loved my grandchildren, Sarah Catherine and Sean. Susan and her children adapted to the spotlights and cameras much quicker than me. Sarah Catherine and Sean thought it was great fun.

After our five-year-old grandson did his first ad, he sat in my lap.

"Papa Tom, I'm a TV star," he said.

"Who told you that?"

"My buddy," he replied.

They liked the attention from their friends at school. We would go into a restaurant, and people would ask if they had seen them on TV. I thought it was a good experience for them — a confidence builder. Who knows, they may one day anchor a nightly news broadcast. Experiencing experiences is the best way to live and grow a notch or two. I certainly did.

At the end of one of the TV ads, our videographer said we were short.

"We need about 10 more seconds of verbiage for this ad to be at 30 seconds," he told me.

"Don't be surprised if someone offers you a fresh-baked cookie as you shop," I responded.

"That's perfect," he said.

After finishing the commercial and driving away, I thought, we're going to be in the cookie business big time. What will Sherry think about serving freshly baked cookies?

We wanted our customers to feel welcomed and at home. We used the employee lounge from fundraising days as a space for shoppers to get soft drinks from vending machines. On weekends, we served free hot dogs. After traveling or shopping for a couple of hours, children could be satisfied with a snack. When we advertised freshly baked cookies for our customers, we added another dimension as to why our store was worth the drive.

***

I can't emphasize enough the importance of our slogan to the success of Henco Furniture. Wherever I went, people I did not know would say, "it's worth the drive," when greeting me. One lady from Memphis telephoned me at the office and said she had forgotten the name of the store. She told me she called her neighbor and asked about the "worth the drive" store. Her neighbor said, "Henco Furniture in Selmer. Here's their number!"

Many families approached me in the showroom.

"I have heard so much about your store," they said. "I wanted to see it, even though I don't need furniture now."

These families were some of our best word spreaders.

"Henco — it's worth the drive" was remembered more than Henco Furniture. Everyone seemed to have fun with the statement. They seemed to feel a part of it.

One Sunday morning, Sherry and I found ourselves in Memphis. I hadn't eaten at an IHOP restaurant in a long time, so I suggested we try the one on Germantown Parkway. It was a beautiful morning, the restaurant was full, and Sherry and I waited to be seated. As the hostess directed us to our table, a group of women stood and gave us a round of applause. They called me Mr. Henco. Then the men stood.

"It's worth the drive!" They shouted.

I had everyone's attention.

"When you lay down those forks, get in your car and head to Henco!" I called. "These people have said it's worth the drive!"

The crowd followed that with laughter and more applause. It was a new, pleasant experience. There wasn't a dull moment in building our business.

***

I have never had a business course, and I certainly have no formal knowledge in marketing. But I do believe marketing is mostly about common sense and empathy. In marketing, you must be a master communicator with a good understanding of people. Also, I prefer a straightforward message to educate people about our service. It's not trickery or cleverness. It's good, honest communication.

When people come to your business, they should not be disappointed — they should be pleasantly surprised. Television ads, in the simplest terms, must describe you and your service without a bunch of hype. Too many times people hype beyond a clear view of their service.

To stay on track, I often surveyed families.

"Do my ads accurately describe our Henco service?" I would ask.

"This store is way beyond what I envisioned," they would reply. "Your ads don't do justice to your store."

These kinds of statements were appreciated because families made the long drive and were not disappointed. They were pleasantly surprised. Their shopping experience began with a positive attitude. Thus, they were more apt to make a purchase and spread the word to their families and community.

We spent up to $50,000 per month on television ads to tell our story to audiences in Jackson, Memphis and Tupelo, Mississippi. It wasn't long before everyone knew Henco Furniture was worth the drive.

We sat in those two glider rockers that first day, frustrated that we didn't have any customers. After our television campaign, I was a household name, and business was booming.

CHAPTER 24
HOMETOWN USA

*"Life is wonderful when you surround yourself
with people smarter than you."*

"It's worth the drive!" the newspaper article began, and continued …
"When you step inside the showroom doors, shoppers are astounded with the sights and sounds of a replica of a small West Tennessee town, Henco's 'Hometown USA' and the aroma of freshly baked cookies. Complete with storefronts, park benches, trees and a waterfall, you feel as if you've gone back in time to the 1950s era. Young visitors are delighted, during the weekends, when Henco's mascot, Happy the Hippo, who is 'big on savings,' meets them on Main Street and blows them kisses or is seen dancing with their Dad to the music of Danny Churchwell, a local musician.

"Just beyond the stone arch of the train trestle topped with a silhouette of a steam train on one side and a red caboose on the other is Henco's Whistle Stop Café featuring gourmet soups, salads and sandwiches while boasting its house specialty — fried green tomatoes … Adjacent to the Café is a 1950s-style soda fountain where homemade ice cream, milkshakes and floats are served to anyone young at heart.

"Rumor has it that you can even buy furniture at the store."

***

Henco Furniture had become more than a furniture store. It was a destination. People could eat, visit with friends, spend a Saturday afternoon or even hold a civic club meeting. And many of them bought furniture. Sherry and I shared the credit, though, for creating a furniture store that offered fun as well

311

as bargains. Our journey to become a destination, where it was "worth the drive" to Selmer's Industrial Park to buy furniture at a bargain, required the vision and hard work of many people.

Sherry and I were fortunate to have talented employees at Henco Furniture. Many were old friends with whom we had worked closely with for 20 or 30 years during Henco's fundraising days. They were just a phone call away and happy to quit their jobs to join our newest mission of service. Like me, they did not know anything about retail furniture, but it wasn't a problem because they understood Henco's long-term service philosophy.

I have often said that a company cannot rise above its people. Henco Furniture's strength was its people. They wanted to be a part of our vision. They were talented and motivated with proven skills. Their attitude of service, doing something special for customers, drove the business.

I couldn't hire all my old Henco colleagues at once. It was important to start small lest we become too big for our britches. I had strong feelings about expanding a profit center and not an activity center. It was important for Sherry and me to learn the furniture business, especially the sales side, before expanding so we could lead people intelligently.

Grady Barnes was with us at the very beginning. Grady came to work at Henco out of high school and had spent his career with the company. With his wonderful attitude, he could do just about anything, or he would give it his best shot. From maintenance work to erecting billboards and delivering furniture, or rescuing me when my car failed or I lost a key, he was there when I needed him. He would help seven days a week if needed, and he was excited about our new furniture store.

The store grew while Sherry, Grady and I did the day-to-day work.

We asked Anita Graham to join us and take care of accounts payables and receivables and payroll. As my executive assistant in the fundraising business, she and I had worked together well for many years. She was a dedicated and loyal assistant in my many ventures, and her responsibilities included a myriad of details.

Anita Graham

Our warehouse and delivery operation was a beehive of activity. I telephoned Jim Tucker and asked him to come for an interview. He was a unique individual and flew the company's jet for years. He had an aeronautical engineering degree and was a naval commander with thousands of flight hours. Jim also was a mathematician who projected product flow. After our meeting, Jim agreed to manage warehouse and delivery and project our furniture purchases.

Bob Brooks came to my office more than once, expressing his interest in helping us carry out our vision for the store. I had put Bob off because we were determined to keep our expenses as low as possible. But he was persistent.

"Pay me what you can afford," he said. "I want to help you build this business."

I was eager for him to join Henco Furniture, so we worked out a plan. After a short time, Bob had learned the business and became general sales manager. He was well-qualified to lead our sales effort, integrating the Henco service philosophy. He was an excellent teacher and had the skills to hire the right people to teach the business.

Bob immediately said that we needed to hire Gene Hébert. Bob and Gene had worked together for years. Gene was a top salesman as a fundraiser, and then a regional sales manager. He had strong sales and management skills, and he was an outstanding band director before joining Henco in 1975.

With leadership from Bob and Gene, I could leave the store for periods of time and rest assured that the operation would run smoothly. They did not call me; they simply made decisions to meet customers' needs. If I did not agree with their decision, we could discuss it later. But that was rare.

So many times when leaving the store, I told them to run the business as if they owned the place. I wanted our Henco team to be decisive, whether I was there or not. After all, they knew as much about the operation as I did.

Again, with outstanding employees, it cannot be a one-man show. Capable and talented people want to be a part of the action, making operational decisions when needed. If they know you will back up their decision, they will be more decisive.

I also called Loretta Hendrix, my sister-in-law. She joined Henco in 1971 to wrap our cylinder candles with the acetate wrappers, and she supervised a sizeable office staff for more than 20 years. Loretta oversaw clerical operations and customer service. She had the experience and confidence to hire and train people. She was an ideal person for this position, and it fit her natural talents. Loretta had an energetic mind and observed the entire company with strong ideas as to how things should be done. She could work well with all the departments for a speedy result and better customer service.

Loretta's experience and business background made her effective with our vendors. She made sure they lived up to their promises to our customers. I knew we would not get it right every time with our customers because there were so many hands in the details. But we would try.

"If it's not right, make it right for our customer," I told her. "We don't want them talking bad about us in their communities."

Loretta walked a tight rope. She was creative and went the extra mile to satisfy customers without driving up costs, because all costs are passed on in the price of the product. She did an amazing job, and in so many cases, her resolution of a customer-service problem resulted in some of our most loyal shoppers. They knew we cared about them and that we would go the extra mile for them.

In my judgment, you cannot build a successful furniture business with repeat business without a sensitive, caring and capable customer service department.

One of our most popular salespeople turned out to be the widow of a friend who rented office space near my office. David Weaver was diagnosed with advanced cancer; the disease had progressed to the point that nothing could be done for him, and his doctor gave him only a short time to live.

"How can I help?" I asked him.

"I just want to come into my office as long as I can," he said. "The days seem better here than spending long hours at home."

We delivered a comfortable recliner to his office so he could stretch out and relax. I made it a practice to ask him questions that encouraged him to think through his situation.

"When you think of death, what are your thoughts?"

"I am a Christian," David said. "I don't fear death, but my biggest concern is my wife's financial situation. We have just gone through a business reversal."

Donna, his wife, had helped him in his business, never working anywhere else. I understood his concern.

"David, Sherry and I need someone to help sell furniture, and Donna could be very good with our customers," I told him.

"Tom, she doesn't have experience as a furniture salesman."

"I think we can teach her how to be a star salesman," I replied.

David died a short time later.

After giving Donna time to grieve, we asked her to interview with us. We hired her, and she was one of the kindest people to ever join our team. When a customer came to the store, she met them with a big, sincere smile and helpful attitude.

At first, she had problems giving the store greeting as outlined, which was an overview to start the sales process. But after a while, she got better. During our sales meetings, she was proud to show off her skills. Many customers asked for Donna to help them when they returned to the store.

The leader of a company does not do the work. The work is done through people. It was a big asset to have talented employees with proven skills help build Henco Furniture. Too many times I received too much credit for the success of the company. When I finish sharing with all our talented people, I don't have much left to gloat over — as it should be. I often have thought that I did nothing to develop the tools I use — telephones, computers, trucks or planes. I share my success with everyone who has had a hand in it. It keeps me humble.

I have thought about how being thankful helps one see more clearly the picture we are trying to paint. None of us are as thankful as we should be.

***

After touring the country in our motor home and visiting furniture stores, we decided on Jordan's Furniture in Natick, Massachusetts, as our model. Inside the store, Jordan's recreated Bourbon Street with realistic-looking facades surrounding entertaining elements that were fun for the whole family. From their Streetcar Named Dessert ice cream bar to their full-sized riverboat, the Natick store was much more than just a store. It was an experience.

Each day, Jordan's staged a Mardi Gras effects show on Bourbon Street. Smoke billowed, lights flashed and animatronic robots put on a musical event worthy of true Louisiana spirit. Occupying a substantial corner of the building was a particularly friendly restaurant — a longtime favorite of patrons. We took note of how shoppers entered the restaurant from the store's Bourbon Street to enjoy a beverage or meal.

We spent a great deal of time exploring possibilities, and so did our operational people. Jordan's system was the most up-to-date we had found, and they were willing to share a great deal with us. They were generous, helpful and patient.

Many of our Henco employees were creative with ideas of their own, and we sent key people to visit Jordan's. Teresa Parris, our interior designer and furniture buyer, went with Bob Brooks to tour it. After two days, they returned with a lot of enthusiasm as their creative minds churned with ideas for our Selmer Industrial Park location.

Loretta Hendrix was the next person to visit, and she delved into details with the store manager and learned as much as possible in regard to the operational side of the business. Sherry and I made one more trip to see the store manager. We asked numerous questions, and once again, the manager was helpful. I always have appreciated the generosity of business people being open with one another. Some trade secrets are held back, but for the most part, they will help you if you know how to approach them.

We took what we learned from Jordan's and set out to create a unique showroom for Henco Furniture. It would be a destination — an experience.

***

Our daughter, Susan, and her husband, Patrick, moved from Nashville to West Tennessee and joined our team to help build the new showroom. Patrick was the ideal person to oversee construction and lead the team. With degrees from Florida State University in finance and real estate, he was a qualified property appraiser. He also had been a regional director in a cellular business with the responsibility of locating sites and overseeing construction of cell towers.

I prepared our staff, as part of their job description, to teach Patrick their departmental job descriptions. I told them I was certain he would be a quick study, and as soon as he was up to speed, he would be our new company president.

Patrick was a welcomed relief for me. It gave me more time to promote the store and greet as many families as possible in the store — a full-time job.

I felt our team was complete, but we had some shortcomings.

Patrick's objectives in the beginning were three fold: furnish leadership to the construction of our showroom, learn the business from our management team and modernize our operation. Our software was not working effectively. It didn't give us the information we needed to run a large furniture operation. This was Patrick's cup of tea — make what had been a weakness into one of our strongest assets. For that matter, everyone was excited about our creative new store and wanted to have their say in what it should be one day. I appreciated their interest and listened attentively.

***

Spurred by the Bourbon Street theme at Jordan's, we brainstormed the idea of a small-town main street, a replica of hometowns in the Mid-South. We wanted to build a park in the middle with a waterfall that carried soothing sounds. The street would be a space to relax, serving as a gathering place and a connecting pathway to different showrooms with entrances that looked like storefronts.

We called our idea Hometown USA. We thought it would be something our customers would enjoy and appreciate. And we felt we were fully capable of building our vision. If we could visualize it, we certainly could build it with Patrick leading the way.

Our showroom was a huge warehouse with no frills in the beginning. We had great prices, quality furniture and attracted many customers. But with so much furniture, it was difficult for our customers to find their way through to what they were looking for. Some families left without buying anything when all along, we had what they wanted.

One of my objectives was to simplify the shopping experience so people could find what they wanted. Our hometown showroom would be designed for people to take a walk down Main Street. On the way, they would pass shops. The "State Theater," for example, offered home entertainment and office furniture. The "Turning Inn Bed and Breakfast" was filled with bedroom suites. "Silver Spoons Fine Dining" offered the best in dining room furniture, while "Reid More Library" was filled with leather furniture. With these different sections of the showroom, people could easily find what they wanted.

We wanted Henco Furniture to be a beautiful store, but we also wanted it to make sense so customers could make smart decisions. Shoppers would be able to access our catalogs with information about the furniture in each section, and we would work to keep the catalog prices current. We were placing an enormous amount of furniture at customers' fingertips.

***

We interviewed architects to find a person who was creative and comfortable thinking outside the squares. We were impressed with Richard Rohn's free flow of ideas as we discussed our vision, and we felt he would work in harmony with our team.

Knowing that our architectural design would require artistic scenes and murals, we began to search for an artist. We telephoned friends, business associates, universities and state leaders and described our vision. We heard Victor Moore's name mentioned several times. He lived in nearby Henderson.

I called Victor and asked him to visit me at Henco. Victor sat on the edge of his seat with intense interest as we told him what we had in mind. At the end of our discussion, I continued a line of questions and learned as much as I could about him. As we talked, we became more comfortable with one another.

"If I can afford you, I think we might be able to work together on this project," I told him.

"Tom, I'm the right person for this project and wouldn't want to miss working on it. Let me go home and put some ideas together for our next meeting."

Teresa Parris joined Patrick and me in our next meeting with Victor to get a glimpse of what he proposed. Afterward, we were convinced that he was the man for us.

I asked Richard Rohn to visit Jordan's to see the bigger-than-life store before sketching a preliminary drawing of our Hometown USA showroom. He returned in a few days and presented a sketch of the Main Street and the storefronts. It was exciting! I shook his hand and said: "Let's build it!"

Patrick and I had been having conversations with building contractors and decided to work with Richard Mitchell because we felt he could work successfully with our assembled team. I knew Richard's family and his good reputation as a builder. He had the necessary equipment to do our construction.

With our team in place and the architectural rendering of the street, we were ready to brainstorm each storefront. We discussed exactly how it would be constructed — examining the overall design, signage and color combinations — to produce what we envisioned.

Patrick and Teresa had several meetings about construction and building materials. When I met with Teresa, her creative ideas were flowing. Sherry was in the loop every step of the way, sharing her thoughts. She chaired the committee to select themes for the different storefronts and whimsical names. It was exciting to see their creative minds at work.

Of course, I was concerned about construction costs, so we met regularly to review them. Because it was a creative trip, it was difficult to bid the construction. Richard Mitchell and Richard Rohn told me what they thought it could be built for and how long it would take to complete. The store remained open throughout construction, and we frequently rearranged our showroom floor and draped sheets of plastic as temporary walls and entrances. We dealt with hammers pounding, saws running and the smell of paint as we worked with customers to keep their experience enjoyable. The project still was a hindrance to the sales effort.

Construction projects of any kind, in my experience, rarely stay on schedule, especially an unusual project like ours. It took almost twice as long to complete as projected, and costs almost doubled. But I am not pointing a finger at anyone. Everyone worked diligently to build the showroom as quickly as possible, and we didn't want to sacrifice quality because customers would see the finished product close up. It had to look great.

The final venue our showroom needed was a café. When we visited Jordan's, it was obvious that its restaurant was well attended by shoppers. Other megastores we visited also had restaurants or snack bars and play areas for children to enhance the shopping experience. The town of Selmer was established after the railroad was built in the late 1800s, so a connecting passageway in our showroom was treated as a train trestle with an artistic faux train engine above the archway. We designed the restaurant to look like a train's dining car, and at Sherry's suggestion, we called it Henco's Whistle Stop Café.

I found Henco's Whistle Stop Café to be special in many ways. As I pictured a couple sitting at a table, I wanted them to view our beautiful storefronts on Main Street to entice them to begin shopping as quickly as they finished their meal. The café's service complemented Henco's good service. We served delicious food and made the experience enjoyable for the entire family. People would make the long drive and head to the Whistle Stop for lunch. After a sale, we would direct them into the café for a complimentary lunch or treat little Johnny to an ice cream cone to keep him happy.

***

Brainstorming a project, with creative juices flowing, is one of the most fun things one can do, and it is amazing what can materialize from freewheeling sessions. We made Henco Furniture one of the most creative stores in the country. We walked around the spotted cow, and people told us how she looked from their side. It was fun!

When we dedicated Henco's Hometown USA, the press and a large crowd of people attended. Cars filled our parking lot, and we had to create overflow spaces on the grassy areas under the pine trees in front of our building. Grady shuttled people to the showroom in a golf cart. Tears came to my eyes as I shared the helpfulness of numerous people who had assisted us in building Henco Furniture. I wished those guiding voices, our mentors, could have been there to witness what they had helped create.

Henco was so different it made good conversation among friends and neighbors. They liked to talk about their furniture finds and our new show-room, and they kept sending us business.

***

As a child walking about on our farmland, I liked the looks and aromas of the timber. As I grew older, hauling and bunching logs, my favorite tree was the oak tree. I wanted beautiful oak trees through the central park area of our Main Street. So I called Victor.

"Have you ever made an oak tree?" I asked.

He laughed. "Tom, I have never made an oak tree."

"Victor, I want you to think about beautiful oak trees up and down our park all night long, and tomorrow, I will call you for some tree talk."

The next day, I called and asked, "Victor, what do you have for me?"

"Tom, the kids and I are headed to the saw mill to gather oak bark, and we are going to make some of the most beautiful oak trees for Henco's park."

"That sounds great!" I exclaimed. "What are you going to do for the tree limbs and branches?"

"We will take them off the trees in our back lot," he responded.

Victor and his family carried those beautiful oak trees in a long trailer behind his car, and his children helped him bring them inside the showroom. They glued bark to a form of heavy cardboard, about 24 inches in diameter, to resemble the trunk. They secured the limbs and attached silk leaves. The trees looked real, just like the oak trees in the forest when I bunched logs as a teenager. They were perfect and certainly received more attention than anything in the showroom. During the holiday season, we attached strings of miniature lights to the branches for a great atmosphere.

I tell this tree story to share credit. I could not make an oak tree, but Victor and his family could. That is the way the magnificent showroom was created. I often say I received too much credit for the development of Henco and Henco Furniture. The talented hands around me always made me look good.

When I walked barefooted behind the mules and plow, I never dreamed I would be able to work with so many creative and talented people to help me reach my goals in life. Life is wonderful when you surround yourself with people smarter than you. They help pave the way so you can follow your mission, and your mission becomes their mission. As an entrepreneur, I realized how dependent I was on help from others.

CHAPTER 25

A MISSION OF SERVICE

*"A person with a servant attitude finds ways
to go beyond the call of duty."*

With work, I have found it best to find something that excites your imagination, something that makes you happy. Find a great service for the benefit of many people and educate yourself to do it well. Making a living never made much sense to me. If you have a service mission in life and dedicate yourself to it, you will live an abundant life with financial freedom.

Henco's objective was to make a customer more than just a sale. I remember when an elderly fellow, who appeared to be about 80 years old, came to me about two or three years after we opened our furniture store.

"Do you realize we buy all our furniture as a family from you?" He said.

"Tell me about your family," I responded.

He told me how he and his wife bought furniture from us. And when his son built a new house, he suggested Henco to his son. "Most of my children have bought here, and now we are working on our extended family," he said.

I shook his hand and let him know that I was grateful. "It is people like you who have built this store. Thank you very much!"

I gave a lot of thought to this conversation, and I looked for ways we could be helpful to dedicated customers. Because furniture is made with human hands, we will not get it right every time. From time to time, there would be an issue with a product. I wanted to know how we could help customers when they had problems so we could show them we cared about them. We made it a policy for the salesperson to explain our commitment after each sale.

"Mrs. Jones, we appreciate your business," they were instructed to say. "The likelihood of your having a problem with your furniture is low, but should you have a problem, we want to be helpful. The furniture manufacturer gives you a warranty and makes certain promises to you. I want to emphasize it's not Henco's promise — it's the furniture manufacturer's promise to you. It's our job to work with you and the manufacturer to make sure they live up to their promise. Our customer service manager is dedicated to making sure they do. If you have a problem, you know whom to call to get the problem solved. Also, even if your furniture is out of warranty, we have a master craftsman here at Henco to repair the damage. All you do is bring the piece to us, and we will repair it for just the cost of labor. You are our customer, and we want you to know how we can work together should you have a problem."

We wanted customers to know that Henco service did not stop with the sale. This policy prevented a tug of war if a warranty issue arose because we had an understanding in writing with the person to contact as to how we would work together. It reinforced an important idea: "You are our customer, and we are in the service business."

Our delivery crews had the last contact with our customers. They were trained as our goodwill ambassadors and dressed in a Henco service uniform. They were taught to place the furniture in the home and inspect it. They made sure no dust was left behind and everything worked, as it should, before asking the customer to make a final inspection. After the customer signed for his or her furniture, the deliverymen was supposed to express their appreciation with our celebrated cookies.

We were determined to raise our service to a level that turned our customers into raving fans. Even our custodians were reminded about our commitment.

"We are in the business of creating raving fans in every community — look for ways to be helpful and create a raving fan," I explained.

I expressed the same message to our warehouse staff. For example, when a person pulled furniture from inventory for a customer and prepared to load it on our delivery truck, I asked them to get involved.

"When you pull an order, I want you to have a chat with Mrs. Jones," I would tell them. "Explain to Mrs. Jones that you noticed she is from Holly Springs, Mississippi, and it's your responsibility to pull her order correctly. Tell her she can count on you to look out for her, and you'll inspect her pieces carefully to make sure every one of them is loaded on the truck. When the furniture is placed in her living room, she'll become one of Henco's raving fans, sending us business. We look out for families in a special way for many reasons — one of which is they furnish a check for you and your family to live the good life."

With Henco's service philosophy, our employees were not simply working and loading furniture. They were pulling furniture for a family in Holly Springs, Mississippi, who could be raving fans of the company, sending their family and friends to Henco. I did my best to help each Henco employee see how it made common sense to live a mission of service to their fellowman.

"You are no longer working when you are on a mission of service, doing something special for people," I often said. "This kind of thinking will put a spring in your step and make you proud. If someone asks you what you do at Henco, tell them your job description is to create raving fans in the neighborhood."

Our employees were dedicated to the mission of service. We knew that a well-trained staff would be good at our mission. We selected our team carefully, and we created a waiting list of talented people in every department who wanted to join our company.

I often think about the outstanding people who joined us through the years to make a major difference in the success of the company. Those are milestones in the life of a business — the days when you hire the right person to do the job.

***

A person of any age who strikes out on his or her own to build a business, whether it is a neighborhood shop or national company, does not have all the answers at the outset. Regardless of the completeness of a plan, it will have gaps, and unanticipated situations will arise. To become an outstanding businessperson, you must remain a student.

One of the furniture stores Sherry and I visited in Dallas was founded more than 60 years ago by J. Ray Weir and his wife, Bea. Today, Weir's Furniture is a multi-store operation. Mr. Weir was a gem, and he cast a long shadow in the furniture business. His family-owned business sold more furniture per square foot than any store in the country.

Sherry and I arrived early one morning and began asking questions of the sales staff. I asked how long they had worked there and was amazed to learn that many of the salespeople had been there for decades. They came to work with the store and spent their life in his business. That is unusual for this day and time. One fellow said he had worked there for about 30 years.

"I worked two years, and then I left for greener pastures," he explained. "But, I found the pasture was not as green as I thought, so I came back, and I've spent my work life with Mr. Weir."

About that time, Mr. Weir, who appeared to be about 85 years old, came into the store walking with a cane. He had a big smile on his face as he greeted his employees. I went over to meet him and told him that we had driven more than 600 miles to learn some things from him.

"Thanks for coming," he said with a smile. "I'll do my best to be helpful."

We had a seat on a sofa close by and I began to ask him some questions.

"Mr. Weir, when did you start in the furniture business??"

"Out of high school," he replied. "I was 18 years old."

"What are you are most proud of in building your business?"

"This business, through all these years, starts each day with a prayer."

"Why?" I asked.

"Opening with a prayer encourages everyone to be more truthful and to be more service-minded. If we can live a Christ-like day, our service will have more quality, and our business will grow faster."

"What do your employees think about coming together for prayer before they start the day?"

"They must like it because they've spent their life with me. We hardly have any turnover."

I liked his response.

"That explains the big gold hand, on the roof of your store's entrance, pointing skyward," I said.

"Exactly," he replied.

"Mr. Weir, I like what I am hearing. What else should I know?"

"I'm a circle-eight guy," he said. "I go to the top stores to learn from them, and I have done that for more than 60 years. I still travel and learn to improve our services. Don't become ingrown. Reach out and learn, because change is constant."

Sherry and I spent most of the day learning from Mr. Weir. After we returned home, Mr. Weir and I exchanged letters about our philosophy of life. He was one of the most mature people we met. It was an education. I can't express enough the importance of remaining a student and reaching out to people to mentor you from their successful experiences in what you need to know.

We built Henco Furniture with top people mentoring us in the furniture business. None of them charged us a dime, but we understood the value of being mentored as we developed the store. Mentoring is about business owners sharing what they have learned and helping others avoid common mistakes that can slow down success.

Why do people give of their busy time? First, it is a way of giving back to their fellowman. Mr. Weir was a good example. Many mentors owe their personal business success to a mentoring relationship, and are eager to pay it forward.

If you are a person striking out on your own, for goodness sake, let people be helpful who are smarter than you. Avail yourself to mentors as long as you live. In my many years of entrepreneurship, I have learned you don't need all the answers up-front as long as you remain a student as you build. Don't be afraid to say, "I don't know." Ask for help. Success is an inside job. Become the person to do the work at hand, and this can best be done through advice from mentors. This is the spirit of a good entrepreneur.

***

Sherry and I created Henco Furniture with the dream of creating a happening in the Selmer Industrial Park. The picture was a bit fuzzy in the beginning, but we knew if we kept dreaming with an open mind, it would take shape. I visualized offering an incredible service and creating a fun shopping experience for the family. It was an experience families would enjoy and then spread the word with their neighbors when they returned home

"You should see what they created," I wanted them to say. "It's amazing!"

The Henco service plan took shape quickly around the idea that we must be a most unusual store in service to get people to talk about the store in their communities. We wanted Henco Furniture to be a part of the conversation: "If you need furniture, go to Henco!"

We could not be successful in the Selmer Industrial Park with just good service. Other furniture stores had a good service, too. Henco's service had to be way better than anyone expected. Our service had to be special for people to make the long drive.

We constantly taught the sales team how to be more customer friendly and ask questions until we knew why each shopper came to our store. Until we knew their need, how could we be an effective helper? We encouraged our customers to let us help. To be most effective, we asked the customers to help us visualize the room before attempting to furnish it. I told our team that the customer must see you as a helper instead of a salesperson.

"Don't make a sale," I explained. "Make a customer. The best salesmen on planet earth are those who have mastered the art of being helpful. Look for ways to be helpful! If the little boy is restless, find a way to pacify him — maybe an ice cream cone or a cookie. If a customer's sizeable order and financing causes a delay, suggest they relax at the café and enjoy a free lunch or a beverage. If they have a flat tire in the parking lot, offer to send someone to jack up the car and change the tire. It takes a creative, thoughtful mind to render a service that people rave about. A person with a servant attitude finds ways to go beyond the call of duty. An unexpected service is the way to get people's attention and develop a long-term customer who tells their best friends about Henco."

***

I recall a couple arriving at the entrance of our store one morning, casually dressed. It didn't appear as if they had two nickels to spend. I greeted them and gave them an overview of how to shop the store. The gentleman, whose name was Jim, never changed his expression as I talked. He just looked me over. As they began walking into the showroom, I called out to them.

"By the way, where are you folks from?" I asked.

The man looked down at his watch with methodical effort.

"Betty and I have driven three and a half hours from Marks, Mississippi."

I thanked them again for making the long drive, and they began their shopping trip. A short time later, I encountered them being helped by Gene Hébert. They were sitting on a leather sofa, and I sat beside them.

"Jim, I can see you and Betty getting in your car early this morning, backing out of your driveway, heading north and driving three and a half hours to Henco Furniture," I said. "Why would you do such a thing?"

"When I saw you on TV, I told Betty we were going to buy from that old man when we get ready to furnish our new home," he explained. "You said it was worth the drive."

"Jim, you and Betty are an interesting couple," I replied. "Tell me about yourselves. What kind of work are you in?"

He shared his story, and I encouraged him to tell me more.

"Betty and I worked hard and saved our money," he began. "When this 200-acre farm came up for sale, the banker worked with us to buy it. The delta land Betty and I now own is more than 3,000 acres, and we have a large crop-dusting operation. Our planes dust farms all over our area."

"When Jim and I get the crops out, I work in town — every little bit helps," Betty added.

They also told me about their son graduating from college with a degree in agriculture to help them manage their operation.

I asked Jim and Betty to accept a complimentary lunch at the Whistle Stop Café. They completely furnished their new house — it was a sizable order. Gene Hébert alerted me as they were leaving. I engaged with them and thanked them for their business.

"We will be back," Jim said. "We have thoroughly enjoyed a wonderful shopping experience, and it has certainly been worth the drive."

We made an effort to get acquainted with our families and encouraged them to share details about their lives with us. Getting to know Jim and Betty certainly changed my impression from what I thought when they first arrived. We were in a much better position to be helpful to them after we became acquainted.

If you want people to like you, encourage them to talk about things that make them proud. Being patient and listening is a great trait in dealing with people. We encouraged our employees to listen and learn and ask timely questions. When you sincerely get to know families, you become a better communicator. You can be more helpful when a customer shares his experience with you. That customer can tell we are truly interested in him and want the best for him.

***

One day as I sat at my desk, a helicopter landed on our campus. A couple stepped out while the blades were still turning, reached for each other's hand and started walking down the drive. I left my desk and met them halfway.

"Welcome to Henco Furniture!" I said. "I generally greet people at the door, but when they come by helicopter, I greet them halfway up the drive."

As we made our way to the showroom, they told me they had built a new home and came to Henco to furnish it. I introduced them to our interior designer and asked her to help them out. The family furnished their home with us and came back several times later to purchase more.

Years later, a fellow came to my table at the Top O' the River Restaurant near Pickwick and shook my hand. He said that he and his wife were the ones who landed on Henco's campus in their helicopter. He said he built custom homes and always recommended that his customers come to Henco for their furniture. Relationships of this kind built our furniture business in the industrial park. I never would have made it without people spreading the word for me.

On another occasion, I met this wonderful lady, who was having lunch with her daughter, and I could tell she was special. She had a big smile and she was glad to see me.

"What brought you to Henco today?" I asked her.

"I am 100 years old today," she said with enthusiasm.

I hugged her neck and wished her a happy birthday.

"I see you on television every day, and I've always wanted to come and meet you and see the place," she said. "My daughter asked me what I wanted to do on my birthday, and I told her I wanted to go to Henco and meet that TV star."

Now, I don't feel like a TV star, but she thought so, and I gave them their lunch as a birthday present. I told her how we started Henco Furniture, and I asked her to tell me about herself. She had lived a most interesting life, raising a good productive family. She had several grandchildren and great-grandchildren.

This is how Sherry and I developed a happening with entertainment for shoppers in the Selmer Industrial Park. We had many helping hands with the same mission. To repeat, it was not a one-man show. The Henco team was on a mission of service, and that was the reason families drove from six states, passing other furniture stores, to shop with us. The way we treated families who came to visit made the difference.

I did my utmost to change attitudes from selling to being helpful. We asked the sales team to read, among other books, *How to Sell to Your Grandmother.* I wanted them to give our customers the grandmother treatment.

"You would never take advantage of your grandmother," I said. "Giving grandmother treatment to families is the best way to create raving fans."

Sherry and I have been on many business ventures, but our furniture experience was the best. We got to know so many families that we would not have known otherwise.

Every so often, we had family reunions in the store. Extended family would meet and spend the day with us. We would set them up in a special place to have lunch together, and the kids would roam through the store eating our popcorn.

We were a frequent destination for other groups, as well.

The UT Martin staff had meetings at the store. I spoke to the university's WestStar group annually, which consisted of future leaders of West Tennessee counties. They toured the store, and I visited with them for about 30 minutes. I enjoyed speaking to the group because they were progressive, community-minded people who were interested in making improvements in their counties.

The McNairy Regional Alliance assembled its leadership class at Henco Furniture to tour our store, and I spoke to young adults about leadership. The Rotary Club met at Henco each Monday at noon and ate lunch in the café. We welcomed church groups, political groups, Red Hat ladies, bridge clubs and other community organizations.

We had customers from all walks of life. We were fortunate to have many FedEx and International Paper employees as shoppers. They were young, well educated, financially free, and they could buy whatever furniture they wished. But regardless of where they worked, we helped families within the reach of their wallets. If a couple had just married and had a limited budget, we helped them stretch their dollars. They might return, within a few years, to furnish their new home with the most expensive furniture in the store.

When you are sincerely helpful to people, they buy more and tell more people about their experience. It's a win-win for everyone!

***

The Henco customer held our employees to a high standard, and we put our best foot forward to live up to their expectations with ongoing training to get it right for them. Henco's team made an honest effort for each family to have a wonderful time.

The teachings of Bob Brooks and Gene Hébert centered on how to be helpful to the families that made the long drive. They explained that people buy more furniture when you are a capable, sincere helper. You must know your product to be helpful. For the customer to understand the value of what they are buying, they needed to see the furniture clearly. Nothing ever outperforms the truth. So tell the truth, even if you lose the sale. We pictured ourselves creating a sales force in every community. Families were excited about Henco's service and told others we were worth the drive.

Our sales team appreciated Bob and Gene for their teaching abilities. The three of us worked together for more than 30 years. They had been teaching Henco's service attitude for decades, and they knew it verse by verse.

We also taught employees to make Henco Furniture a happy place. We wanted to hear laughter as we helped customers. We told them to be entertaining and make it a pleasant shopping experience.

"Let's make it so much fun the kids will cry when they have to leave," I'd say.

Repeatedly, when the parents took their child out of the kiddie car with a bag of popcorn in his hand, the child would scream.

"No, I don't want to go!"

And I thought: what a shopping experience we have created in the Selmer Industrial Park. Our vision was a reality, and our sales grew at a rapid clip.

CHAPTER 26

BROADENING AVENUES

W ith Henco Furniture's less-than-desirable location, we knew we needed to reach out to a broader market. We reached many people through television, but a 30-second advertisement was not ample time to communicate our extensive professional services, our wide selection of home furnishings and our great prices.

Home shows, tours of homes and trade shows in our surrounding area provided another way for us to reach thousands of our customers. It was a way for me to personally meet families and thank them for making the drive to Selmer. It added a personal touch to our marketing.

The home shows also were a way to showcase our quality furniture and our interior design department's capabilities. Henco's interior designers partnered with homebuilders to make recommendations, especially in the kitchen and bathrooms, on interior design and paint colors for buyers. Henco's breadth of products enabled us to outfit and furnish the entire house — whether it was a starter home or a million dollar dream home. And with our discounted prices, families saved a lot of money.

Some home shows presented awards in various categories, such as Best of Show, Best Interior Design, Best Kitchen and so forth. Henco Furniture won several awards. The time and expense in setting up and staffing a show house were tremendous, and we put a lot of effort into making an award-winning home.

During the tour of homes, we did our best to greet families just as warmly as if they were shopping our store in Selmer. I personally interacted with as many people as possible.

Many times, people came through the front door talking about our house. "This is the Henco house, and there's Mr. Henco!"

We made it fun for families coming through our show house. We placed Henco people at different locations to be helpful and answer questions. I worked from the master bedroom. My greeting had to be brief, especially on weekends when we had so many people coming through. I explained Henco's uniqueness to families and invited them to shop with us. Many times a family within earshot would speak up and say: "We bought furniture at Henco — it's worth the drive!" That always was heartwarming to hear. I seldom got a complaint. We had a great reputation. The home tours were helpful in broadening our reach and spreading the word.

In 2008, we became a Mohawk Floorscapes dealer. Tennessee had only three at the time, which gave us a big advantage. The Mohawk Floorscape Home Centers provided more selections in flooring, carpet and tile. We also added a full line of custom cabinetry for every part of the home. We hired designers to custom fit the cabinets in the home, coordinating all the colors. The home shows gave us an opportunity to showcase our kitchens, bathrooms and utility cabinets.

Henco Furniture, in conjunction with Henco's Home Center, had become a one-stop shop with everything under one roof. We could completely furnish homes with top brand furniture, accessories, flooring, carpet, light fixtures and cabinets. We were the only company around with a full line to accomplish it all. We had more services than almost anyone, and that set us apart.

Our sales reached $1 million per month.

***

Immediately after we launched the Mohawk Floorscapes Home Center, the financial crisis of 2008 hit the country. Our furniture sales dropped 50 percent overnight. The home building industry fell flat on its face, and I wondered whether we were headed for a temporary or a more extended recession.

Furniture is purchased with discretionary money. A family can put off replacing their bedroom suite, and people did just that. Fuel prices also rose to more than $4 per gallon. That was especially difficult for Henco because most of our shoppers drove long distances to get to our store.

These situations called for tough decisions. We were faced with cutting our expenses to match our sales. We had no choice. We made a list of people who had to be laid off. So many of them were dedicated people who believed in our service mission. It also was necessary for the people we kept to take pay cuts. Sherry and I stopped our weekly checks to set the example that these are tough times that call for tough decisions so the company can survive. Patrick and I met several times each day to discuss our situation and make sure our decisions were fair.

Furniture sales everywhere dropped, and stores across the country made major cuts. Henco Furniture was not alone.

Did anyone see the recession coming? I don't think so. Maybe an adjustment was to be expected, but not a fall off the financial cliff.

**

The government bailed out Wall Street, automobile companies, banks and Freddie Mae with billions of dollars to prevent economic collapse. In my opinion, federal officials used the wrong recipe to revive the economy. We should have cut taxes and left more money in the pockets of the American people. Our free enterprise system is fueled by free people exchanging their services. With more money in their pockets, people can ex-change more services and expand the economy. The federal government is the clumsiest organization when it tries to create jobs. In most cases, Washington doesn't have a clue. It wastes billions of dollars trying to claim credit for something it is totally inept at accomplishing.

When Ronald Reagan was elected President, he came to Washington with a financial mess on his hands. I liked President Reagan's approach. He said it was difficult for businesses to plan with the economic uncertainties. He acknowledged that the country was in financial straits with inflation at 12 percent and interest rates at 20 percent. Most Americans couldn't afford to purchase a car or home, and consumers are the lifeblood of the economy. If they don't buy goods, companies can't produce them. He also said that because Washington didn't know how to create jobs, he would leave that task to the people, and he armed us with a 30-percent income tax reduction. He put policies in place to reduce regulation and squeeze out inflation. President Reagan got out of the way and compelled businesses to ramp up production and start hiring.

After about one year, the policies began to take effect, and we had a big surge in our economy, and it grew at a rapid rate. The economy remained strong for many years to come.

Reagan had a common-sense approach and relied on the American people instead of big government. Meanwhile, the 2008 recession was prolonged by the federal government trying to be Mr. Fix-it!

I disagreed with how the government handled General Motors and Chrysler. I think they should have gone into Chapter 11 and taken their medicine, adjusted their expenses to match their revenue and got rid of dead wood. The companies should have reduced their pay and made sense out of their bloated pension plans. They were living beyond their means, and it was time for a common-sense correction.

To me, the talk of those automakers going out of business was nonsense. They would have been allowed to continue to operate as they made changes. After they faced reality, banks would have loaned money for a lean profitable company going forward. After that, it would have been more appropriate for them to receive the government's loan. But, I don't think that would have been necessary if they had cut their expenses to be a profitable company. The banks would have gladly loaned them money. I believe in doing things the old-fashioned way: giving free enterprise a chance to work its magic.

Business people fill needs. When customers zip their wallets closed, we must make adjustments to fulfill a lesser need. The American people call the shots. That's the good thing about the free enterprise system. Companies make adjustments, in a timely manner with common sense, and cut expenses to match the revenue.

So many times, people forget that when a company is laying off employees, the American people are calling for the adjustment. The public, essentially, demands the layoffs when people realize they have overspent and must cut back to live within their means.

Again, business people never know what is around the bend. That's why it's called risk taking. Henco Furniture had been profitable from the outset, but we, like everyone else, had to make adjustments to survive.

***

In 2013, I was 81 years young, contemplating the future of Henco Furniture. I had both my knees replaced two years earlier. One of my biggest blessings in life is good health, but getting older is a sloppy trip.

Susan and Patrick joined the business with plans to take over the store one day, giving Sherry and me some continuity. But, with a prolonged recession, they questioned whether they wanted a business they would have to manage seven days a week. They decided to accept another offer.

"Dad, this furniture store is just like having a dairy farm," Susan told me. "You have to milk the cows seven days a week. Patrick and I don't want to milk the cows seven days a week."

I was thankful that Susan and Patrick could earn more than they needed in their careers to live the good life. Today, they are doing quite well rearing a wonderful family. Our children and grandchildren are our greatest accomplishment.

I had planned to write a book one day about my journey in life. I was encouraged to get started when Dr. Claude Gardner, past president of Freed-Hardeman University, came for a visit.

"Tom, you must write your book," he said. "If you don't get started, you'll forget some of the chapters. Every day you put it off, you're dumbing it down."

Sherry and I had long talks about our future. I had been an entrepreneur making business decisions for more than 55 years. Retirement was calling, but we did not want to think about closing the store. Was there another way? I spoke with possible investors about purchasing the store, and every one had the same thought.

"We don't think we can get people to make the drive as you have," they told me. "Your store is built around your personality."

I was positive I had a plan to regain our profit, but it would require an expansion and a significant amount of my time. My family wanted me to slow down.

"Tom, at your age, you need to admit you should not be working long hours for an extended period of time on an expansion of the store," Sherry said.

So we began to discuss closing Henco Furniture, which would be a tough thing for us to do. We loved the store. It had become a part of our life. We cherished so much about it — our team, the townspeople and the families who came on a regular basis. Our customers loved the store, too. Some drove for miles without making a purchase. They just wanted to visit and see what was new.

Henco Furniture was more than a store. It was a destination. It was shopper entertainment. It was a part of who we were. Diverse groups met at the store on a regular basis. We were on stops for tour buses, and two or three of them at a time would pull into our parking lot to spend a couple of hours. The tourists would enjoy refreshments, and in some cases, they came together as a group for me to speak to them.

Closing the doors of our unique furniture store was one of the toughest decisions we have ever made. Sherry and I still miss it. We disappointed many people, and we are truly sorry it became necessary to end our dream.

Our employees were a big concern, but I knew they were the kind of people the marketplace wanted. We gave them plenty of notice to make a smooth transition, and the people who wanted to work found work quickly. Some drew their unemployment, and some retired.

Closing our store was a bittersweet experience. We had the opportunity to talk to families and learn how much Henco Furniture had meant to them. We thanked them all for their business. They expressed how they would miss visiting and promised it had definitely been worth the drive. Some customers came to me with tears in their eyes and embraced me as we said goodbye.

***

When the doors of Henco Furniture closed, I opened another door and began another path — writing a book about my journey. My life has been an interesting road, as I pressed forward from one project to another. I've enjoyed returning in my mind to the days when I was a little boy on the farm, milking cows and hooking up mules to the plow. I also have enjoyed contemplating my entrepre-

Tom, in his sunroom, works on his autobiography.

neurial life. I didn't know much about most of my projects in the beginning. I learned on the job. I made mistakes. I earned successes. Recording my entrepreneurial and family journey in my memoir has been above my pay grade, but also one of the true joys of my life.

One of my objectives in writing about my journey is to help young people who are searching for what they want to do with their life. I hope you have enjoyed my book, and I hope you will pass it off as a gift to a young person who is trying to find his or her way. I hope that my life journey will help them find their way.

Above all, I hope my experiences will motivate people to find the courage to live a bold life in service to people, to take the risk to achieve a dream.

By now, you can see why I loved business and devoted my life's journey to being an entrepreneur with a mission of service — whether I was selling watermelons, Bibles, fundraising projects, emus or furniture. It is a constant, unfolding story of working with people. Business is a people trip — a most interesting trip. It's worth the drive!

ADDENDUM
CHAPTER 27

MY FAITH, MY MORAL COMPASS

"Success is an attitude that Christ tried to describe — a life
of faith, hope, confidence, service, generosity, integrity, love
and forgiveness — the moral truths that lead the way to a good life."

I cannot write about my life's experiences without acknowledging my debt to my faith. From my early childhood of going to the small Buena Vista Methodist Church in the back of a wagon with my family, I was taught that we must do what Christ said if we were to live happy, successful lives. These simple teachings stick in my mind; I believe them today as much as my parents believed when they were teaching me many years ago.

My faith is not an imitation of others. My faith is my beliefs formed from my upbringing and my life's experiences since then. My beliefs have proven good for me, and I share them for that reason. I certainly don't think I have all the answers. All of us see things differently because our lives are different. That is a good thing because we can share what we believe, and, together, hopefully get closer to the truth.

Education helps us to better understand our universe and how it works. Education, though, is just information unless we can implement it for someone's benefit. The best-educated people are those who understand how to achieve what they want by helping other people get what they want. If it is that simple, why aren't more people successful?

Success is an attitude that Christ tried to describe — a life of faith, hope, confidence, service, generosity, integrity, love and forgiveness — the moral truths that lead the way to a good life. This successful attitude enables us to put our education to work to have almost anything we want within reasonable limits. This attitude enables us to effectively use a greater percentage of what we know because we are not controlled by fear, but by hope and faith to activate our good ideas in service to people.

We observe and learn about God by observing His physical laws and His moral laws. His physical laws, also known as scientific laws, are the most direct expression of His will. We learn as much about God's will through His physical laws as we do His moral laws. They are both His handiwork. We must comply with these truths for the results we seek.

Christ came to give us the moral side of the equation — the lessons of love and forgiveness that enable us to get along with each other and work together for progress. I like to think of it as a success recipe. We cannot be successful without practicing good moral values. Whether we acknowledge Christ or not, we had better pay attention to what he said.

***

"Everyone who hears these words of mine and does them is like a wise man who built his house on rock. The rain fell, the flood came, and the winds beat against that house, but it did not collapse because it had been founded on rock. Everyone who hears these words of mine and does not do them is like a foolish man who built his house on sand. The rain fell, the flood came, and the winds beat against that house, and it collapsed; it was utterly destroyed!"

Matthew 7:24-27

***

Since I am a Christian, I state my views based on being a Christian, and, certainly, I do not apologize for my Christian beliefs. Christianity, though, is not the only religion that teaches moral values for a good life. I don't think we Christians should be so smug in our beliefs, thinking we have all the answers and everyone else is wrong. In my opinion, we form our beliefs from the way we are reared, the churches we attend, the religion we are taught. We are a product of our upbringing and our circumstances.

I have many non-Christian friends whom I admire very much. One friend, who is special to me, is Jewish. "Ed," as I will call him here, is one of the most caring, sensitive, generous, loving, service-minded men I have ever been around. He called me one Sunday to tell me of a human need that was not being met, and he wanted me to help him solve the problem.

"Ed, where are you calling me from?" I asked.

"My office," he replied.

"What are you doing at your office on this Sunday afternoon?"

"I set aside a day each week to look for unmet human needs," Ed answered, "and this is the day for me to do that kind of work."

Ed was busy being helpful to others. We completed our phone conversation, and I thought, "what a guy!" I wish I were more like him.

I had another close friend, "Bob," who was in Rotary Club with me. Bob did not believe in organized religion. He never said he was an atheist, but he certainly seemed to be one. My description of Ed also describes Bob perfectly. Bob was a respected gentleman in our community, and he was doing what he could to make it a better place in which to live. He was as honest as any person you would find. I asked him once why he did not go to church.

"I have been turned off with all the religions, how preachers on television and radio are going to jail because of their behavior," he replied.

I think about how the three of us were living basically the same kind of life, practicing the same moral values. One of us was a dedicated Christian, one was Jewish, and one did not believe in organized religion. With our moral beliefs being much the same, our lives were much the same. If a person observed us in action, not knowing anything about our religious background, one might think we all went to the same church.

Because we all lived the same kind of life, how will we be treated in our next life? Will we be judged the same? Is the objective to abide by the moral laws that give us a good life, in service to our fellowman? How much emphasis will be placed on the religion we practice? I don't know the answers, so I will leave this question for your consideration according to your beliefs.

I do believe that to be successful here on planet Earth, we must comply with God's laws, both physical and moral — however we go about it. It goes back to how a person is reared and what he or she believes. I have always been enthusiastic about the teachings of Christ because He taught a recipe based on moral laws that enable us to live successfully with our fellowman to achieve our goals. Therefore, it behooves us to get a good education and make a study of Christ's teachings for a good value system, knowing God's laws enables us to live in harmony with our universe, our neighbors and ourselves.

In my opinion, Christ did not come to this Earth to make us more religious. He came to change the conduct of man. Simply, He wanted us to be Christ-like, to enjoy our time here on Earth, to express our love through service to our fellowman.

***

"So then, if anyone is in Christ, he is a new creation; what is old has passed away — look, what is new has come!"

II Corinthians 5:17

***

If everyone on planet earth followed Christ's teachings and lived a Christ-like life, armies would not have a reason to exist. There would not be an FBI or CIA, and we would reduce a policeman's work to directing traffic. Bank employees could go to lunch and leave the money on the counter, and it would all be there when they returned. Doors would not have locks; we could leave them wide open at night and sleep in peace. Congress would work part-time because we would need few laws to regulate a moral people.

Think about the standard of living we would enjoy if we did not waste our resources on securing our nation and communities with armies, intelligence agencies and law enforcement personnel. We would live in abundance, going beyond ourselves in service to others, eliminating government welfare.

Christ makes a request of us in the Lord's Prayer, when He says, "Thy kingdom come, thy will be done on earth as it is in heaven." He is saying to us, "Follow my teachings and live in my kingdom here on earth, living just like you will in heaven. And, when you get to heaven, you will fit right in because you will have been practicing on earth, the way things are done here in heaven."

Christianity makes so much common sense to me — a life of hope, love, forgiveness, patience and generosity. These beliefs enable us to live an unbelievable life here on earth. God knew, if we behaved ourselves according to His teachings, the floodgates of abundance would open up and pour over us greater than we ever dreamed possible.

Christ was enthusiastic about us living a life of faith and hope, admonishing against fear. He wanted us to be positive, hopeful and courageous people striving to reach our God-given potential in service to each other. He knew fear would be our greatest challenge, and for that reason, He spoke of fear often to help us see the devastating effects it could have on our lives. It seems to me that Christ emphasized faith and hope for us to believe in our ideas — to take the risks to develop the cures for our diseases, to learn his physical laws, to fly our planes, develop computers, and create the Internet to give us the conveniences of life. He wanted us to learn the truths of the universe.

Why would God build the truths into His plan had He not wanted us to take advantage of them? I can see God giving Thomas Edison a big hand when the light bulb gave light, applauding Jonas Salk when he found a vaccine to eradicate polio, and grinning with pride when Nelson Mandela found a way to unite his country without violence.

God wanted to inspire successful living. He wanted us to take on bold projects, to unlock the secrets of the Earth for the good of people. Dr. Salk is an excellent example of what God wanted. Dr. Salk went into his lab with faith and hope. Through trial and error and many disappointments, but with faith, he persevered until he had the vaccine to save children from polio. On the other hand, if Dr. Salk had gone into the lab doubting himself or with fear, his ideas would never have worked. Children would have continued to contract polio, resulting in twisted bodies, shattered dreams and, in many cases, death. Surely,

God didn't give us faith and hope to make us more religious, but to make us more successful in service to people.

I don't think God wanted children to have twisted bodies. Instead, He wanted us to develop the vaccine to save children from polio. Think about all the prayers, and children still came down with polio. Too many times we ask God to change His plan, instead of realizing that we must get in step with His plan. Thank goodness for people like Dr. Salk, who had the perseverance to find the answers to God's plan concerning polio.

That's one example of why I believe our prayers should express our desire to develop wisdom, faith and hope, to continually strive to learn God's laws for the good results we seek. Our prayers should not be to change God's laws, but rather to get in step with them.

***

"If I had not found encouragement in your law, I would have died in my sorrow. I will never forget your precepts, for by them you have revived me."

Psalm 119:92-93

***

Don't get me wrong. I'm certainly not against prayer. But it might have been better to pray that we find a cure instead of praying that God vaccinate the children.

I think of Thomas Edison as he worked on the light bulb, trying different ideas thousands of times before one produced light. A newsman asked how he felt about failing thousands of times, and Edison said, smiling, "I have not failed. I've just found 10,000 ways that won't work."

Now that's the kind of faith that gave us light.

As I write, the media has just announced the death of Nelson Mandela. I laid my pen aside to think about the impact of his life and to celebrate his contribution to mankind.

Mandela's life embodied much of what Christ taught. Here was a man who sat in prison 27 years, much of it in solitary confinement. He came out of prison with a smile on his face and determined to unite a country without bloodshed.

If that happened, he said, his prison term would be worth it. He did exactly that to become the president of the country.

Regardless of our occupation, the challenge will always be to live a Christ-like life as we do our work. Mandela, certainly, set a good example for us to follow as he became a powerful leader through the practice of what Christ taught. His faith, hope, love, forgiveness and courage were more effective than all the guns in South Africa.

I have been asked to speak on leadership many times through the years. Leadership is an interesting subject. You can ask 100 different people their definition of leadership, and you will get 100 different answers.

We should go to Christ to learn about servant leadership. At the Last Supper, Christ knew His time was short. Since He had spent three years with His disciples, He wanted to consolidate their energy going forward. He chose to wash their feet. We certainly don't think of a strong leader washing the feet of the people he is to lead, but Christ thought it to be important. You can see Him now placing their dirty, dusty feet in His hands and into a pan of water and looking up at His disciples, saying, "we have a job to do, and we are in this together. I believe in you and I will do anything for you."

Having the humility to wash their feet left a lasting impression on the disciples, a time they would never forget — a lesson in servant leadership. How could you not follow a person like Christ, someone who wants the best for you, someone you can trust and admire, someone who loves you? That is real leadership, the same kind of leadership Mandela demonstrated to the world as he went about uniting his country, black and white, without bloodshed.

When I started Henco, we wrote in our sales manual that we would do our best to base our leadership and management on the teachings of Christ. We made sure not to get into personal religious beliefs, not to stir the passions of argument, but to speak of Christ's teachings in non-emotional terms. We did so to have more trust, more forgiveness, and more faith and hope as we worked together.

Since we were in the service business, helping schools raise money for their different school projects, we believed a Christian attitude of unselfishness would translate into a more quality service. It makes common sense. If a school sponsor knows you want the best for the school and want to help them solve financial problems, they are more apt to pay attention to what you are saying. If you work with them unselfishly, they more likely will work with you in future years. Our philosophy was, "let's not just make a sale, but let's make a long-term customer." I have always said, "our best salesmen are those who have mastered the art of being helpful, of doing something special for others." This kind of selling is a much better service and will build a business over time.

I wanted Henco to have a heart and soul, and we chose my good friend and mentor, Jack McConnico, to push the heart and soul wheelbarrow.

Jack read constantly — history books, autobiographies and, especially, business books. He wanted to learn how management could include and mo-tivate employees, how to elevate people to be a part of the decision-making process, how the use of everyone's brain power could make the company more successful and how to help employees see how they fit into our company's service and success. He would share the important lessons from his readings to encourage everyone to grow to his or her full potential.

Jack had strong feelings about Henco employees growing to their full po-tential as we rendered our service. He kept his ear to the ground to make sure we were fair, to create more harmony and enthusiasm, and to put a spring in our step for a quality service with more company *esprit de corps.* Jack had un-believable influence on the people of Henco.

This is a good example why we should practice the teachings of Christ. Whether it is building a business, uniting a country or teaching school, we are better servants if we follow Christ's lead in achieving our goals.

In the early years of Henco, as I traveled across the country, I read the New Testament each January to help guide my steps for the year. I wrote all over the pages with examples of how the ideas could be used. Every time I read the New Testament, I found more ideas that I had not thought about. I am totally amazed how much wisdom is in the New Testament to guide us to live a good life, from the cradle to the grave. I strongly feel that what we believe determines what we do, and what we do determines what happens to us. The life we live goes back to what we believe. Christ came to help us get our heads screwed on properly.

***

"The thief comes only to steal and kill and destroy; I have come so that they may have life, and may have it abundantly."

John 10:10

***

We should believe in Christ to the extent we become doers of His teaching. We should do our best to live what he said in whatever we are doing. It's not something to talk about on Sunday mornings; it is to be lived 24, 7.

Millions of God's physical laws cause our universe to behave in a predictable way. These physical laws are the most direct expression of God's will. For example, if I comply with God's physical laws that cause a combustible engine to run, it will run every time. It also will run for everyone else regardless of his or her beliefs or where they live because it's God's law, and you can bet on it.

Our universe works the same for everyone; it's predictable. We can drop a ball, and it will always fall because of God's law of gravity. Anyone in the world, rich or poor, fat or skinny, American or European, can drop the ball, and it will fall. Preachers everywhere can get on their knees praying until they wear holes in their pants to suspend the law of gravity. Governing bodies worldwide can pass laws to suspend the law of gravity. But when all of these people are finished, we can drop the ball, and it will fall. These physical or scientific laws are immutable and unchanging. We should understand that once and for all, and for that reason we can trust God.

I also think God built into our universe an answer to every problem and a cure to every disease. It might be the seaweed in Africa, but it's here someplace.

***

"For the Lord God is our sovereign protector. The Lord bestows favor and honor; he withholds no good thing from those who have integrity."

Psalm 84:11

***

I like to define God as truth and love. There has to be some kind of intelligence behind the creation of this beautiful universe other than chance. If we accept the idea God created the universe, we must also accept the laws of nature or God's laws that cause the universe to behave in a predictable way. This is a truth that we must respect, learn about and get in step with if we are to live a successful life.

Many religions and denominations have done the physical laws a disservice by implying that they can be changed through prayer. Instead of teaching sensible respect for God's laws through compliance, they indicate that if we don't like them, we can petition God to change them. All you have to do is believe, have faith. I have a great deal of faith, but not to change God's laws.

In many cases, religion sends mixed signals. For example, in our Rotary Club, a Presbyterian preacher was called on to ask the blessing. A terrible storm was coming ashore near Mobile, Alabama. It had been on the news for a couple of days, and the storm was at the top of our minds. So, the preacher prayed about the storm. He first mentioned turning the storm toward Mexico, but that would not do, so in a loud voice, he called out.

"God, stop the storm!"

When we sat down, I tapped the preacher on the arm.

"Let's go to a TV set and see if the storm stopped," I said.

"You are making fun of my prayer," he responded.

"You bet!" I replied. "It makes more sense to pray that those people find protection. Maybe they can get into a hole because the storm is coming ashore. People can protect themselves because God gave them a good mind to do so."

The minister did not expect the storm to stop. That would have been a huge news story that night: "A minister, in a Rotary Club in Selmer, Tennessee, asked God to stop the storm, and the winds stopped."

Simply put, this is not the way God designed our universe. For, if He did change his physical laws, we could not trust Him.

I don't think the preacher appreciated the good of the storms. Our universe has weather patterns that water fertile soil to feed people. The storm the preacher was praying about watered the eastern part of the United States from Tennessee to the Atlantic, increasing crop yields and making farmers happy. God didn't tell us to build unsafe houses or poorly constructed high-rise buildings and thus have people unsafe in a bad storm.

A 12-year-old boy was killed when an oncoming car hit his four-wheeler. At the funeral service, the preacher made the statement, "God loves little children so much; he came and took him to his own." That kind of talk is very confusing to a family. I think God wanted the boy to grow up as a great Christian and to rear a Christ-like family, but God would not suspend his universal laws to save the boy. We lay too much on God unfairly.

Since God's universal laws are immutable, the little boy must abide by these laws for his safety. For that reason, we tell our children to wear their helmets and to not get on the highway. Let's say God changed the universal laws that were involved in this wreck, just to make an exception for the little boy. For example, with the law of gravity suspended, everything on earth would go sailing from the earth. Our houses would go to pieces in seconds. If God's plan was not predictable with an off and on plan, would we buckle our seatbelt or expect God to grant us an exception?

With all the exceptions, we would live in an unpredictable world, a world of chaos. We would not have the faith to make progress. Edison's light bulb would be unpredictable; we would not be sure the light would burn when we flipped the switch. Edison would never try 10,000 experiments for the light to burn if God's physical laws were unpredictable. Simply put, we would not have faith in God's plan. We would not make progress if one day the light bulb burns and the next day it doesn't.

We are the only creatures that God saw fit not to program for success. He set us aside as being special. He programmed all of the other creatures for success, to live the good life. They don't have to go to college; success is in their DNA. Look at a squirrel. She climbs the tree, builds her nest, gathers the nuts and jumps from tree to tree. Squirrels have done that for thousands of years. Man is not programmed like the squirrel, but has been given a free will, a great opportunity to program his own life as he seeks the truth, solves problems and grows toward God through service to people. We are just getting warmed up for the progress of tomorrow.

When we were laid in the cradle, God blessed each of us with almost un-limited potential. Unlike the squirrel, if we want a life of success, we must do the programming. Our computer is useless until we program it to do the work. We are no different. If it's to be, it's up to us! God would not have given us all the potential if He had not wanted us to develop it. With few exceptions, we have the potential. The problem is that it lies dormant because we don't set high goals or have a plan for our life. I don't think God picked one person to fail and one to succeed. He is not in the business of picking winners and losers. He wants every single one of us to invent a light bulb. He did not give us the potential to be a loser, but to be a winner. If we believe we are created in the image of God, we believe we are pretty darned special.

He gave us free will to make something of our life or make a mess of it. It's our choice. He gave us free will to make mistakes, learn from those mistakes and learn from the mistakes of others to grow a notch or two as we go through the ups and downs of life.

I often told my daughters as they were growing up, "good decisions, good life; crummy decisions, crummy life."

If you were to walk down the street and ask a hundred people, "Do you have a well thought-out plan for your life?" only a small percent would respond that they have programmed their life to carry out a mission in service to people, that they have a life plan they feel strongly about. Many times we spend more time planning our two-week family vacation than we do our annual plan for the year.

What a difference it would make if everyone had a mission for his or her life. The most successful people are the people with a mission. We need more of those people.

Because of our free choice and because we are blessed with so much potential, man has made great strides in solving many problems, curing diseases, making a better life for everyone. The little squirrel still is operating like 2,000 years ago. This makes God's plan for us very fascinating. I am thankful that I'm not a little squirrel. I am thankful I have a free choice to make mistakes and to learn from those mistakes. We comply with God's plan, we get a good result. We go against God's plan, we get a bad result.

***

"In the same way, every good tree bears good fruit, but the bad tree bears bad fruit. A good tree is not able to bear bad fruit, nor a bad tree to bear good fruit."

Matthew 7:17-18

***

It seems to me, too much emphasis is placed on making a living or joining a company with a good benefit package for early retirement. Too much focus is placed on what I can get instead of what I can contribute. The Bible does not speak of an individual reaching a point, regardless of age, where he or she is commissioned to occupy the stool of "do nothing" — where they cease to contribute to society. This may be the reason why the New Testament does not have a chapter on retirement. If Christ was on earth, would He retire or would He continue to "chop his wood" in service to people? My guess is that He would continue on his mission of service.

***

"So we must not grow weary in doing good, for in due time we will reap, if we do not give up. So then, whenever we have an opportunity, let us do good to all people, and especially to those who belong to the family of faith."

Galatians 6:9-10

***

We can travel the world and see God's plan at work in the minds of people. They are from all different kinds of churches and religions, but a moral tone guides their thinking. As we go forward, with the fast pace of technology, we will be challenged to maintain our moral bearings. It behooves us to teach our children and grandchildren Christ's practical lessons to help them keep their moral balance in order to handle the swift changes they will be facing.

The scientists tell us we will see 1,000 times more advances in the 21st Century as we did in the 20th Century when we went to the moon and developed the Internet with its universal library of information at our fingertips.

Our future has changed! In the beginning of time, nothing much dramatically happened in a million years. But that's not so today. My grandfather and my father's lives were about the same. My father pictured my life as being like his had been, but to many people's surprise, my generation was a part of a big change, particularly with technology and improving life's comforts.

We have made great progress learning about God's physical laws. From the moral standpoint, we have some catching up to do to manage technology for the good of people. Our children must be grounded in a solid set of beliefs and morals if they are to handle this fast-moving world for a happy life. Parents are struggling to pass off a solid set of beliefs that will enable their children and grandchildren to live a happy, productive life. We need more families teaching values across the kitchen table.

***

"The wicked are overthrown and perish, but the righteous household will stand."

Proverbs 12:7

***

Selling Bibles to work my way through college gave me the opportunity to observe how more than 2,000 families interacted with their children. I would see chaos and disrespect, and I would see love and well-behaved children. I decided the most important thing I could do was to rear a good child because she would go and rear good children, and that's what you stock a good neighborhood with — good people. So, Sherry and I worked diligently doing what we could while Susan and Leigh Anne were still living at home.

As we would head to church when Susan and Leigh Anne were about 12 and 14, I would give them an assignment.

"I don't care whether you pay attention to the preacher, but I want you to come away with at least two good ideas that will help you be a better person."

In the car, on the way back home, I would ask them for their good ideas. We would discuss what the preacher said.

Sometimes, the young girls had unusual insights. I remember one Sunday, we went to Memphis to attend Central Church where my friend, Jimmy Latimer, was the pastor. Jimmy had been one of my Bible salesmen, and he became a successful preacher with one of the most successful churches in our area. After the service, I asked Leigh Anne to share her best idea.

"Dad, I was fascinated with all those beautiful lights in the ceiling of the church. There were about 200 lights."

We all had a big laugh! Leigh Anne wasn't very intent that day on what the preacher said.

***

"Train a child in the way that he should go, and when he is old he will not turn from it."

Proverbs 22:6

***

When Susan and Leigh Anne got to the age of being able to discuss ideas in abstract terms, we would have family time at our evening meal — no television, no phone calls. It was a time we could share with each other.

"Any person who ever amounts to anything must decide what he or she believes, because what we believe determines what we do, and what we do determines what happens to us," I would say. "It all starts with what we believe. I think it is important for this family to reduce to writing what we stand for, what we believe. We will each bring a universal truth to the table for discussion three times a week. Obviously, some of these ideas will come from the Bible."

If that universal truth, principle or value was important enough for us to write it into our book of family values, the person bringing it to the table would have his or her initials written beside it. We would discuss these values and ask how they would help us live a better life. Many times, we would give examples on how a value could be a part of our decision making.

We wanted these discussions to be sensible and practical so they could easily base their life on them as they progressed through high school and, especially, when they went away to college. Young people are exposed to a lot of ideas, but we wanted our children to appreciate their family values and to know they had a lot to live up to. We wanted them to be grounded in a set of good values to see them through the high temptation years of college and young adulthood. I am happy to say we have never had a family meeting to deal with a moral problem or behavior. This is not to say that they led perfect lives, but I never doubted they would make good decisions because of their rearing. They did, and Sherry and I are very proud.

When Susan and Leigh Anne were in college, I wrote letters about what was taught across our kitchen table, mentioning who brought the idea for our discussion. They seemed to be glad to get those letters. This gave me an opportunity to give them a refresher course as they dealt with their college life.

Christ's teachings of love told us how to have a happy and successful life. Children need to understand the value of what Christ said and why His teachings are just as important today as they were 2,000 years ago. They may even be more important today in our fast-paced world.

I believe our universe is guided by a moral purpose and governed by laws designed to affect that purpose. It is easy to think our world is on a sinful course, but I still believe God's moral and physical laws guide it.

I believe there is a plan for mankind; that the plan grows and evolves through the centuries as does any flower, tree or other thing, according to the immutable laws of God that govern the universe. I think God will always be in the driver's seat as we go through the vast changes coming our way. These ideas are taken from our Henco Faith, which we compiled many years ago, with Jack McConnico's guiding hand. I believe we determine our own fate by the degree to which we cooperate with or oppose the will of God. I believe to cooperate with the will of God is to live. This entails a lot of struggle and growth. To cease growing is to die.

We live our lives in service to people doing as much good as we are capable, then we get older and our bodies play out; we step aside, a child is born to replace us. Each generation stands on the shoulders of the giants of the previous generation, seeing farther into the future to advance the cause for man. It is part of God's plan. When we are old and have done our best in service to our fellow man, we give up our space for more progress. Therefore, death is a generous event — a renewal for progress.

When people ask me what I think about heaven and hell, I tell them I have never been to either place, so I am not an authority on either one. I have all I can say grace over today trying to live the life Christ asked me to live. I like the second statement in the Lord's Prayer, "thy kingdom come, thy will be done on earth as it is in heaven." Christ, I think, is saying to us, "do your best to live what I have taught you; living in my kingdom here on earth as you picture heaven being." To me, that's pretty good advice.

I have never thought of heaven as a location but as a state of mind, a consciousness. I don't know if it does us any good to see the place, but I can get excited about living in the warmth of love. Now, that fits my thinking.

If we awake surrounded by greed, selfishness, dishonesty, pride, envy, malice, jealously, intolerance, hate, anger, fear and worry, we would still be living in hell. Heaven must be made up of love, forgiveness, hope, faith, unselfishness, intelligence, tolerance, patience, kindness, justice, peace and joy. If we can live this kind of life, we will be living in God's kingdom here on Earth, making for a smooth transition to our next life.

My beliefs have shaped my life and helped me achieve success. Everyone is entitled to their own, but I am confident in mine.

***

"As for me and my household, we will serve the Lord."

Joshua 24:15

CHAPTER 28

THE ROAD TO GOOD HEALTH

*"Do you not know that your bodies are temples of the Holy Spirit, who
is in you, whom you have received from God? You are not your own;
you were bought at a price. Therefore, honor God with your bodies."*

I Corinthians 6:19-20

For many years, I have been interested in living a healthy lifestyle. In observing myself and others, it seems to me that too many people ruin their health before they even start to take care of it.

Growing up on the farm, it was natural to eat what Mother prepared for us, which included many homegrown vegetables and typically meat at every meal. As I grew older, I found myself eating what I liked. It was all about what tasted good, and many times the foods were not particularly healthy.

After Sherry and I married, we became health conscious and paid more attention to what we ate. We took heed of health charts, government health information, the food pyramid and the general flow of health information.

During the 1970s and 1980s, we spent most of our weekends on our boat in one of the beautiful coves on the Tennessee River. Many times our friends tied their boats alongside ours, and we would enjoy good food, swimming and skiing. Those fun-filled days consisted of grilling too many steaks, hamburgers and pork chops, which created a high-fat weekend, gumming up our vascular systems. And we thought nothing of it. If you could afford it, you ate the best cuts of meat as often as you wanted.

I have often said that if we were to take care of our body as well as we take care of our automobile, we would have much better health. If the car's service manual recommended five quarts of oil, we would not consider adding seven or eight. If the manual recommended a certain grade of oil, we would not consider adding a different kind. If we ignore these recommendations, we can expect problems from our car, many trips to the garage and expensive repair bills.

The approach to our body should be no different. Our body requires certain foods in certain amounts. In fact, a fatty diet will send us to the butcher shop early for open-heart surgery, stents and more, simply because we do not respect our body as much as our automobile.

To know how to fuel our body to achieve good health requires a serious study of foods and their effects.

In the Korean War, more than 30,000 service members were killed in battle. Specialized military doctors examined the hearts of 300 of them. These young men, with an average age of 22, were healthy when they died. But during the autopsies, doctors found that 77.3 percent had gross evidence of heart disease, and one in 20 had so much plaque that 90 percent of an artery was blocked. They were active young men in the prime of their lives with no indication of the beginning stages of a serious heart condition. When we are young, we think we can eat anything we like, with no consequences. Obviously, that is not true.

In my early 60s, I began annual exams with doctors who were truly interested in wellness. These exams used advanced technology and clearly showed that my vascular system was gumming up.

These health facts prompted me to make a serious study of how to live a longer, healthier and energy-filled life well into my 80s and 90s.

The first book I read was Dr. T. Colin Campbell's "The China Study." The study reviewed the consequences of foods based on solid science instead of selling a fad diet. The book made so much sense to me. I read it two or three times, underlining the parts where I intended to change my habits.

When I first read the book, my cholesterol was 190. Within a few months,

I lowered it to 100. I thought: "Wow — I can reverse a potential heart attack." It was exciting to realize how foods were affecting my body.

I adopted a plant-based diet, which gave me an abundance of energy. I also felt much better, especially after a meal. Sherry read Dr. Campbell's book and joined me in a healthier diet. We gave more thought to the preparation of our foods and selected items meant to sustain our bodies for better health. We enjoyed our food just as much as ever, and it gave us both satisfaction knowing we were choosing meals for more energy and a longer life absent of chronic diseases.

I find it interesting that 2,500 years ago, Plato warned us to eat animals at our own peril. Hippocrates, the father of Western medicine, advocated diet as the chief way to prevent and treat disease. The Old Testament advocated eating vegetables. A plant-based diet for good health has been around through history.

Are we fanatics? No! We eat red meat occasionally, but we certainly don't make it a habit. I am in my 80s now. I exercise every morning and have plenty of energy to do the things we enjoy in life. I just recently sold our motor home, but I was very comfortable driving it, with our car in tow, through New York City at night. Sherry and I do what we have always done to live the good life.

Why am I talking about health? It just makes sense for each of us to do what is right to achieve and maintain good health. A healthy body is completely necessary for a good life.

I observe people every day who have ruined their health with poor health habits. They are not able to enjoy their golden years simply because they did not make a serious study of how to live a healthy lifestyle. We're not getting this information in school or most doctors' offices. The airwaves are full of confusing health information, and many of the books written on how to live a healthy lifestyle confuse the issue and are garbage.

I have found that many doctors show an interest if you tell them you are interested in practicing wellness.

"Tom, most people are not interested in doing the things necessary for wellness," a doctor once told me. "They are more interested in a Band-Aid for whatever ails them at the moment."

Another doctor, when he saw how I controlled my blood-work numbers with the foods I ate, told me I was one in a thousand.

Well, that was a nice compliment. But perhaps doctors could be more direct about the problems brewing inside a patient's body so the patient would fully understand the consequences of not turning to a healthier lifestyle.

"Your vascular system is closing," the doctor could say. "Your blood flow is being restricted. You can do one of two things. Continue on with your choices of foods, and you will go to the butcher shop for open-heart surgery with a $50,000 price tag. And open-heart surgery is not a cure. It is just a temporary Band-Aid. It will take some time to recover from the surgery, and you may not ever resume full strength. Your other option is to see my dietician, who will work with you to develop a sensible diet, and with an exercise program, your vascular buildup will reverse. You can live an energy-filled life. Eating properly and working with our dietician is pennies on the dollar compared to open-heart surgery."

"What will it be?" The doctor could ask. "The butcher shop or the dietician? It's up to you."

Perhaps a good percentage of people would choose the dietician for a long-term cure if they were convinced by the doctor's explanation that it just makes common sense to eat sensibly.

Our health providers should lead the parade with a wellness practice. Insurance companies can play a big role selling wellness policies. Medical schools should adopt a wellness approach and move away from doctoring our ailments with a handful of pills and surgery. Too much money is spent doctoring sick people after they have ruined their health. This doesn't make sense, and I maintain it will change over time when people cannot afford the doctor's office visit or when insurance deductibles get so high that people will be forced to think in terms of living a healthier lifestyle.

Elizabeth Holmes is a bright woman who studied chemical engineering at Stanford University. She quit school as a freshman to start a business and change the way we deliver health care in this country. Part of her plan is to do blood work using only two or three drops of blood for about a 10th of the cost. She has convinced the chairman of Walgreens to join her in testing small wellness centers inside stores with pleasant background music, providing a relaxing atmosphere as blood is taken for lab work. Because these tests will be inexpensive, a person might have his or her blood work done each month to observe how their diet moves the numbers. For example, a person can eat a big cheeseburger with French fries and watch it change his blood work numbers. Miss Holmes hopes to give patients videos of the blood work trends to spot any problems that might be brewing — preventive medicine can save us a lot of heartache later.

During my years of working with people, I have observed that the ones who live a healthy lifestyle have much more energy to pursue their goals and have a better sense of wellbeing. We promoted healthy lifestyles with our Henco employees and offered fitness programs and facilities.

When I returned home from my service in Korea, I wore pants with a 32-inch waist. Then I grew to a 34-inch waist. I told myself I would never buy a pair of pants over 34 inches. Through the years, if my pants got too tight, I knew exactly what to do to adjust the size. Today, I wear 34-inch pants. That is my size, period! I eat and exercise to make it so. This decision has controlled my weight through the years.

After you have read Dr. Campbell's book, you might consider reading Dr. Caldwell B. Esselstyne's book, "Reversing Heart Disease." It is quite an impressive read. These books can be purchased for less than $10, and a used book can be bought for only a few dollars. I hope you will read "The China Study" for sure, because it could save your life and enable you to live an energy-filled life late into your golden years. The doctors will hardly know you exist.

I am often quoted as saying: "If we drink eight glasses of water, exercise each day, get a good night's sleep and make a serious study of how to eat properly, the doctors would get very bored."

We also have a problem ending our life in a responsible way. After all, death is not an option. The world-famous neurosurgeon, Dr. Ben Carson, states in his book, "America the Beautiful," that 40 to 50 percent of our health dollars are spent in the last six months of life. Dying patients are placed in intensive care and tested, prodded and poked until their last breath. The doctor never knows when a lawsuit will be filed over a test he should have ordered, but didn't.

A few weeks before my mother passed away at 89, I visited her early one morning. The sun was shining into her room, and she had a big smile on her face as she greeted me. I asked her how she was doing, and she was frank.

"Tom, the nights are so long," she said. "Then I struggle through the day."

Then she paused and looked me straight in the eye. "I raised seven children — a great family — but I am fouling up my life here at the last. I have lived my good life, and I am ready for the next one."

"Mother, are you saying that you do not want us to take extraordinary steps to keep you alive?" I asked.

"Exactly," she replied, with emphasis. "Let me die in peace."

Not long after, I was informed that she was being taken to the hospital. I rushed to her hospital room to carry out her wish. Luckily, I met her doctor in the hallway.

"I don't want you to hook my mother up to any life support," I said adamantly. "No tubes running out of her."

He was uncomfortable with my request. "We must do something," he said.

I reiterated that she definitely did not want life support. Our family and her doctor agreed to make sure she was not in pain. And we arranged it so she could spend her last days at home. She returned to her home and passed away the next night with my brother, Carlton, at her bedside. She died in peace, as she requested.

In this day and time, doctors are placed in uncomfortable positions at the end of a person's life. I am convinced they could have kept my mother in intensive care and kept her alive and unhappy for several months. I am so thankful we did not travel that road.

A Speech to University of Tennessee at Martin Graduates, Class of 1990

This graduation day is special to you, and I am honored to be your speaker. When I was here studying agriculture, never in my wildest dream did I think I would be speaking to the 1990 graduating class.

It is an exciting world out there, and many good things will come your way as a result of your experience here at UTM. We all love this university and what it stands for. You are fortunate to be graduating from UTM, and I congratulate you.

I want to say three things to you that I hope will make a positive difference in your life.

My first thing I want to discuss with you is your occupation — your work must be worth your life. Life is made up of "x" amount of time, and when you give time to something you are simply giving away a part of your life. Your life is special. Your work should take on that same kind of importance.

We have far too many people working for a living. We need missionaries in the marketplace — people who base their lives in service to other people by rendering service in wholesale quantities, and I say to you there is absolutely nothing wrong with getting rich in service to people.

When you do good, you feel good. Your enthusiasm is determined by the way you feel, and that is the stuff that makes for success.

For the most part, we make our contribution in this life through our work. If we want to live a successful life, a quality life and an exciting life, our work must be all of these things. They are inseparable.

Secondly, I want to suggest and persuade you to become a risk taker. Most people play their cards too close to their chest.

You will not live but one time. Live your life to the fullest, being a courageous person, and taking action on what you believe. Be secure enough to understand there will be some failures as you climb your mountain.

Failure is no disgrace. How do we know our limits without failure? I am convinced that the real winners in life will be those who try the most and fail the most.

Risk must be taken, because the greatest hazard in life is to risk nothing. The person that risks nothing becomes nothing, has nothing and is nothing. We may avoid suffering and sorrow, but we cannot learn, feel, change or love without some risk. If we seek the certainties of life, we will become a slave. There has been a lot of research on risk taking.

During World War II, psychologist Paul Torrance, studied the outstanding pilots and what made them outstanding. To his surprise without exception, they were risk takers. When they encountered the enemy, they were take-charge people. They would go after the enemy. They were decisive — they were risk takers.

These risk takers were the most effective pilots with the best safety records. They suffered fewer casualties than the play-it-safe pilot.

In all walks of life, the most successful people are the risk takers. By that I mean, they risk believing in themselves and their ideas: striking out toward their own goals and standing up for what they believe to be right. They take the risk of being different.

Folks, when you stand for what you believe, you run the risk of creating short-term problems, but in the long run you will win. Risk takers realize there is nothing wrong with an occasional setback because that is the stuff a successful life is made of. Risk takers are not fool hardy.

Getting back to the flying aces for a moment, it was found that these men were very fussy about their equipment, their planes had to be right, they were painstaking in their preparation and they were highly disciplined in following instructions and what they had been taught.

But when they encountered the enemy, they flipped the switch to take the calculated risk to win the battle. So I say to you, be an intelligent risk taker.

I want to sell you on the idea of making a study of success. What makes folks successful? You need to get your arms around that successful attitude that will enable you to be all you can be in life.

Your degree is wonderful, but it won't in itself make you successful. There are mountain climbers and slope climbers. It is up to you as to how high you want to aim.

This universe works the same for everyone. The universe is impartial, it doesn't care whether you succeed or fail. For the most part, it is a level playing field.

My last year in college, I became interested in why some people were highly successful while others made a living. I read every book I could get my hands on having to do with success. I read *Think and Grow Right, Acres of Diamonds, As a Man Thinketh, The Magic of Believing, The Power of Positive Thinking, Wake Up and Live* and the list went on. Then I started reading about some of the great people of our time: John D. Rockefeller, Henry Ford, Dr. Jonas Salk, Dr. Norman Vincent Peale, Thomas Edison and Abe Lincoln to find out what they believed. What made them so darned successful?

I wanted to know what these men stood for, what they believed and what their value system was because I wanted to do my best to copy the winners. I found a common thread in their thinking. These are some success traits that I found in every one of them.

To begin with, they were honest people — men of integrity. They understood the value of integrity for good communications. Integrity is essential if you are to work through other people successfully.

They each had a mission that was bigger than life. Henry Ford was determined to build an inexpensive car with his production line concept paying his employees more than anyone on the block. In fact, he paid $5 per day, which was unheard of at that time. He wanted his employees to buy his cars and they did. Folks, I can't imagine this country without Henry Ford. I can't imagine there not being a Ford Motor Company with all the good that has come from it.

The mission of John D. Rockefeller, with Standard Oil, was to produce inexpensive energy. At that time, we had depleted whale oil. By the way, Mr. Rockefeller gave about $550 million away to charitable causes. Now that is generosity!

Dr. Salk wanted to stop the kids from dying with polio. That was his goal. He wanted to immunize the world's children against polio. He was sick and tired of seeing parents live in dread of their sons and daughters contracting the disease.

These people were on the go, and they knew where they were going. They were self-directed people.

Yes, they were risk-takers. They not only put their ideas on the line, they mortgaged their homes and everything they had to get to where they were going.

My senior year after having done extensive reading on success, I knew exactly what Tom Hendrix would be about. Even though I had studied agriculture, I was determined to build a business, and I wanted it to be national in scope. I didn't have any money, but that didn't make any difference. I would find a way. These successful people had stretched my mind. I no longer was interested in making a living, I wanted to climb a mountain that was worth my life.

I am convinced if you will act on these suggestions, the floodgates of abundance will open up and pour over you greater than you ever dreamed possible. May God bless you along the way.

LETTER FROM ANDERS WIDESTRAND

I n 1983 I arrived in the Hendrix home as a 17-year-old exchange student from Sweden. With a new set of sisters, Susan and Leigh, and a new set of parents, Tom and Sherry, I was immediately welcomed as a brother and son in an exciting, active and intellectually stimulating lifestyle from the moment I arrived.

Thanks to their lifestyle, even as a teenager I got to see and experience the United States in a way that most Americans never get to in their lifetime. My exposure to life in the United States covered the entire spectrum, from entertainment to business and politics, to history and religion.

In the summers we spent many weekends on Pickwick Lake. During those weekends and with family and friends frequently visiting, the entire family taught me to become an experienced boater and water skier. A winter trip to Vail, Colorado, later on gave me the opportunity to return the favor by teaching them how to snow ski down the slopes of the Rocky Mountains.

These are just a few examples but they are a testament to the Hendrix's active and open-to-new-experiences lifestyle that they shared with me.

An accomplished businessman, Tom would sometimes let me sit in on Henco Inc. board meetings. When Tom traveled to business meetings across the United States, he would occasionally take me out of school for a day or two to let me join him on trips to Dallas, Las Vegas or other interesting locations. As fun and interesting as these meetings and travels were, they taught me a lot about how business is conducted in the United States. I didn't know it at the time, but this would be an invaluable experience for my later professional career working for a European company in the United States.

Although my grandfather had been a Lutheran minister in the Sodra Vi parish in southern Sweden, going to church on Sundays was a new experience for me. Attending church service with the Hendrixes at Selmer's First United Methodist Church fostered a community spirit that was very different from the one I knew in Sweden.

Most importantly, Tom ensured that attending a church service was not only a social and religious experience but an intellectual exercise as well. I soon learned to pay attention to the minister's sermon because after church, mostly in the car on our way to Sunday brunch, we kids would often be quizzed on our personal interpretation of that day's sermon. It would lead to engaging family discussions with Tom serving as the family moderator.

These family discussions helped me grow and reflect upon my own moral values. My values were shaped in a way that would not have happened under other circumstances during that formative time in my life.

Dinnertime was the time when the Hendrix family came together after everyone's busy day of school and work activities. Always delicious and nutritious, Sherry's home-cooked dinners were the best. Our daily family dinner routine with engaging dinner conversations was one of the most beneficial and enjoyable parts of my experience as an exchange student. It usually started with us kids sharing our experiences from school and after-school activities. After the most intriguing school gossip had been covered, Tom often steered our dinner conversation to thought-provoking topics on personal values, current affairs, politics, economics or philosophy. In these discussions, everyone was engaged, and everyone's opinion mattered equally.

To me personally, these discussions taught me to structure my own thoughts and to express them as clearly as I could.

Living with the Hendrix family set my life on a completely different path from what it had been until then. I benefited from the experience both in my personal life and in my professional career. The Hendrix family's generosity and hospitality to me were truly exceptional. They always treated me like a true member of the family.

Being a member of the family included taking on responsibilities (such as occasionally washing the cars, mowing the lawn and taking care of the swimming pool) as well as receiving privileges appropriate for a boy of 17. But no matter how you look at it, for this exchange student, the family privileges easily outnumbered the family responsibilities.

As a successful businessman, Tom gave me exposure to entrepreneurship and how the free enterprise system works and brings out the best in people. We had many one-on-one talks on how taxation, inflation, welfare and other public policies affect the business environment. Often we compared the American system with European countries and noticed how these factors affect individual opportunities for employees and employers, and how they determine the productivity and wealth of a society.

These insightful talks sparked my interest in business and economics and were a major contributor to my later studying business and economics at the University of Tennessee. What I realized at the university was that many of the lessons Tom had taught me were very applicable to our coursework, but more practical and insightful than much of the economic theory I learned in business school.

During summer breaks in college, Tom gave me the opportunity to experience real life, practical entrepreneurship by helping to run the Hendrix Orchard, the largest peach orchard in Tennessee.

My entrepreneurial responsibilities included hiring college students as sales people, running the sales team that was dispersed at various locations throughout Knoxville and delivering peaches from our orchard to our sales stands. These experiences set the stage for me to build my career with successful global companies, such as Reuters and SAP, the world's largest enterprise software company where I am currently running the software partner co-innovation program for the banking and insurance industry sectors.

In many ways, Tom was a father, friend and mentor all wrapped up in one person. From a practical perspective, he taught me many things, such as how to drive a car and operate a ski boat and a yacht. He taught me how to tie a cleat hitch to dock the boat and a necktie to go to church. When washing a car, Tom's advice was to "always hose it down from the top, never from the bottom." Thirty years later, I still remember that advice every time I wash my own car.

Most of all, I am extremely grateful for the opportunity Tom gave me by sponsoring my studies at the University of Tennessee in Knoxville. It was a wonderful four years to be studying at the same university with my two sisters and spending family time together during ball games and school breaks, and being peach entrepreneurs during the summers.

Double-majoring in finance and German with a minor in economics at UT Knoxville enabled me to hit the ground running in my graduate studies in England. I started my career working for multinational corporations in Germany before returning to the United States about eight years ago. Much of the success I have had can be attributed to the lessons and the opportunities Tom gave me at a very crucial and formative period of my life. It is not an overstatement to say that Tom truly changed my life.

COOL SCHOOL STOOL SONG

Words and music by Rip Reagan

Verse I

All cool cats
Who really swing
Have a Cool School Stool cause
That's the thing;
With their own school color
And design to rule
Get with it "Big Daddy," get
Cool School Stool.

Don't be a pauper
Don't be a fool
Don't spend your loot
A shooting pool.
A real sharp cat
Will stay in school
And spend his loot
On a Cool School Stool.

Verse II

It's furniture
It's a souvenir
It's a foot prop, baby
Like a rocking chair; you can
Use it as a ladder
Use it as a tool
Be a wise old cat
Get a Cool School Stool.

Verse III

You can hit it with a hammer
You can hit it with your fist
You can stand up on it and
Do the twist.
You can clap your hands
And stomp your feet
But a Cool School Stool
Just can't be beat.

Get your own school color
Get your own school name
Put your own John Hancock
Or get it plain.
Put your club mascot
Or the name of your school
Put the name of your chick on your
Cool School Stool.

Chorus

As a rule
It's a fool
Like a stubborn old mule
Who has no chair like a
Cool School Stool.
You can stack 'em to the ceiling
Store 'em like a spool,
Be a real gone cat and get a
Cool School Stool.

Index

NOTES

NOTES